PRAISE FOR BEN SHAPIRO'S *N*   ER

BULL

HOW THE LEFT'S CUL
INTIMIDATION SILENCES AMERICANS

★

"Ben Shapiro is a warrior for conservatism. I've never known him to back down from a fight and, in *Bullies*, he shows us all exactly why that fight is necessary."

—Glenn Beck

"Don't let the left shut you up—read *Bullies*, and learn how to fight back!"

—Sean Hannity

"Ben's premise about the left's silencing tactics is absolutely correct. . . . Please read *Bullies* and consider his advice. . . . We must not allow ourselves to be frightened into silence."

—Sarah Palin

"Meticulously documented and deeply personal, *Bullies* will infuriate AND inspire you."

—Michele Malkin

"You don't know the left until you've read *Bullies*. And you won't be able to beat them unless you do."

—David Limbaugh

"Irresistibly readable. . . . Ben Shapiro has nailed the left right where it lives."

—David Horowitz

THE PEOPLE

★★★ VS. ★★★

BARACK OBAMA

THE CRIMINAL CASE AGAINST
THE OBAMA ADMINISTRATION

BEN SHAPIRO

THRESHOLD EDITIONS

New York   London   Toronto   Sydney   New Delhi

Threshold Editions
A Division of Simon & Schuster, Inc.
1230 Avenue of the Americas
New York, NY 10020

First Threshold Editions paperback edition April 2015

THRESHOLD EDITIONS and colophon are trademarks of Simon & Schuster, Inc.

For information about special discounts for bulk purchases, please contact Simon & Schuster Special Sales at 1-866-506-1949 or business@simonandschuster.com.

The Simon & Schuster Speakers Bureau can bring authors to your live event. For more information or to book an event, contact the Simon & Schuster Speakers Bureau at 1-866-248-3049 or visit our website at www.simonspeakers.com.

Interior design by Akasha Archer

Manufactured in the United States of America

10 9 8 7 6 5 4 3 2 1

Library of Congress Cataloging-in-Publication Data

Shapiro, Ben.
  The people vs. Barack Obama : the criminal case against the Obama administration / Ben Shapiro.
     pages cm
  1. Obama, Barack. 2. Executive power—United States. 3. Abuse of administrative power—United States. 4. United States—Politics and government—2009– I. Title. II. Title: People versus Barack Obama.
  E907.S43 2014
  342.73'06—dc23
                                      2014009187
ISBN 978-1-4767-6513-6
ISBN 978-1-4767-6515-0 (pbk)
ISBN 978-1-4767-6514-3 (ebook)

To my daughter, Leeya Eliana, who deserves the country of God-given rights promised in our Declaration of Independence and Constitution

CONTENTS

★

INTRODUCTION

★

THE CASE AGAINST
THE PRESIDENT

On November 4, 2008, Barack Obama was elected president of the United States. It was a time of hope. It was a time of restoration. Three months later, President-elect Obama stood at the podium before cheering throngs, and he raised his right hand. "I, Barack Hussein Obama, do solemnly swear that I will faithfully execute the office of President of the United States, and will to the best of my ability, preserve, protect and defend the Constitution of the United States."

Fast-forward five years. White House press secretary Jay Carney takes to the podium in the press briefing room. The Obama administration, now in its second term, has been plagued by scandal after scandal:

- On September 11, 2012, the American consulate in Benghazi, Libya, was attacked by terrorists after months of desperate pleas for more security from Ambassador Christopher Stevens and his staff; Stevens and three other Americans were murdered as American forces remained mere hours away. Now State Department witnesses from Libya have testified that higher-ups at the department tried to stifle them from speaking with Congress.

- The IRS has admitted that its nonprofit division targeted conservative groups in the years leading up to Obama's reelection effort; further evidence showed that conservative nonprofits were subjected to costly audits.
- The Associated Press has revealed that the Department of Justice had secretly obtained months' worth of call logs from its reporters. A few days later, reports emerged that the Department of Justice had obtained a warrant for Fox News reporter James Rosen's personal emails and tracked his movements at the State Department.
- Within a few days of *that*, Congress sends a letter to the secretary of the Department of Health and Human Services, Kathleen Sebelius, asking why she had solicited donations from nonprofit organizations to push Obamacare—the same organizations responsible for directly implementing Obamacare and therefore subject to HHS oversight.
- At virtually the same time, Republican lawmakers send a letter to the Environmental Protection Agency asking why the EPA has forced conservative groups to pay fees for Freedom of Information Act requests while simultaneously waiving those fees for liberal groups.
- In early June, former Booz Allen Hamilton employee Edward Snowden, who worked with the National Security Agency, reveals that the NSA PRISM program is tracking all American phone calls. Soon, revelations emerge that the NSA collects "nearly everything a user does on the Internet." Snowden says that the government has the ability to collect your keystrokes as they appear.

Facing down this cornucopia of political horror, Carney peers through his MSNBC glasses and begins to speak. Carney has already become infamous for spewing gobbledygook at the press—so infamous that the left-leaning parody site *The Onion* prints a mock op-ed by Carney playfully titled "Well, Time to Go Out in Front of a Bunch of People and Lie to Them."[1]

On this day, July 22, President Obama is preparing to relaunch another failed attempt at economic mumbo jumbo, a desperate try at shifting the narrative from the bevy of scandals. Unprompted, Carney spouts that thanks to "some phony scandals that have captured the attention of many here in Washington only to dissipate, there has not been enough attention paid, in the President's view, to this central idea that we here in Washington ought to be doing everything we can to help the middle class. . . ."[2]

Phony scandals. All phony scandals.

A few hours later, President Obama himself repeats the "phony scandal" meme. "With an endless parade of distractions, political posturing and phony scandals, Washington has taken its eye off the ball. And I am here to say this needs to stop. Short-term thinking and stale debates are not what this moment requires," Obama intones.

What, exactly, made these scandals "phony"?

According to the administration, these scandals are phony because they say so. According to the White House, White House–initiated investigations had shown that President Obama didn't personally engage in any of them. Though the White House still hasn't revealed President Obama's whereabouts during the seven-hour Benghazi attacks, Obama, his investigative team assured us, did everything necessary to save the men in harm's way. And Secretary of State Hillary Clinton assured us that while there was negligence, there was no need for firings—for, after all, "what difference, at this point, does it make?" Meanwhile, Secretary of the Treasury Jack Lew told Fox News that there was "no evidence" that the White House was involved with improper targeting—as though absence of evidence were evidence of absence, especially given the fact that the investigators were from the Obama administration itself. Attorney General Eric Holder lied to Congress about targeting the Fox reporter, then somehow got away with claiming it wasn't a lie at all. Director of National Intelligence James Clapper did the same with regard to the NSA's surveillance programs. Sebelius and the EPA didn't even bother making excuses for their actions.

All of this was nobody's fault. Wrongdoing, if it existed at all, took place at the individual level. Low-level staffers were responsible. Mistakes were made. We don't know what happened, but we'll initiate an investigation. We can't comment on pending investigations, even if we control them. These are not the droids you're looking for. Move along.

Only nobody ever got fired, many people got promoted, and all of those mistakes by all of those low-level staffers just happened to synchronize precisely with the wishes of the White House. Every day, Obama's knights were ridding him of meddlesome priests—but that was all just a big coincidence.

There's only one problem with Obama's routine: it's not just a lie, it's a crime.

The Obama administration has become a full-fledged criminal enterprise. Riddled up and down with executive branch appointees engaged in high crimes and misdemeanors, the administration has not merely failed to cleanse itself, it has incentivized ambitious bureaucrats throughout the government to take action on behalf of the Obama political agenda.

PROSECUTING THE OBAMA ADMINISTRATION

The crime of conspiracy has typically been defined at the state level as the agreement of two or more people to commit a crime. There is little question that some of the crimes of the Obama administration have been coordinated at the highest level, as the evidence will show. But when it comes to huge organizations, conspiracy has historically been tough to charge. That's because large organizations rarely have direct chains of command—and in an organization as enormous and classified as the United States executive branch, tracing such chains of command becomes nearly impossible.

Which is not to say that legal responsibility does not exist. In 1946, the U.S. Supreme Court legally established the principle of "command responsibility"—the idea that a commander bears responsibility for the actions of his subordinates during times of war.[3] As the commander in chief, President Obama bears responsibility for the acts of his subordinates, particularly with regard to crimes against Americans under the auspices of war.

That would be difficult to prove in a court of law. What *isn't* difficult to prove is that the Obama administration is a quasi-criminal syndicate, a top-down system in which policies are decided at the highest levels, signals are sent, and low-level bureaucrats receive and implement them.

In 1970, in an attempt to curb organized crime in general and the mafia in particular, Congress passed the Racketeer Influenced and Corrupt Organizations Act, also known as the RICO Act. The goal of RICO is to make it easier for prosecutors to cast the net in indictments, placing evidence in "the broader context in which the crime was committed, along with the pattern of conduct that led up to the crime," according to Professor Samuel Buell of the Duke University School of Law.[4] In other words, it was designed to fill a loophole in the law—the problem of plausible deniability, in which the man at the top can foist responsibility off on his subordinates (or plausibly call everything under the sun a "phony scandal").[5] RICO, according to former Department of Justice director of research Donald J. Rebovich, provides the prosecutors the ability to "abandon a reliance on discrete statutes. Instead, they can prosecute patterns of criminal acts committed by direct and indirect participants in criminal enterprises."[6]

RICO provides that any person who is part of an organization that commits any two on a list of crimes can be prosecuted for racketeering, fined up to $25,000, and sentenced to twenty-five years in prison per count. Those charges include murder, kidnapping, gambling, arson, robbery, bribery, extortion, dealing in obscene material, dealing in drugs, bribery, counterfeiting, embezzlement, extortionate credit transactions, wire fraud, witness tampering, retaliating against a witness, victim, or informant, and dozens of other crimes—some of which, as we'll see, have been committed by the Obama administration. RICO, according to its language, was supposed to be "liberally construed to effectuate its remedial purpose."[7] The U.S. Court of Appeals for the Third Circuit has described the list of predicate offenses under RICO as "exhaustive."[8]

Politicians aren't immune to RICO charges. When Detroit mayor Kwame Kilpatrick conspired with contractor Bobby Ferguson, he was charged with RICO Act violations. Together, Kilpatrick; his father, Bernard Kilpatrick; and Ferguson faced forty-five charges, including racketeering, extortion, bribery, and mail fraud. As the *Detroit Free Press* reported, "The most weighty of the charges was the one levied under the Racketeer Influenced and Corrupt Organization Act (RICO), a 1970 law that was initially designed to combat organized crime but has since been used in several public corruption trials. In the Detroit case, prosecutors charged the group they called the 'Kilpatrick Enterprise' engaged in a pattern of criminal activity—one of the requirements of RICO—that included at least two criminal acts."[9]

While prosecutors routinely use RICO to go after criminal enterprises, RICO extends beyond criminal prosecution to include civil suits. That means that you can sue a criminal enterprise, and receive triple your damages—you don't have to wait for President Obama's corrupt Department of Justice to do the work they're being paid not to do. The victims of Bernie Madoff, for example, have targeted Madoff's associates under RICO. (It's worth noting that Bernie Madoff's fraud pales in comparison to the federal government's fraudulent social programs.) As the Supreme Court has written, the goal of civil RICO filings is to deputize the public to enforce the law against corruption, to make citizens into "'private attorneys general' on a serious national problem for which public prosecutorial resources are deemed inadequate."[10] Plaintiffs in civil RICO actions must show by a "preponderance of the evidence" that defendants bear guilt. That's different than "beyond a reasonable doubt"—it's a much lower burden of proof.

To bring a RICO case, plaintiffs must be able to show that an "enterprise" exists, and that there is a "pattern" of criminal activity. To show that an "enterprise" exists, plaintiffs must demonstrate that there is a "continuing unit that functions with a common purpose." That unit, in this case, can't be the entire federal government or the entire executive branch—it has to be separate and apart from the normal functioning of those organizations. That's a problem in and of itself, given that with the massive growth of government, it's arguable whether the executive branch has become a quasi-criminal syndicate, no matter who runs it (when is the last time a president didn't oversee massive corruption and criminality?). But if a pattern of criminal activity is shown by members of a group, and that activity always benefits their common interest, it will be difficult to argue that there was no "enterprise" in place.[11]

Now, prosecuting an administration as a criminal syndicate presents certain challenges—first and foremost, the fact that the Department of Justice is responsible for administering the RICO statute. That puts any RICO prosecution in the hands of the Eric Holder Justice Department, which is to say, it kills any chance of real consequences for the Obama administration. But that's not to say that Holder *shouldn't* investigate. Under the law, the attorney general is supposed to investigate whenever there are "reasonable grounds to believe there has been a violation of criminal law." That's an incredibly low bar.[12]

But let's take this out of the hands of Eric Holder. Assume for a moment that President Obama's administration were in the private sector. He'd be in court so fast it would make his head swim. Were Obama a civilian in the business world he so despises, and were he stripped of his executive privilege, there is no doubt that not only would many of his bureaucrat lieutenants find themselves in jail, but that he would be hard pressed to prove his innocence. Either he would be culpable of presiding over a criminal enterprise, participating in obstruction of justice and becoming an accessory after the fact, or he would be the kingpin.

THE ANOINTED ONE

The first secretary of the Treasury, Alexander Hamilton, worried in *Federalist No. 70* that if America were to embrace a council of executives, that would leave room for virtually any wrongdoing to go unpunished. Nobody would be able to be held accountable, because there would be too many people with conflicting areas of responsibility.[13] Accountability was the hallmark of the founding ideal. As Harry Truman would later put it, the goal was for the buck to stop on the president's desk.

That vision went out the window with the rise of Woodrow Wilson and the administrative government. Wilson believed that the legislative branch was an obstacle to change (sound familiar?) and that the presidency represented the collective will of the people. But the president couldn't do everything on his own. He needed helpers. Lots of helpers. America, he wrote, should be run not by millions of citizens, but by "hundreds who are wise." Those hundreds would not be selected by the people. They would be selected by the president. "Self-government," Wilson scoffed, "does not consist in having a hand in everything, any more than housekeeping consists necessarily in cooking dinner with one's own hands."[14] This vision would usher in a glorious age in which the Constitution was scrapped and the executive branch experts would run things.[15]

It took a hundred years, but Wilson got his wish: a president with almost ultimate power and a huge cadre of agents to implement it, a horde of servants so huge that the president can always place blame with a low-level flunky. The number of agencies of the federal government has increased exponentially; there are literally thousands of agencies and subagencies of the federal government, not to mention the nearly 2.8 million civilian employees of the executive branch.[16] In 1900, there were approximately 300,000 such employees.[17]

That's a lot of people to hide behind.

And President Obama is an expert at hiding from his own crimes. That's doubly true, given the bizarre worship of Obama himself.

There has never been worship for a president like the worship for President Obama. It is not merely political admiration; it borders on the psychosexual. The 2012 Democratic National Convention featured the wholesale abandonment of the donkey logo for the Democratic Party, supplanted instead by the fascist-nouveaux Obama logo, complete with a blue *O* overarching a subjected-but-celebrating red population. A giant sand statue of Obama adorned the sidewalk near the arena. Teary-eyed women wearing homemade Obama T-shirts thronged together, cheering wildly for abortion—not for the right to choose, but for the moral righteousness of the murder of the unborn. Street vendors selling gear plastered with Obama's visage—illegally, no doubt, and without any taxes paid—grinned as they passed out the outerwear of redistributionism. Posters of Barack and Michelle adorned the streets like paintings of Mary and Joseph in Rome. While Bill Clinton drew attention for his presence, it was Obama who drew obeisance.

And when Obama appeared onstage, the atmosphere in the room was near orgasmic. Women screamed and jumped up and down as though they had just seen Jim Morrison reappear from the dead. Hands reached out as though to touch him, to put their fingers on the cult figure who could lead them to the promised land. And Obama did not disappoint. He turned himself into a Messiah-mirror who could grant salvation simply by allowing citizens to believe in him: "So you see, the election four years ago wasn't about me. It was about you. My fellow citizens—you were the change."

This was the message Obama put forth in his second inaugural address as well. He was the wellspring from which liberty could be drawn. He was the source of all rights. He could change human nature—and he could grant absolution, for in joining him, you embraced that world-altering Change: "When times change, so must we. . . . Being true to our founding . . . does not mean we all define liberty in exactly the same way or follow the same precise path to happiness. Progress does not compel us to settle centuries-long debates about the role of government for all time, but it does require us to act in our time." Liberty means whatever Barack Obama thinks it means. But we can all join him in his quest for meaningless liberty. For it is the quest itself that grants meaning, and cleanses sin.

Thus the Blessed One spake.

Worship for Obama is the only thing that has prevented him from imploding in personal approval polls. The historically large gap between disapproval for a president's policies and approval for the president during this administration personally boggles the mind. His personal job approval numbers have never dropped below 41 percent, according to poll averages.[18] Yet his job approval numbers on the economy routinely drop below 40 percent, hitting their low in September 2011, when less than 34 percent of the public approved of his performance.[19] His job approval numbers on health care, his signature issue, have been in the toilet consistently since the launch of Obamacare, hitting their low in August 2011, when just 20 percent of the public approved of his policies.[20] Foreign policy is the president's best-polling area, and even there, his approval ratings dropped dramatically in the summer months of 2013.[21] Yet he remains largely popular, especially among Democrats, who treat their Sun King as Justin's Beliebers treat their icon. His approval rating has never dropped below 70 percent among Democrats, and generally hovers well above 80 percent.[22]

Compare those numbers with the numbers for President George W. Bush. His last positive job approval numbers appeared in February 2005. From there, he saw a drop-off so dramatic that by the time he left office, just 28 percent of Americans approved of his job performance.

Just a bare majority within his own party approved of his job performance in those polls.

How can Obama continue to ride high in the public opinion polls when nobody really likes his policies?

The answer is that nobody holds Obama responsible for his policies. They see him merely as a figure, a principle, a talisman of good feeling. As sycophant rapper Jay-Z put it, President Obama's "presence is charity. . . . Obama provides hope. Whether he does anything, the hope that he provides for a nation, and outside of America is enough. Just being who he is."[23]

THE DUALITY OF SUPERMAN

This is an air Obama cultivates. He projects an air of übercompetence, a willingness to go it alone; his White House Flickr account routinely features hero shots of him, back to the sun, gazing toward the future in full Mao style. Simultaneously, however, he portrays himself as the victim of circumstance, a mere cork bouncing merrily along the surface of politics, a target of enemies both without and within.

World-beater Obama is the campaign guy—the man who begins to speak the moment he sees a light go on (which makes trips to the refrigerator particularly lengthy). This is the fellow who suggests that he can single-handedly fix Americans' problems. Upon entering office, Obama portrayed himself as a transformative figure, the messenger of Hope and Change. He pledged a new day for American government. Transparency? He would run the "most transparent administration in history." Ethics? He would preside over the most "ethical administration in U.S. history." Success? Why, he wouldn't just solve unemployment, the national debt, and financial malfeasance, he'd reverse the rise of the oceans and make the world safe for our children's children (so long as they could escape the uterus unharmed). Congress wouldn't stand in his way. The Supreme Court wouldn't stand in his way. Neither would state power, religious institutions, charitable institutions, the business community, or the family unit.

Then there's President Obama—the man who is supposed to govern.

When it comes to actual matters of government, Obama suddenly becomes invisible. Again and again, Obama has fostered the impression of individual power by claiming that he can act alone, without Congress. Then again, he contends on the *very same issues* that he can't act alone, and ultimately isn't responsible for action or lack thereof.

Here's Obama on gun control: "I am constrained . . . by the system that our founders put in place."[24] And here's Obama on gun control: "Even without Congress, my administration will keep doing everything it can to protect more of our communities."[25]

Here's Obama on immigration: "This notion that somehow I can just change the laws unilaterally is not true. The fact of the matter is there are laws on the books I have to enforce. And there is a great disservice done to the cause of getting the DREAM Act passed and comprehensive immigration reform passed by perpetuating the notion that somehow by myself I can just go and do these things."[26] And here's Obama on immigration: "If Congress is unable to move forward in a timely fashion, I will send up a bill based on my proposal and insist they vote on it right away."[27]

Here's Obama on tax policy: "So where I can act on my own, I'm going to act on my own. I won't wait for Congress." And again: "That means whatever executive authority I have to help the middle class, I'll use it." And again: "We're going to do everything we can, wherever we can, with our without Congress."[28] And here's Obama on tax policy: "The one thing about being president is, after four years, you get pretty humbled. You'd think maybe you wouldn't, but actually you become more humble. You realize what you don't know. You realize, you know, all the mistakes you made. But you also realize you can't do things by yourself. That's not how our system works. You've got to have the help and the goodwill of Congress. . . ."[29]

President Obama has contended, over and over, that he is *surprised* by the actions of his own executive branch. Over and over, he has contended that the way he has learned about scandals within his own administration is from the nightly news. Dan Pfeiffer, a top White House adviser, said in May 2013 that President Obama was personally unaware of the IRS scandal. "No one in the White House was aware," he said on national television.[30] When the Obamacare website began disastrously with glitches lasting weeks, White House press secretary Jay Carney blithely informed the press that Obama didn't know "until the problems manifested themselves" after reports in the press.[31] Similarly, President Obama found out about the Department of Justice targeting reporters from "the news reports,"[32] and the Solyndra scandal from "some news accounts."[33] He was supposedly unaware that his own NSA was spying on foreign leaders with whom we are under treaty.[34]

So, which is it? Is our president a helpless naïf, wandering door to door in search of aid? Or is he an aspiring authoritarian in control of his operation?

In the end, it doesn't matter. President Obama's executive branch is *his*. As he himself said about 2012 Republican presidential candidate Mitt Romney, "if he aspires to being president one of the things you learn is, you are ultimately responsible for the conduct of your operations."[35]

The fact is that when Barack Obama said he would act alone, what he really meant is that he would act with hundreds of agencies, dozens of czars, and millions of federal employees to back him. In our system, thanks to a hundred years of executive branch growth, the president *does* bear outsize power. Thanks to Supreme Court decisions stretching back decades, the president has the ability to unilaterally change policy through executive orders; the limits on executive orders are quite vague. The president also has the ability to appoint regulatory bureaucrats, whose authority is only constrained by statute—and in many cases, whose administrative judgments are virtually unreviewable. The power of the legislative branch has declined since the rise of Wilsonian progressivism, but the power of the executive branch has expanded dramatically.

Which is why President Obama's claims of impotence ring hollow. On gun control, President Obama ended up acting alone by signing several executive orders curtailing Americans' Second Amendment rights. President Obama unilaterally refused to enforce immigration law with regard to young illegal immigrants. President Obama unilaterally shifted cash during sequestration in order to harm taxpayers in a blatant political attempt to create impetus for tax and spending increases.

That doesn't mean the president can do everything he'd like to do.

Congressional action is still necessary for the most epic federal encroachment. And it's just those constitutional boundaries that force the Obama administration into the realm of illegality.

The Obama administration is honeycombed with criminality. Yet the administration routinely claims that investigations are under way, that low-level staffers are responsible for all the problems, and that the president remains pristine, clean from the taint of scandal. As we will see, however, the Obama administration has shown a peculiar willingness to overlook the criminality of those who help its agenda. Promotions are in store for those who break the law to benefit the Obama platform. Even those who are moved out of positions of power are handed cushy jobs outside the administration, helping to push forward the Hope and Change externally.

So why doesn't anyone seem to notice?

WHO WATCHES THE WATCHMEN?

Let's go back to those dreaded days Before Barack, when a benighted dunderhead who didn't maintain dominion over the seas or the English language held the Oval Office. The press routinely climbed all over George W. Bush. Every scandal went all the way to the top. Every whiff of nastiness spread all over the administration. Bu$hitler was a war profiteer willing to trade American blood for oil. He supposedly signed off on Abu Ghraib. He was responsible for the political scouring of the Department of Justice, the outing of a CIA agent, the illegal torture of detainees, racist-driven slow response time to Hurricane Katrina, bribery of journalists, and much, much more. The *New York Times* approvingly reported on former prosecutor Vincent Bugliosi's book accusing George W. Bush of premeditated murder.[36]

This was the press doing its job—seriously. Yes, the press is leftist. Yes, the press hates Republicans. Yes, the press attempted to draw every possible inference from every possible Bush administration screwup, justified or not. But better an overzealous press than an underzealous one. As Thomas Jefferson said, "The only security of all is in a free press. The force of public opinion cannot be resisted when permitted freely to be expressed. The agitation it produces must be submitted to. It is necessary, to keep the waters pure."

The press is no longer free, however. Or at least, they have forged their own fetters, and shackled themselves to a corrupt president. Blinded by their own godworship for the first major party black candidate in American history, charmed by his speech patterns and bloviating language, the press decided early on that this man, Barack Obama, held potential for change unparalleled in American history. The wild celebration with which the press met Obama's initial nomination finds no match in the history of the media. As Chris Matthews put it four years into Obama's failed tenure, "Everything he's done is clean as a whistle. He's never not only broken any law, he's never done anything wrong. He's the perfect father, the perfect husband, the perfect American. And all they do is trash the guy." According to Matthews, like the rest of his compatriots in the media, criticism of Obama could be explained only by appeal to racism.[37]

The press, like the good flunkies for the Obama they have become, now abide by the crucial mob rule: snitches get stitches. When legendary journalist Bob Woodward criticized the White House's strategy on the mandatory spending cuts known as sequestration, he was told by Gene Sperling that he would "regret" speaking out with that perspective. Woodward said, "It makes me very uncomfortable to have the White House telling reporters you're going to regret doing something you believe in."[38] Instead of the media jumping to Woodward's defense, they jumped to the attack, accusing him of exaggerating the White House's behavior—even as major journalist after major journalist, from Ron Fournier of the *National Journal* to David Jackson of *USA Today*, confirmed the general notion that the White House routinely treated reporters with hostile intent.[39] When it emerged that the Department of Justice had targeted both the Associated Press and Fox News, the press responded with a united front of faux indignation . . . which promptly faded away, leading the media to begin speculating about whether all of the Obama administration scandals had been overblown.

Obsessed with their hand-chosen One, the press have ignored scandals that would have sunk any Republican below Richard Nixon in the public mind. The mainstream media did not uncover any of the major scandals of the Obama administration. Not a single one. Virtually all were revealed by foreign press, bloggers, Fox News, or government document dumps.[40] In fact, the media have gone out of their way to cover up those scandals, turning the stories into laments about Republican overreach and unjust attacks on President Obama. The audacity of Jay Carney and President Obama in declaring their myriad scandals "phony" springs from their well-grounded assumption that the media will never allow those scandals to coagulate into anything truly damaging.

After all, there's progressive work to be done.

THE OBAMOB

The RICO statute was designed to target the mafia—an organization that top law enforcement officials including FBI boss J. Edgar Hoover insisted for years didn't exist. According to the Department of Justice, "Congress found that organized crime, particularly La Cosa Nostra, had extensively infiltrated and exercised corrupt influence over numerous legitimate businesses and labor unions throughout the United States, and hence posed 'a new threat to the American economic system.'" Congress expressly worried in the RICO law itself that organized crime was using its money and power to "subvert and corrupt our democratic processes."[41]

Clearly, those worries were understated. Now the chief threat to the democratic process comes not from the mafia but from within the government itself.

President Obama is that threat. It's safe to be an ally of President Obama's. It's very dangerous to be an enemy. That isn't chance. That's design. "If they bring a knife to the fight," then-candidate Obama said in 2008, "we bring a gun." The executive branch is President Obama's gun. But gangster John Gotti had a rule about guns that President Obama makes sure to follow: "It's nice to have them close by, but don't carry them. You might get arrested."

In *The Godfather*, new mob boss Michael Corleone meets with his soon-to-be wife, Kay. He has just taken over day-to-day operating duties from his father, Don Corleone.

"My father is no different than any other powerful man," he says. "Any man who is responsible for other people, like a senator or a president."

"You know how naïve you sound?" Kay shoots back.

"Why?"

"Senators and presidents don't have men killed."

Michael shakes his head. "Oh. Who's being naïve, Kay?"

We've been naïve. And thanks to that naïveté, President Obama is getting away with murder.

COUNT 1

★

ESPIONAGE

Whoever, with intent or reason to believe that it is to be used to the injury of the United States or to the advantage of a foreign nation, communicates, delivers, or transmits, or attempts to communicate, deliver, or transmit, to any foreign government, or to any faction or party or military or naval force within a foreign country, whether recognized or unrecognized by the United States, or to any representative, officer, agent, employee, subject, or citizen thereof, either directly or indirectly, any document, writing, code book, signal book, sketch, photograph, photographic negative, blueprint, plan, map, model, note, instrument, appliance, or information relating to the national defense, shall be punished by death or by imprisonment for any term of years or for life. . . . If two or more persons conspire to violate this section, and one or more of such persons do any act to effect the object of the conspiracy, each of the parties to such conspiracy shall be subject to the punishment provided for the offense which is the object of such conspiracy.

—18 U.S. CODE § 794

OPENING ARGUMENT

Their bodies were carried slowly off an American military jet by stiffly starched Marines in their dress blues. Their coffins were covered in American flags. And as they were loaded into the waiting hearses, which sat underneath an enormous star-spangled banner, the president of the United States and the secretary of state comforted one another. He wore a black suit and a striped tie; she wore a black pantsuit and a three-layered pearl necklace. Both wore solemn faces.

The president spoke first from the podium, flanked by the maternal-looking secretary of state. "Their sacrifice will never be forgotten," he said. "We will bring justice to those who took them from us." He continued, "The United States of America will never retreat from the world. We will never stop working for the dignity and freedom that every [person] deserves. . . . That's the essence of American leadership. . . . That was their work in Benghazi, and that is the work we will carry on."

"Four Americans, four patriots," he concluded. "They loved this country. They chose to serve it, and served it well. . . . Their sacrifice will never be forgotten."

Then the secretary of state stepped to the microphone. "Today we bring home four Americans who gave their lives for our country and our values," she said. "To the families of our fallen colleagues, I offer our most heartfelt condolences and deepest gratitude . . . we will wipe away our tears, stiffen our spines, and face the future undaunted."[1]

As the bodies of Ambassador Christopher Stevens, State Department employee Sean Smith, and former Navy SEALs Glen Doherty and Tyrone Woods lay before them, the president and secretary of state were already planning their own futures. President Barack Obama was planning a reelection campaign event in Washington, D.C.[2] Secretary of State Hillary Clinton was already planning her 2016 run for the presidency.

They were both planning a cover-up. For the people responsible for taking the lives of those four brave Americans were not merely the Islamist terrorists of Benghazi, Libya. They were present in that Andrews Air Force Base hangar. They were speaking from the podium.

THE CHARGES

The crime of espionage is a difficult one to charge. Historically, the government has reserved espionage charges for agents of foreign countries acting in the interests of those countries. Kenneth Wayne Ford Jr. was sentenced under the Espionage Act for carrying six boxes of National Security Agency papers back to his house. Former CIA agent Jeffrey Alexander Sterling was charged under the Espionage Act for leaking national security information to *New York Times* reporter James Risen. And most famously, both Private First Class Bradley Manning of WikiLeaks fame and NSA leaker Edward Snowden were charged under the Espionage Act.

But these crimes pale in comparison to the espionage of the Obama administration itself. American law still places us at war with "nations, organizations, or persons [who] planned, authorized, or aided the terrorist attacks that occurred on September 11, 2001, or harbored such organizations or persons." Obviously, that would include al-Qaeda and other assorted terrorist groups. But, as we will see, the Obama administration has completely reversed field, not only backing such groups, but supplying them with weaponry. One consequence of that supply chain, which likely ran through Benghazi, Libya: the caskets at Andrews Air Force Base.

That isn't just illegal under the Espionage Act. Gunrunning is banned under multiple provisions of American law, including the Arms Control Export Act, which calls for a maximum sentence of twenty years.

Failing to protect U.S. diplomats abroad by refusing to arm protective forces—a situation that ended with Ambassador Chris Stevens's body being carried through the streets of Benghazi—wasn't just negligence, but part of an overall policy plan. That makes his death involuntary manslaughter, also known as negligent homicide. Typically, negligent homicide is governed by state statute, which is where Obama administration officials would be charged. Conviction for the crime requires three elements: someone was killed, the act leading to the death was inherently dangerous or recklessly disregarded human life, and the defendant knew that the conduct threatened the lives of others. Those elements describe Benghazi to a T.

And then the administration covered all of this up by silencing witnesses and threatening agents. Those are all predicate offenses under the RICO Act.

In contradiction to what you see on *Law & Order*, motive is not a necessary element to convict someone of a crime. Motive *does*, however, increase the probability that a jury will find a defendant guilty: it is important to understand just *why* someone in a position of power would break the law.

In this case, the motive is clear: the Obama administration's vision of foreign policy required a defenseless presence in Libya, gunrunning to enemies of America, and, by consequence, the death of four brave Americans that fiery night of September 11, 2012.

PRESIDENT OBAMA'S "ARAB SPRING"

Shortly after taking office, President Obama traveled to Cairo, Egypt, to tell the Islamic world that the United States was turning over a new leaf. Obama had already made clear to Muslims around the world that he was not merely comfortable with Islam, he had a cultural affinity toward it; in March 2007, sycophant *New York Times* columnist Nicholas Kristof reported, "Mr. Obama recalled the opening lines of the Arabic call to prayer, reciting them with a first-rate accent. In a remark that seemed delightfully uncalculated (it'll give Alabama voters heart attacks), Mr. Obama described the call to prayer as 'one of the prettiest sounds on Earth at sunset.'" Obama campaigned, at least in part, on the basis of understanding Islam in a way that other candidates could not, given that he had studied the Koran while growing up in Indonesia.[3]

In Cairo, Obama took that cultural affinity to a whole new level. "I have come here to seek a new beginning between the United States and Muslims around the world; one based upon mutual interest and mutual respect; and one based upon the truth that America and Islam are not exclusive, and need not be in competition. Instead, they overlap, and share common principles—principles of justice and progress; tolerance and the dignity of all human beings," Obama stated. "There must be a sustained effort to listen to each other; to learn from each other; to respect one another; and to seek common ground. As the Holy Koran tells us, 'Be conscious of God and speak always the truth.' . . . I know civilization's debt to Islam. . . . Islam has always been a part of America's story." Then he added, "I consider it part of my responsibility as President of the United States to fight against negative stereotypes of Islam wherever they appear."

In that speech, Obama also called for liberalization of rule in Muslim countries, regardless of who came to power. "America respects the right of all peaceful and law-abiding voices to be heard around the world, even if we disagree with them," Obama said.[4] To underscore that principle, the Obama administration reportedly coerced the Egyptian government, led by dictator and American ally General Hosni Mubarak, to invite members of the Muslim Brotherhood—the ideologically Islamist group that routinely works with terrorists around the Middle East—to the speech. "I can tell you that invitations have gone out to the full range of actors in Egyptian political society," said Obama adviser Denis McDonough.[5] Middle Eastern news networks reported that the administration actually told the Egyptian government that at least ten Muslim Brotherhood members had to be sitting in the audience for Obama's rigmarole.[6]

Obama's commitment to hitting the reset button with the Muslim world was accompanied by signals of American pullback from strategic alliances. Because he ran as an antiwar candidate, Obama now engaged in a precipitous pullout from Iraq that allowed the Iranian regime to fill the gap. He began making overtures to the Taliban in Afghanistan. "If you talk to Gen. [David] Petraeus, I think he would argue that part of the success in Iraq involved reaching out to people that we would consider to be Islamic fundamentalists, but who were willing to work with us because they had been completely alienated by the tactics of al Qaeda in Iraq," Obama said in March 2009 to the New York Times. "There may be some comparable opportunities in Afghanistan and Pakistan."[7]

When protests broke out in Iran in June 2009 over election fraud in the reelection of President Mahmoud Ahmadinejad, resulting in a mass crackdown allegedly including murder and rape, President Obama remained silent for several days before announcing that it was "up to Iranians to make decisions about who Iran's leaders will be," then stated that he believed that the Iranian government would "look into irregularities that have taken place." Obama added that he was still seeking diplomacy with Iran. Even ten days later, Obama was still repeating that the United States had not decided on a real strategy for dealing with the protests in Iran.[8] The United States had spent much of the Bush administration funneling money to antiregime groups in Iran. Obama undercut those groups.

Obama's strategy of leading from behind while spouting platitudes about democracy culminated in the so-called Arab Spring—a massive Islamist uprising resulting in the overthrow of several pro-American regimes in favor of popular Islamist ones. The Islamist Winter led off with a self-immolation by a fruit vendor in Tunisia, which culminated in an uprising resulting in the ouster of dictator and American ally President Zine El Abidine Ben Ali in January 2011. The United States had provided Ben Ali some $347 million in aid since his rise to power in 1987. Ali had imposed stability and market reforms, despite his repressive regime.[9]

Initially, the United States said nothing about the protests in Tunisia, with Hillary Clinton announcing just three days before Ben Ali's ouster, "We are not taking sides, but we are saying we hope that there can be a peaceful resolution."[10] Behind the scenes, though, the United States was signaling that Ben Ali should go. Internal U.S. government documents regarding Ben Ali had been released by WikiLeaks, and they showed that America wasn't keen on its erstwhile ally. Recognizing the signals, the Tunisian revolutionaries seized their moment.

The left reacted to the news as though Ben Ali's deposing were an unfettered good. Christopher Alexander of *Foreign Policy* wrote, "Once it became clear that the Islamists no longer posed a serious threat, many Tunisians became less willing to accept the government's heavy-handedness."[11] Now the Obama administration responded with sunny optimism; Obama released a statement explaining that Americans "applaud the courage and dignity of the Tunisian people" and called for the new authorities "to respect human rights, and to hold free and fair elections in the near future that reflect the true will and aspirations of the Tunisian people."[12]

Tunisia promptly elected an Islamist government led by the Ennahda Party, which had been banned by Ben Ali. Islamists began assassinating opposition leaders.[13]

The Arab Spring was under way.

A similar scenario played itself out in Egypt, where protests against longtime American ally Mubarak ended in the United States supporting his ouster. After initially doing nothing to support the protesters—Hillary simply called for restraint from "all parties," and actually called the Egyptian government "stable," saying it was "looking for ways to respond to the legitimate needs and interests of the Egyptian people"[14]—the United States ended up joyfully celebrating Mubarak's resignation. Ignoring the rise of the Islamist role in the opposition, the rapes in Tahrir Square, the hints at repressions of Christians, Obama began applauding. "There are very few moments in our lives where we have the privilege to witness history taking place," Obama cheered. "This is one of those moments; this is one of those times. The people of Egypt have spoken. Their voices have been heard and Egypt will never be the same. By stepping down, President Mubarak responded to the Egyptian people's hunger for change."[15]

Mubarak's government was quickly replaced with an elected Islamist government under the oversight of Muslim Brotherhood president Mohammed Morsi, a terrorist supporter and ally. Later, certain reports would link Morsi and the Muslim Brotherhood directly to the attacks in Benghazi.[16]

The Obama administration was finally getting the hang of this thing. And so they helped bring the Islamist traveling road show to Syria, where thug Iranian ally Bashar Assad was in power. Up until the Syrian civil war broke out, the Obama administration had done its best to prop up Assad. Hillary Clinton appeared on national television on March 27, 2011, explaining, "There's a different leader in Syria now. Many of the members of Congress of both parties who have gone to Syria in recent months have said they believe he's a reformer." Two days later, she reversed course, stating, "I referenced opinions of others. That was not speaking either for myself or for the administration."[17]

The United States began debating the wisdom of arming the opposition to Assad. Ignoring all the evidence that the Syrian opposition was heavily in league with al-Qaeda, the United States eventually jumped in with one foot, deciding to arm the rebels. And as later events would show, one of the key links in the arms chain to Syria was in Benghazi—in violation of the Arms Control Export Act, and the Espionage Act.

"WE CAME, WE SAW, HE DIED"

If the Obama administration was willing to let allied dictators like Ben Ali and Mubarak fall on behalf of Islamists around the Middle East, it had no qualms about the uprising in Libya against neutered dictator Muammar Qaddafi. After the United States' invasions of Afghanistan and Iraq, Qaddafi—a man with a history of ties to terrorism, including the Lockerbie bombing in 1988, and who had been bombed by the Reagan administration—decided to abandon his pursuit of nuclear weapons. He also renounced support for terrorism.[18]

In February 2011, an uprising against Qaddafi began. Qaddafi cracked down violently, using snipers and helicopter gunships, prompting British prime minister David Cameron to condemn his actions as "appalling and unacceptable." President Obama waited eight days to say that the violence was outrageous—at which point the United States jumped into the fray with both feet. On February 26, the United Nations imposed sanctions on Qaddafi, and on March 17, voted to authorize a no-fly zone against Qaddafi's air force. The rebels began gaining ground steadily, until on September 20, Obama called for Qaddafi's forces to surrender, and announced the return of a U.S. ambassador to Tripoli.[19]

On October 9, 2011, Hillary visited Tripoli, where she pledged millions to the Libyan opposition. She told the leaders of the National Transitional Council, "I am proud to stand here on the soil of a free Libya. The United States was proud to stand for you in your fight for freedom and we will continue to stand with you as you continue this journey. This is Libya's moment. This is Libya's victory and the future belongs to you."

Two days later, as video broke across the Internet of Qaddafi being sodomized with a knife and then murdered, and written reports hit the Web, Clinton was caught on camera reacting: "Wow!" Later, Hillary appeared laughing hysterically on camera, her thumbs up, crowing, "We came, we saw, he died!" The reporter questioning her laughed along with her.[20]

Hillary missed a step. The truth was far more sinister than her triumphalist guffawing. America came. We saw. We gave arms to the rebels. Qaddafi died. Then, so did four Americans in Benghazi.

It was all fun and games for Hillary, appearing on national television to chortle over Qaddafi's demise. But the same actions taken by the Obama administration that resulted in one dead dictator would lead to the deaths of four Americans in Libya, and the deaths of thousands more around the Middle East. For while Qaddafi's death was undoubtedly good news for the world, those who had opposed him were openly associated with al-Qaeda. And the Obama administration ensured they were armed.

In late February 2011, Al Qaeda in the Islamic Maghreb (AQIM) released a statement: "We declare our support for the legitimate demands of the Libyan revolution. We assert to our people in Libya that we are with you and will not let you down, God willing. We will give everything we have to support you, with God's grace."[21]

The Libyan rebel leader Abdel-Hakim al-Hasidi told Italian newspaper *Il Sole 24 Ore* that some members of the core of his jihadist movement sprang from those who had fought American troops in Iraq. His soldiers, he claimed, were "patriots and good Muslims, not terrorists," but he also stated that "members of al-Qaeda are also good Muslims and are fighting against the invader." Al-Hasidi said he had fought Americans in Afghanistan, then was captured in Pakistan, handed over to the United States, and held in Libya until his release in 2008. The United States said that al-Hasidi was a member of the Libyan Islamic Fighting Group (LIFG), which is a group cooperative with al-Qaeda.[22] Admiral James Stavridis, NATO supreme commander for Europe, said, "We have seen flickers in the intelligence of potential al Qaeda, Hezbollah." Former CIA officer Bruce Riedel said, "There is no question that al Qaeda's Libyan franchise, Libyan Islamic Fighting Group, is a part of the opposition. It has always been Qaddafi's biggest enemy and its stronghold is Benghazi."[23]

The rebel leader Abdel Hakim Belhadj, who would eventually become commander of security in the Libyan capitol of Tripoli, was captured by the CIA and given to Qaddafi in 2004. He admitted to *Time* that he "was a member of the Islamic Fighting Group"—in other words, a jihadist, although he denied that he was a member of al-Qaeda.[24] Other reports suggested that Belhadj was lying—he was the "emir" of the LIFG, and reportedly became close to al-Qaeda leader Abu Mussab al-Zarqawi. Overall, LIFG members became security leaders in virtually all major Libyan cities, including Tripoli, Benghazi, and Derna.[25]

While the Obama administration was reaching out to Libyan rebel groups and al-Qaeda affiliates across the Middle East in an attempt to move beyond the Bush presidency, the al-Qaeda-affiliated groups were happy to take the West's help in ousting Qaddafi in order to consolidate power, weapons, and cash for that war. In essence, the Obama administration began arming America's enemies in order to get rid of repressive regimes that had historically quashed those enemies.

Many in Congress opposed action on behalf of the Libyan rebels. Obama never bothered to get authorization at all. Democratic representative Jerrold Nadler of New York said, "Briefing Congress is not the same as authorization. Briefing is nice, but authorization is required under law." Representative Greg Walden (R-OR) added, "I can't think of a time in our nation's history where we put our men and women in combat like this without an administration of either party coming to Congress first." But the Obama administration didn't really care. Representative Geoff Davis (R-KY) said, "The implication was very strong that they saw no need for any authorization at any time regardless of how long this were to continue."[26]

Even President Obama himself, when he was a U.S. senator, opposed attacking foreign forces without congressional authorization: "The President does not have power under the Constitution to unilaterally authorize a military attack in a situation that does not involve stopping an actual or imminent threat to the nation."[27] Libya was no such threat, of course. Congress declared as much when, after sixty days, a bipartisan resolution passed with three-quarters of the House of Representatives condemning Obama for not even bothering to ask for authorization for his action, in direct contravention of the War Powers Act.[28]

Probably thanks to the public's tepid original approval of the Libyan action—tepid approval that turned to heavy disapproval over time[29]—the Obama administration never got specific about defining its public position on arming the Libyan rebels. In testimony before Congress, Secretary of Defense Robert Gates said that the United States would provide communications, surveillance, and nonlethal support to the rebels, but would allow other countries to ship such weapons in. Even that position was arguably illegal under international law, according to NATO secretary general Anders Fogh Rasmussen, who told reporters that he believed the UN resolution authorizing an air campaign to help the rebels did not allow weapons shipments directly to the Libyan rebels.[30]

But behind closed doors, the administration prepared to act alone. On March 30, 2011, ABC News reported that President Obama had secretly signed a presidential finding to send covert aid to the al-Qaeda-linked rebels. This would be a violation of the Arms Export Control Act (22 U.S. Code § 2780), which specifically prohibits supporting terrorists. Those provisions are waivable by the president, but President Obama did no such thing at the time. He waited until 2013 to do so, and even then, he did so with regard to Syria, not Libyan rebels.[31]

The same day as the ABC News report, the *Washington Post* announced that Obama's secret finding included an authorization to the CIA "to carry out a clandestine effort to provide arms and other support to Libyan opposition groups." The authorization came in spite of the fact that the Obama administration was still busily sending "teams of CIA operatives into Libya" to find out who exactly the rebels were.[32]

The White House insisted that such aid was not lethal—"no decision has been made about providing arms to the opposition or to any group in Libya," said the White House press office. "We're not ruling it out or ruling it in. We're assessing and reviewing options for all types of assistance that we could provide to the Libyan people." Meanwhile, Obama himself told ABC News' Diane Sawyer that he would not rule out providing arms to the al-Qaeda-linked rebels. Hillary was more cautious: "We don't know as much as we would like to know and as much as we expect we will know."[33]

Those cautions didn't last long. Not only did the United States allow arming of Libyan rebels from abroad, but the Obama administration tasked the CIA with ways of helping to accomplish that goal. If performed without congressional approval, such covert actions amounted to violations of the so-called covert action statute (50 U.S. Code § 413b).

Libyan terrorist groups began receiving arms shipments and money via Qatar. The Obama administration approved such operations. That was due to the administration's unwillingness to get too involved directly with the Libyan uprising—they recognized that they had no domestic support for such involvement, and instead attempted to find a backdoor way to support Libyan terrorist groups. So the United States green-lit a gunrunning operation via Qatar to those groups. One of the people looking to arm the Libyan terrorists was an American arms dealer in communication with one of the men who would be killed in Benghazi.

His name was Marc Turi, and he was an arms merchant who lives in Arizona and Abu Dhabi in the United Arab Emirates. In March 2011, he emailed then-special representative to the Libyan rebel alliance Chris Stevens, applying to help smuggle weapons. Stevens said he would pass the request up the chain. That application was originally turned down because it openly specified desire to ship weapons into Libya. A few months later, he applied again, this time saying he wanted to ship weapons via Qatar. This request was approved. Turi told the *New York Times* that his only job was to get the weapons to Qatar; what "the U.S. government and Qatar allowed from there was between them." A few months after the United States okayed Turi's gun dealing, the Department of Homeland Security raided his home.[34]

The United States' policy of winding down the war on terrorism played right into the hands of such terrorists. Take, for example, the case of Sufyan Ben Qumu. Qumu drove a tank in the Libyan army, spent time in prison in that country, and was a known drug addict; he fled Libya in favor of Egypt before heading to Afghanistan and joining Osama bin Laden's al-Qaeda. Then he moved on up to the Taliban before being captured in Pakistan and sent to the United States, which imprisoned him at the U.S. naval base at Guantanamo Bay, Cuba. At the time, he was considered a "medium to high risk . . . likely to pose a threat to the United States, its interests and allies." In 2007, the Bush administration sent Qumu back to Libya to be handled by Qaddafi, on the condition that Libya and the United States could find a "satisfactory agreement . . . that allows access to detainee and/or access to exploited intelligence." In 2008, Qumu was released as the Qaddafi regime attempted to parley with the burgeoning rebellion.

All of that was on Bush. But it was President Obama who turned Qumu from enemy of the United States into, as the *New York Times* put it, an "ally of sorts." What changed? The "remarkable turnabout," the *Times* stated, "result[ed] from shifting American policies rather than any obvious change in Mr. Qumu." Qumu led the Darnah Brigade, which received support from NATO. The *Times* quoted unnamed Western observers as stating that Qumu wasn't much of a threat: "We're more worried about Al Qaeda infiltration from outside than the indigenous ones. . . . Most of them have a local agenda so they don't present as much of a threat to the West."[35] Giving guns to those folks, the Obama administration believed, wasn't a problem. Legally, of course, it was: it was a violation of the Espionage Act, given that we were *literally handing guns to terrorists without congressional approval.* On September 19, 2012, Bret Baier of Fox News reported that intelligence sources believed that one Sufyan Ben Qumu had masterminded the attack on the compound in Benghazi—the same Qumu the United States had released from Guantanamo Bay, then helped attain weapons.[36]

PUTTING GUNS IN THE HANDS OF "SOME VERY UGLY PEOPLE"

There was more involved than the United States merely green-lighting other countries' shipping weapons into Libya to Islamist terrorists. The United States played a direct role in arming such enemies of America. And that role continued long after Qaddafi's fall, as the United States worked to arm al-Qaeda-linked rebels in Syria.

The U.S. operation in Benghazi was apparently crucial to American gunrunning into Syria. In January 2013, Senator Rand Paul (R-KY) asked Secretary of State Hillary Clinton whether she had any knowledge of a CIA gunrunning operation in Benghazi. She responded, "You'll have to direct that question to the agency that ran the annex," claiming not to know whether such an operation had in fact been in place.[37]

But according to Joe diGenova, attorney for one of the whistle-blowers in Benghazi, four hundred U.S. missiles were "diverted to Libya" just before the September 11, 2012, attacks; diGenova said that the missiles were stolen and fell into "the hands of some very ugly people." He said that the U.S. complex in Libya "was somehow involved in the distribution of those missiles," sourcing his information to a "former intelligence official who stayed in constant contact with people in the special ops and intelligence community." The British newspaper the *Telegraph* reported as well that thirty-five CIA operatives were in Benghazi working "on a project to supply missiles from Libyan armories to Syrian rebels."[38]

On September 14, 2012, three days after the attack on the Benghazi annex, the *Times of London* reported that a Libyan ship loaded with the single "largest consignment of weapons for Syria since the uprising began has docked in Turkey and most of its cargo is making its way to rebels on the front lines. Among more than 400 tonnes of cargo the vessel was carrying were SAM-7 surface-to-air anti-aircraft missiles and rocket-propelled grenades (RPGs), which Syrian sources said could be a game-changer for the rebels."[39]

All of this was allegedly part of a broader operation. In March 2013, the *New York Times* reported that the CIA had been shipping weapons to Syria for a year or more: "The airlift, which began on a small scale in early 2012 and continued intermittently through last fall, expanded into a steady and much heavier flow late last year, the data shows. It has grown to include more than 160 military cargo flights by Jordanian, Saudi, and Qatari military-style cargo planes landing at Esenboga Airport near Ankara, and, to a lesser degree, at other Turkish and Jordanian airports."[40] In June 2012, the *Times* reported that a coterie of CIA officers was working in southern Turkey, attempting to funnel weapons to particular groups. "The weapons," the *Times* reported, "including automatic rifles, rocket-propelled grenades, ammunition and some antitank weapons, are being funneled mostly across the Turkish border by way of a shadowy network of intermediaries including Syria's Muslim Brotherhood and paid for by Turkey, Saudi Arabia and Qatar, the officials said."

The White House continued to claim that all aid was "nonlethal."[41] Ben Swann of Full Disclosure did a one-on-one interview with President Obama. "You mentioned about al Qaeda in your speech," Swann asked. "Going after al Qaeda in Afghanistan, certainly going after them in Yemen as well. And yet there's some concern about the U.S. funding the Syrian opposition when there are a lot of reports about al Qaeda heading up that opposition. How do you justify the two?" Obama answered: "I shared that concern, so what we've done is said we will provide nonlethal assistance to Syrian opposition leadership that are committed to a political transition, are committed to an observance of human rights. We're not going to just dive in and get involved in a civil war that in fact involves . . . some folks who would over the long term do the United States harm."[42]

Obviously, that wasn't true.

Arms poured into Egypt, too. In August 2013, after a military coup ousted erstwhile Obama friend Muslim Brotherhood president Mohammed Morsi, the military reported on Muslim Brotherhood terrorist action . . . using U.S. weapons. Jihadists, the military reported, were using U.S. Hellfire missiles against government buildings in the Sinai Peninsula. Pictures showed an AGM-114F Hellfire missile with the label "U.S." on the side. "Reports of U.S.-made weapons turning up in the Sinai date back to at least January, when six U.S.-made missiles were found in a cache of weapons bound for Gaza," Fox News reported. Just a few months earlier, Fox News reported that "weapons left over from the revolution in Libya were being sold at clandestine auctions in the Sinai Peninsula."[43]

Where did all these weapons end up? With virtually every major affiliate of al-Qaeda in the Arabian Peninsula. The *Times* reported that the administration never could determine where all the weapons from the various programs had gone, although "[s]ome of the arms since have been moved from Libya to militants with ties to Al Qaeda in Mali, where radical jihadi factions have imposed Shariah law in the northern part of the country, the former Defense Department official said. Others have gone to Syria, according to several American and foreign officials and arms traders."[44] As early as March 2011, al-Qaeda, according to the president of Chad, Idriss Déby Itno, had been raiding weapons in the Libyan rebel areas for their own use internationally.[45] Hillary admitted as much in her final Senate testimony before leaving as secretary of state: She blamed Libya's liberated storehouses of weapons for the gun smuggling that had become so common. "Libya was awash in weapons before the revolution," she said.[46] But not quite as awash as after the United States government began violating its own law in order to arm those Libyans.

"THE TALIBAN IS ON THE INSIDE OF THE BUILDING"

The attempt to minimize American involvement in arms smuggling in Libya rested on the secrecy of the mission in Benghazi.

The U.S. operation in Benghazi apparently rested on the CIA gunrunning operation. While initial reports suggested that there was a "consulate" in Benghazi, there was no official consulate—there was merely the CIA annex that was allegedly funneling weapons to the Libyan terrorists. According to reporter Aaron Klein, the U.S. diplomatic mission "actually served as a meeting place to coordinate aid for the rebel-led insurgencies in the Middle East, according to Middle Eastern security officials." Both President Obama and Secretary of State Clinton called the Benghazi complex a "mission." As Klein points out, diplomatic missions, unlike consulates, are given a wide variety of responsibilities unrelated to immigration issues. The State Department website did not list Benghazi as a location for a consulate.[47] Klein also reports that Ambassador Chris Stevens, who headed up the mission, was an integral spoke in the gunrunning wheel. "Stevens served as a key contact with the Saudis to coordinate the recruitment by Saudi Arabia of Islamic fighters from North Africa and Libya. The jihadists were sent to Syria via Turkey to attack Assad's forces, said the security officials," Klein wrote.[48]

Such a gunrunning operation would necessitate high security. After all, funneling thousands of weapons through a heavily terrorist area would seem to require a few guns of your own to protect those shipments. In the months leading up to September 2012, the *New York Times* reported, "the Obama administration clearly was worried about the consequences of its hidden hand in helping arm Libyan militants." Within weeks, the United States was receiving reports of arms going to out-and-out terrorist groups. The administration never figured out where within the country the weapons, which included machine guns, automatic rifles, and ammunition, went. This supposedly provoked consternation within the administration.[49] But it did not provoke more security for the Benghazi complex.

It should have. As early as July 2011, Britain's *Sunday Telegraph* reported that Benghazi's security situation was controlled by Islamist terrorists—specifically, the Abu Obeida al-Jarrah Brigade, an element of the anti-Qaddafi forces. Abu Obeida was even responsible for killing General Abdel Fattah Younes, one of the leaders of the Libyan opposition who had switched sides from the Qaddafi regime. That assassination came the day after France, the United States, and Britain decided to endorse the Libyan opposition as the legitimate government of Libya. "Unlike the other militias, the Brigade seems to exercise considerable power within the rebel movement," the *Telegraph* reported. "[I]t has emerged that the group was in charge of internal security in Benghazi, essentially operating as a secret police force."[50] That's right—Islamist terrorists ran the *security forces* in Benghazi.

Those who were in Benghazi understood the threat. According to Eric Nordstrom, former regional security officer at the U.S. embassy in Libya, in the full year before September 11, there were fifty violent incidents against American targets in Benghazi alone.[51] On May 22, 2012, terrorists launched a rocket-propelled grenade at the Red Cross building; the Red Cross abandoned Benghazi in July. On June 6, terrorists hit U.S. facilities in Benghazi with an improvised explosive device.[52] On June 11, a convoy carrying the British ambassador was attacked in Benghazi. The British abandoned Benghazi, leaving their weapons in the charge of the U.S. mission. The weapons went missing. "We are working with the U.S. to establish what, if anything, has happened to this equipment," said a Foreign Office spokesman.[53] In August, there were attacks on Benghazi military intelligence offices. On August 10, a Libyan army general was assassinated. On August 20, terrorists bombed a car belonging to an Egyptian diplomat.[54] Even the United Nations abandoned Benghazi. Lieutenant Colonel Andrew Wood, who handled U.S. military supplementation of diplomatic security, recommended a pullout from Benghazi. "It was apparent to me," he said, "that we were the last [Western] flag flying in Benghazi. We were the last thing on their target list to remove from Benghazi."[55]

But the Obama administration was deeply fearful of offending the locals, especially given the administration's newfound willingness to work with al-Qaeda across the Middle East. This was part and parcel of the administration's pusillanimous approach to the Arab Spring: in building a new coterie of supposed Islamist allies, the United States could not afford to offend. The principle of nonoffense was the rationale behind the Obama administration's befuddling and sickening decision to leave American personnel in Benghazi virtually unprotected.

And so security at the mission was disastrous. Nordstrom told Congress that the State Department had hired Libyan militia members to provide security—they called themselves the "17th of February Martyrs Brigade." That group is al-Qaeda sympathetic, and for months before September 11, 2012, carried the al-Qaeda black flag on its website. As Newsmax reported, "Several entries on the militia's Facebook page openly profess sympathy for Ansar al-Sharia, the hardline Islamist extremist group widely blamed for the deadly attack on the mission. . . . Just a few days before Stevens arrived in Benghazi, the Martyrs Brigade informed State Department officials they no longer would provide security as members of the mission, including Stevens, traveled through the city."[56]

In the spring of 2012, Nordstrom stated, "we saw and noted an increasing number of attacks and incidents targeting foreign affiliated organizations." Nonetheless, "because of Libyan political sensitivities, armed private security companies were not allowed to operate in Libya. Therefore, our existing, uniformed static local guard force, both in Tripoli and Benghazi were unarmed. . . ."[57] Unarmed guards in the middle of Benghazi, a terrorist haven, thanks to politically correct concerns about Libyan sensitivities.

In his written testimony, Nordstrom expressed confidence in the security plan. But in his spoken testimony, Nordstrom told Congress that security was "inappropriately low" and said that he, along with Lieutenant Colonel Andrew Wood, was worried about the flow of terrorists into Benghazi. Nordstrom worried, too, that he didn't think he could rely on the "17th of February Martyrs Brigade." They weren't experienced and hadn't been paid in months. According to Nordstrom, he had "no idea if they would respond to an attack."[58]

Documents released by the State Department show repeated requests for more security. On November 30, 2011, Nordstrom wrote to Deputy Chief of Mission Joan Polaschik and State Department staffer G. Kathleen Hill, complaining about the security dropping precipitously in Benghazi. "Is there a plan for a closure of operations in Benghazi or will we be at this level for some time? If we have such a small footprint, we could really utilize the armored vehicles that are there," Nordstrom wrote. Hill wrote back, irked at Nordstrom: "This came up in conversations with Chris Stevens as well. . . . The plan for Benghazi staffing calls for 3 State (PO, IM/Mgmt reporting officer) plus DS (3–5) plus 1–2 TDYs (temporary staffers) at any given time. With that how many cars does Benghazi need?" On February 11, 2012, Shawn P. Crowley, a foreign service officer at the U.S. mission in Benghazi, wrote, "Apologies for being a broken record, but beginning tomorrow Benghazi will be down to two agents. . . . We have no drivers and new local guard contract employees have no experience driving armored vehicles. . . ."

On February 12, 2012, Nordstrom wrote to James Bacigalupo, regional director of the Diplomatic Security Service, expressing frustration that he couldn't get more security personnel in Benghazi: "I've been placed in a very difficult spot when the Ambassador tells me that I need to support Benghazi but can't direct [Mobile Security Detachment, specially trained to operate in high threat environments] there and been advised that [Diplomatic Security Service, DSS] isn't going to provide more than 3 DS agents over the long term."[59]

Despite Nordstrom's worries, and the worries of then-ambassador Gene Cretz, Hillary Clinton personally signed a cable in April 2012 approving a drawdown of security assets in Benghazi. Clinton actually asked for a "joint reassessment of the number of DS agents requested from Benghazi"—in other words, Clinton wanted the numbers to drop even *more*. In May 2012, when Stevens replaced Cretz, he asked for more security, too. The State Department replied that such a request could not be fulfilled.

On June 25, 2012, Ambassador Stevens wrote a cable explaining that rising attacks in Benghazi "were the work of extremists who are opposed to western influence in Libya. A number of local contacts agreed, noting that Islamic extremism appears to be on the rise in eastern Libya and that the Al-Qaeda flag has been spotted several times flying over government buildings and training facilities in Derna." The Libyan hesitance to okay a security presence in Benghazi, Stevens wrote in another cable, "has created the security vacuum that a diverse group of independent actors are exploiting for their own purposes."[60]

In July 2012, Nordstrom told the diplomatic security (DS) officials in Washington that he wanted to submit a request for an extension of the security teams. Charlene Lamb, deputy assistant secretary for diplomatic security, however, was "reluctant to ask for an SST [Security Support Team] extension, apparently out of concern that it would be embarrassing to the [State Department] to continue to have to rely on [Defense Department] assets to protect our Mission." Lamb shot back, "NO, I do not [I repeat] not want them to ask for the MSD [Mobile Security Deployment] team to stay!"

On July 9, 2012, Stevens asked for more security. Undersecretary Patrick Kennedy rejected the request.[61]

On August 16, 2012, Stevens signed a cable and sent it to the State Department. It explained that the Benghazi mission could not stop a "coordinated attack."[62]

On September 11, 2012, the day of the attacks, Stevens wrote a cable describing how commander Fawzi Younis, acting principal officer of the Supreme Security Council in Benghazi, had "expressed growing frustration with police and security forces (who were too weak to keep the country secure). . . ."[63] Overall, Stevens asked the State Department for more security four times.[64] Apparently, Stevens asked the Libyans for more security, too. He didn't get it.[65] His diary, found four days after the attack, reportedly demonstrated his worries about security in Benghazi.[66] After the attack, journalists from *Foreign Policy* found documents lying on the floor of the consulate. One was a letter from September 11, 2012, informing Mohamed Obeidi, head of the Libyan Ministry of Foreign Affairs in Benghazi, of the deteriorating security situation (apparently Stevens wanted the Libyans to provide more security, as the State Department hadn't): "Finally, early this morning at 0643, September 11, 2012, one of our diligent guards made a troubling report. Near our main gate, a member of the police force was seen in the upper level of a building across from our compound. It is reported that this person was photographing the inside of the U.S. special mission and furthermore that this person was part of the police unit sent to protect the mission. The police car stationed where this event occurred was number 322."[67]

Nordstrom testified before the House Oversight and Government Reform Committee about his frustration with lack of security and reliance on local security. Relating a conversation with another State Department staffer, Nordstrom said, "I said, 'Jim, you know what [is] most frustrating about this assignment? It's not the hardship, it's not the gunfire, it's not the threats. It's dealing and fighting against the people, programs, and personnel who are supposed to be supporting me. . . . For me, the Taliban is on the inside of the building."[68]

Representatives Darrell Issa (R-CA) and Jason Chaffetz (R-UT), both leaders on the House Oversight Committee, said that they had been told that the Obama administration did not just reject requests for extra security, but "systematically decreased existing security to dangerous and ineffective levels . . . to effectuate a policy of 'normalization' in Libya after the conclusion of its civil war."[69] This was reckless disregard for human life, an element of involuntary manslaughter. And the manslaughter followed.

THE ATTACK

September 11, 2012, marked the eleventh anniversary of the September 11 attacks that toppled the World Trade Center towers, tore a gaping hole in the Pentagon, and ended some three thousand American lives. American embassies throughout the New Obama Middle East came under attack.

While the United States mourned, al-Qaeda acted. On September 10, al-Qaeda released a video of leader Ayman al-Zawahiri calling for revenge against America for the drone strike on jihadist Abu Yahya al-Libi. The next day, in Egypt, Mohammed al-Zawahiri, younger brother of Zawahiri, helped organize protests at the American embassy in Cairo; the Egyptians, thoroughly infiltrated by al-Qaeda, stormed the walls. "Obama! Obama! We are all Osama!" they chanted. In Yemen, on September 13, al-Qaeda fighters stormed the U.S. embassy after Sheikh Abdul Majeed al-Zindani called for action. In Tunisia, on September 14, al-Qaeda terrorist Seifallah ben Hassine led an assault on the U.S. embassy, storming it and raising the black al-Qaeda flag on top.[70]

The *Wall Street Journal*, however, reported that the protests weren't based on pure terrorism, but on Muslim rage over a ridiculous YouTube video titled "Innocence of Muslims," which had already been up on the Internet for months, and which had received virtually no attention. The video portrayed the Prophet Muhammad as a homosexual engaging in slavery and extramarital sex. Pastor Terry Jones in Florida, who famously burned the Koran on several occasions, said that he would screen the film on September 11.

This prompted apologetics from the State Department for the First Amendment. "The United States deplores any intentional effort to denigrate the religious beliefs of others," Hillary Clinton said, adding, "But let me be clear: There is never any justification for violent acts of this kind."[71] Meanwhile, in Egypt, the U.S. embassy began signaling its own sorrow over "Innocence of Muslims." "The Embassy of the United States in Cairo condemns the continuing efforts by misguided individuals to hurt the religious feelings of Muslims—as we condemn efforts to offend believers of all religions," the embassy said in a statement on September 11. "Respect for religious beliefs is a cornerstone of American democracy. We firmly reject the actions by those who abuse the universal right of free speech to hurt the religious beliefs of others."[72]

The odd focus on a bad trailer for a never-produced Muhammad movie would become the sole basis for an enormous cover-up by the Obama administration.

Meanwhile, Ambassador Chris Stevens was visiting Benghazi. Stevens, who became ambassador to Libya in May 2012, had come to

Benghazi on September 10, 2012, for vague reasons—supposedly to connect with contacts. According to the House Oversight Committee, Stevens could also have been visiting to assess the security situation. On September 11, twenty-eight U.S. personnel were present at the mission and at the annex.

That night, Stevens met with the Turkish consul general Ali Sait Akin. He escorted him from the building at approximately 8:35 p.m. It is worth noting again that just three days later, the single biggest shipment of weapons from Libya designated for Syria arrived in Turkey.[73]

Less than an hour later, armed terrorists breached the front gate of the mission, setting the guard house and diplomatic building on fire. These were members of Ansar al-Sharia and al-Qaeda—the presence of whom the United States government was well aware. A State Department officer at the mission notified the CIA annex nearby, the Tripoli embassy, and the State Department headquarters of the assault.

During the attack, Stevens, Information Officer Sean Smith, and a diplomatic security agent were in the main mission building; within twenty minutes, Stevens, Smith, and the DS agent had been incapacitated by smoke inhalation. They tried to escape by crawling to a window. The DS agent crawled out the window, but realized he'd lost Stevens and Smith. Under heavy fire, he went into the building over and over again searching for them. He also used his radio to request help, which came in the form of security officers from elsewhere in the complex.[74]

According to Fox News, former Navy SEAL Tyrone Woods was at the CIA annex when he heard the violence break out at the mission, which was about a mile away. He and others told their superiors and asked for permission to help. They were reportedly told to "stand down" twice. Eventually, Woods and others ignored the orders and headed over to the mission.[75]

By 10:05 p.m., the CIA team including Woods had left for the mission. The team faced down gunfire and RPG attack while trying to find Stevens and Smith. They found Smith's body, but couldn't find Stevens. At 11:15 p.m., they began an evacuation of the remaining staff.

The higher-ups at the American government had to know what was going on at this point. At 10:32 p.m., an officer at the Pentagon's

National Military Command Center relayed a message to Secretary of Defense Leon Panetta and the Chairman of the Joint Chiefs of Staff General Martin Dempsey. At 11:00 p.m., Panetta and Dempsey met with President Obama.[76]

By 11:10, Defense Department drones were monitoring the situation from overhead.[77] According to CBS News, Defense Department officials considered sending in troops to help save the Benghazi survivors, but ultimately decided not to; thanks to the drones, U.S. military officials could watch the attack in real-time.[78]

At midnight, the CIA team reportedly returned to the CIA annex and called for more military support because they were taking fire there, too. Fox News reported, "The request was denied. There were no communications problems at the annex, according to those present at the compound. The team was in constant radio contact with their headquarters. In fact, at least one member of the team was on the roof of the annex manning a heavy machine gun when mortars were fired at the CIA compound. The security officer had a laser on the target that was firing and repeatedly requested back-up support from a Spectre gunship, which is commonly used by U.S. Special Operations forces to provide support to Special Operations teams on the ground involved in intense firefights." The CIA denied Fox News's report.[79]

Meanwhile, the State Department was considering whether to send the so-called Foreign Emergency Support Team to Benghazi. FEST, known as "the U.S. Government's only interagency, on-call, short-notice team poised to respond to terrorist incidents worldwide," was ready to go. According to officials, Hillary's deputy, Patrick Kennedy—the same man who had rejected additional security requests in August—said no. FEST was already "packing" to leave when they were "told they were not deploying by Patrick Kennedy's front office. . . . In hindsight . . . I probably would've pushed the button," the official told CBS News. The National Security Council also failed to convene the Counterterrorism Security Group (CSG) to discuss the situation—the CSG likely would have recommended sending FEST. But NSC spokesman Tommy Vietor said that the CSG was unnecessary because "[f]rom the moment [President Obama] was briefed on the Benghazi attack, the response effort was handled by the most senior national security officials in government. Members of the CSG were of course involved in these meetings and discussions to support their bosses."[80]

At 12:30 a.m., seven U.S. personnel—six security personnel and a translator—departed Tripoli, arriving in Benghazi at 1:30 a.m. By this point, Panetta was back at the Pentagon meeting with Dempsey and General Carter F. Ham, commander of U.S. Africa Command (AFRICOM), the branch responsible for military activities in Libya. Panetta then ordered deployment of two Marine Corps Fleet Antiterrorism Security Team (FAST) platoons from Rota, Spain, to Benghazi; a U.S. European Command (EUCOM) Combatant Commander's in-Extremis Force (CIF) to a staging base in southern Europe, within flight distance of Libya; and a special ops force to a staging base in southern Europe. Only at 2:53 a.m. did the special ops force receive authorization to deploy.

At 5:15 a.m., the seven-man team arrived at the annex, at which point terrorists opened fire with mortars, killing Navy SEALs Woods and Glenn Doherty, and wounding two other Americans. At 6:05 a.m., thirty-one survivors were evacuated.[81]

During this entire time, President Obama and Secretary of State Clinton were virtually absent. Neither has spelled out their activities that night. Secretary of Defense Leon Panetta admitted that the president met with him and Dempsey once for half an hour that night, then never checked in the rest of the night.[82] Deputy Chief of Mission in Libya Greg Hicks—the man who became the top State Department official in Libya the moment Stevens was killed—testified that he spoke with Clinton directly at 2 a.m. Benghazi time. He told her about the terrorist attack, and was concerned that Stevens might be in terrorist custody, necessitating a rescue operation. Hicks didn't yet know that Stevens was dead. At no point was a YouTube video mentioned. That was the last time Hicks spoke with Clinton. She never called him back.[83] There is likely a tape of the 2 a.m. call between Hicks and Clinton. It has not been released.

The immediate aftermath of the attack in Benghazi turned to bureaucratic infighting. Defense secretary Panetta blamed the State Department and said that President Obama had ordered that "all available DOD assets" be made available for protection of personnel on the ground. So why weren't the assets present? According to Panetta, the State Department never asked for them.[84] But Hicks testified that he requested that four Green Berets fly to Benghazi for additional protection. "People in Benghazi had been fighting all night," Hicks explained. "They were tired, exhausted. We wanted to make sure the airport was secure for their withdrawal." The team leader, Lieutenant Colonel Steve Gibson, called Special Operations Command Africa to tell them that his unit intended to head to Benghazi. Instead, he was told to remain in Tripoli. "Colonel Gibson and his three personnel were—were getting in the cars, he stopped. And he called them off and said—told me that he had not been authorized to go. The vehicles had to go because the flight needed to go to Tripoli—I mean, to Benghazi. Lieutenant Colonel Gibson was furious. I had told him to go bring our people home. That's what he wanted to do," Hicks testified.[85] The Defense Department claimed "there was nothing this team could have done to assist during the second attack in Benghazi."[86]

The fact that no military was deployed to the hot zone during the seven-hour attack was unthinkable. Military assets were just hours away in Italy. Nordstrom testified, "The ferocity and intensity of the attack was nothing that we had seen in Libya, or that I had seen in my time in the Diplomatic Security Service."[87] Yet aside from that one team from Tripoli, which included Glenn Doherty, there was no show of force from outside Benghazi. A special ops whistle-blower told Fox News that the military had a team ready to scramble from Croatia. That would have taken some four to six hours. The attack lasted for seven hours.[88]

THE YOUTUBE COVER-UP

So far, the Obama administration had committed violations of the Espionage Act and the Arms Control Export Act, and had participated in involuntary manslaughter. Now it was time for the cover-up, which would require witness intimidation, among other crimes.

In the aftermath of the death of four Americans, including the first ambassador killed since 1979, the Obama team knew that they had to cover up what had happened. After all, their leader was in the midst of a dogfight with Republican presidential nominee Mitt Romney—the two were neck and neck in the polls—and one of Obama's chief talking points was his supposed devastation of al-Qaeda around the globe. Between September 11, 2012, and November 1, 2012, Obama said some thirty-two times that al-Qaeda was "decimated" or "on the path to defeat." The day after the Benghazi attacks, on September 12, 2012, Obama appeared in Las Vegas at a campaign event, where he triumphantly announced, "A day after 9/11, we are reminded that a new tower rises about the New York skyline, but al Qaeda is on the path to defeat and bin Laden is dead."[89]

The need to downplay the events in Benghazi led the administration to a fateful decision: they would pretend that what had happened in Benghazi was not the result of American support for al-Qaeda affiliates throughout the Middle East; they would pretend that what had happened was unrelated to the administration's widespread gunrunning, and use of the Benghazi facility as a go-between for such operations; they would pretend that the Benghazi attacks were not the result of a cowardly foreign policy putting America in league with Islamists. Instead, the administration would play Benghazi as a sort of inexplicable black swan attack—the result of a crazy YouTube video. Then the administration would claim that the buck stopped with the White House, even while they shunted all blame aside.

Speaking in the Rose Garden on the day after the murders, Obama carefully parsed his language. "Since our founding, the United States has been a nation that respects all faiths. We reject all efforts to denigrate the religious beliefs of others. But there is absolutely no justification to this type of senseless violence. None," he solemnly intoned. The attack, he was implying, sprang from offensive language used in a YouTube video nobody had seen. Obama never used the word *terrorists* to describe those who had attacked the mission and annex. His only reference to terrorism came in a vague one-liner: "No acts of terror will ever shake the resolve of this great nation, alter that character, or eclipse the light of the values that we stand for."[90] He made clear later that night in an interview with CBS News' Steve Kroft that he was unwilling to call Benghazi specifically an act of terrorism—although CBS News didn't air that footage until nearly two months had passed.[91]

Hillary Clinton, meanwhile, issued a statement repeating the notion that a YouTube video had caused terrorists to murder four Americans. "Some have sought to justify this vicious behavior as a response to inflammatory material posted on the Internet. The United States deplores any intentional effort to denigrate the religious beliefs of others. Our commitment to religious tolerance goes back to the very beginning of our nation," the statement read. Hillary cut a video that was distributed in Pakistan condemning the YouTube video. It cost seventy thousand dollars to run on Pakistani television.[92] Two days after the attack, according to Representative Adam Kinzinger (R-IL), Hillary screamed at members of Congress who suggested that Benghazi had been a terrorist attack.[93]

When Mitt Romney had the temerity to rip the Obama administration's response—he called it "disgraceful" that the administration's "first response was not to condemn attacks on our diplomatic missions, but to sympathize with those who waged the attacks"—the media quickly pounced on him, suggesting that he was politicizing the event. All of this was part and parcel of the Obama campaign's effort to distract from the real issues at stake in Benghazi.[94]

The administration went whole hog in pushing the narrative that Benghazi had sprung from the YouTube video. At the event at Andrews Air Force Base greeting the bodies of the slain, Clinton approached Charles Woods, the father of murdered Navy SEAL Tyrone Woods. "She said we will make sure that the person who made that film is arrested and prosecuted," Woods describes.[95] Obama, said Woods, couldn't look him in the eye. On September 27, the YouTube filmmaker, Nakoula Basseley Nakoula, was arrested and labeled a "danger to the community."[96]

On the Sunday after the attacks, UN ambassador Susan Rice appeared on all five Sunday morning news shows in place of her unavailable boss, Hillary Clinton. It was one thing for Hillary to sit before the cameras to crow about Qaddafi; it was quite another for her to answer questions about Benghazi. Rice told ABC's *This Week*, "[O]ur current best assessment, based on the information that we have at present, is that, in fact, what this began as, it was a spontaneous—not a premeditated—response to what had transpired in Cairo . . . folks in Benghazi, a small number of people came to the embassy to—or to the consulate, rather, to replicate the sort of challenge that was posed in Cairo. And then as that unfolded, it seems to have been hijacked, let us say, by some individual clusters of extremists who came with heavier weapons, weapons that as you know in—in the wake of the revolution in Libya are—are quite common and accessible. And it then evolved from there." A spontaneous protest that appears in precisely zero of the cables or phone calls from Benghazi suddenly became the source of the terrorist assault.[97] Rice repeated this language on CBS's *Face the Nation, Fox News Sunday,* NBC's *Meet the Press,* and CNN's *State of the Union.*[98]

There was only one big problem for the Obama administration: it was obvious to everyone with half a brain that the terrorist attacks in Benghazi had nothing to do with a YouTube video. Almost immediately, reports began surfacing that there was no spontaneous demonstration, and that this had been a precalibrated terrorist action. So how did Rice end up on television as the mouthpiece for such lies?

The administration manipulated the talking points handed to Rice. More specifically, Hillary Clinton's State Department changed the talking points. The talking points went through twelve revisions; one version, which contained CIA warnings about mission insecurity, so upset State Department spokeswoman Victoria Nuland that she emailed back that the warnings "could be used by Members [of Congress] to beat the State Department for not paying attention to Agency warnings so why do we want to feed that? Concerned . . ." After another round of changes, Nuland wrote, "These don't resolve all my issues or those of my building leadership." Assistant Secretary of State for Legislative Affairs David S. Adams agreed with Nuland: "That last bullet especially will read to members [of Congress] like we had been repeatedly warned."

All twelve versions of the talking points said that the Benghazi attacks were "spontaneously inspired by protest in Cairo"—that language came from the CIA, the same entity allegedly responsible for administration-approved gunrunning in Libya. But then the administration morphed the talking points further to mislead the American people, removing language stating that Ansar al-Sharia was involved in the attack and that the CIA had warned of the attack. Another line removed from the talking points: "The wide availability of weapons and experienced fighters in

Libya almost certainly contributed to the lethality of the attacks."[99] As the House Oversight Committee found, "The Administration's talking points were developed in an interagency process that focused more on protecting the reputation and credibility of the State Department than on explaining to the American people the facts surrounding the fatal attacks on U.S. diplomatic facilities and personnel in Libya. . . . This process to alter the talking points can only be construed as a deliberate effort to mislead Congress and the American people."[100] Jay Carney, however, would later label the talking points manipulation apolitical.[101]

It took more than a week before the administration began calling the attacks in Benghazi terrorist attacks.[102] Even then, President Obama continued to blame the YouTube video for what had happened in Benghazi. On September 25, 2012, in an attempt to put a lid on the Benghazi scandal, Obama appeared at the United Nations. He did not label the Benghazi attacks terrorist in nature. He reemphasized America's new pro-Islamist "lead from behind" strategy—the same strategy that brought about Benghazi in the first place: "Just as we cannot solve every problem in the world, the United States has not and will not seek to dictate the outcome of democratic transitions abroad. We do not expect other nations to agree with us on every issue, nor do we assume that the violence of the past weeks or the hateful speech by some individuals represent the views of the overwhelming majority of Muslims, any more than the views of the people who produced this video represents those of Americans." He equated the violence of the Muslim world with the YouTube video: "The future must not belong to those who target Coptic Christians in Egypt. . . . The future must not belong to those who slander the prophet of Islam." Over the course of the speech, he mentioned the YouTube video six times.[103]

In the end, of course, the YouTube video had nothing to do with anything. The administration essentially knew that all along. When push came to shove, however, the administration's perspective on its lies about the YouTube video was simple: push Benghazi beyond the election, blame it on a YouTube video, then pretend it made no difference anyway. Even before the election, President Obama derided Benghazi as a "bump in the road" to CBS News' Steve Kroft and deigned to admit that the death of four Americans was "not optimal" in an interview with Jon Stewart.[104] The administration truly didn't care all that much. As Hillary Clinton put it when testifying before a Senate committee in May 2013, "Was it because of a protest or was it because of guys out for a walk one night and decided they'd go kill some Americans. . . .What difference—at this point, what difference does it make?"[105]

It made a hell of a lot of difference, considering that the nature of the attack meant the difference between involuntary manslaughter and simple negligence: if the attack had been a spontaneous black swan, the administration could credibly claim no one could have stopped it. But the administration knew full well the situation on the ground in Benghazi, and for base political reasons, decided to do nothing.

Hicks told Congress that the administration's decision to blame everything on the YouTube video—a decision he said made his "jaw hit the floor"—completely undercut relations with the government of Libya. Libya had claimed immediately that this was a terrorist attack. "President [Mohamed] Magariaf was insulted in front of his own people, in front of the world," Hicks said. "His credibility was reduced. His ability to lead his own country was damaged. . . . He was angry. A friend of mine who ate dinner with him in New York during the UN sessions told me he was still steamed about the talk shows two weeks later." That anger, Hicks said, led to an eighteen-day delay in the FBI's access to Benghazi.[106]

THE COVER-UP CONTINUES

While the Obama administration was trotting out lies about YouTube and obscuring any hint of gunrunning in Libya, they had to keep everyone quiet. They accomplished this in two ways. First, following a pattern established in every major Obama scandal, the administration appointed a group of flunkies to perform an investigation—an investigation that naturally exculpated the administration. Second, the administration actively worked to silence witnesses who knew anything.

First, the investigation. White House press secretary Jay Carney did admit shortly before the election that Obama didn't care too much about the investigation; Carney said, "He has not participated in the investigation."[107] But the State Department, led by Hillary, quickly announced an Accountability Review Board (ARB) led by Hillary allies. Four were picked directly by Hillary: former UN ambassador Thomas Pickering, former chairman of the Joint Chiefs of Staff Admiral Mike Mullen, Catherine Bertini, and Richard Shinnick. The fifth was selected by the intelligence community—the CIA. Clinton, needless to say, was never interviewed by the ARB. And the report did not even bother trying to lock down President Obama's timeline during the attacks.[108] Pickering later defended the decision not to interview Hillary by stating that there was no need to do so: "We knew where the responsibility rested." And they did: anyplace but Hillary.[109]

Whistle-blowers including Mark Thompson, the deputy assistant secretary in charge of coordinating the deployment of a multiagency team for hostage taking and terrorism attacks, were not interviewed. Even those who were interviewed were not allowed to review their comments afterward, and the interviews were not performed with a stenographer. And those performing the ARB were obviously biased in favor of Hillary—when Hicks was interviewed and informed the ARB that Stevens was in Benghazi at Hillary's direct behest, Pickering "visibly flinched and said; 'Does the 7th floor know about this?'" Hillary's office was on the seventh floor of the building. The ARB ignored Hicks's remarks and instead wrote, "The Board found that Ambassador Stevens made the decision to travel to Benghazi independently of Washington, per standard practice. Timing for his trip was driven in part by commitments in Tripoli, as well as a staffing gap . . . in Benghazi."[110]

The ARB *did* find plenty of blame to go around. "Systemic failures and leadership and management deficiencies at senior levels within two bureaus of the State Department resulted in a Special Mission security posture that was inadequate for Benghazi and grossly inadequate to deal with the attack that took place," the ARB stated. But all of the blame could be relegated to low-level employees. And those low-level employees were not to be punished: "the Board did not find that any individual U.S. Government employee engaged in misconduct or willfully ignored his or her responsibilities, and, therefore did not find reasonable cause to believe that an individual breached his or her duty so as to be the subject of a recommendation for disciplinary action."[111] A congressional report

THE PEOPLE VS. BARACK OBAMA ★ 49

would later find that the ARB report was not independent, and that it was designed to exculpate those in charge: "The ARB blamed systemic failures and leadership and management deficiencies within two bureaus, but downplayed the importance of decisions made at senior levels of the Department. Witnesses questioned how much these decisions influenced the weaknesses that led to the inadequate security posture in Benghazi. . . . The ARB's decision to cite certain officials as accountable for what happened in Benghazi appears to have been based on factors that had little or no connection to the security posture at U.S. diplomatic facilities in Libya."[112]

Nonetheless, Jay Carney said the report was the gold standard in investigations: "The Accountability Review Board which investigated this matter—and I think in no one's estimation sugarcoated what happened there or pulled any punches when it came to holding accountable individuals that they felt had not successfully executed their responsibilities—heard from everyone and invited everyone. So there was a clear indication there that everyone who had something to say was welcome to provide information to the Accountability Review Board."[113] Mullen and Pickering released a statement: "From the beginning of the ARB process, we had unfettered access to everyone and everything, including all of the documentation we needed. Our marching orders were to get to the bottom of what happened, and that is what we did."[114] The White House continued to refuse to release photos of the Obama team during the Benghazi attack, though the White House had been all too eager to trot out pictures of the entire Obama crew in the aftermath of the killing of Osama bin Laden.[115]

Throughout all of this, Hillary claimed ignorance: ignorance about the security situation, ignorance about what was really going on on the ground. "I have made it very clear that the security cables did not come to my attention or above the assistant secretary level, where the ARB placed responsibility. Where, as I think Ambassador Pickering said, 'the rubber hit the road,'" she told Congress. She added, "You know . . . it was very disappointing to me that the ARB concluded there were inadequacies and problems in the responsiveness of our team here in Washington to the security requests that were made by our team in Libya. And I was not aware of that going on, it was not brought to my attention. . . . 1.43 million cables a year come to the State Department. They are all addressed to me. They do not all come to me. They are reported through the bureaucracy." But she had signed a cable herself approving a drawdown in April, and Stevens had sent her a signed cable in August.[116] Perhaps all of this got lost in the shuffle. Or perhaps, and more likely, it was part of an administration policy not to up security lest they offend the locals by doing so.

Senator Rand Paul questions whether Clinton is as ignorant as she claims. He wrote in August 2013, "Does anyone really believe that Hillary Clinton, said to be the leading supporter of arming the Islamic rebels, did not know of the CIA operation?"[117]

If the administration was not guilty of a cover-up, they certainly did an excellent job looking guilty. On August 1, 2013, CNN reported that "dozens of people working for the CIA were on the ground" the night of the Benghazi attack, and that the CIA had been systematically attempting to shut them up ever since. According to CNN sources, "the agency is going to great lengths to make sure whatever it was doing, remains a secret." Those lengths reportedly included polygraph examinations on a monthly basis, with the purpose of finding out if anybody had leaked to the media or Congress. "It is being described as pure intimidation," CNN observed, "with the threat that any unauthorized CIA employee who leaks information could face the end of his or her career." One CIA insider told CNN, "You don't jeopardize yourself, you jeopardize your family as well." Naturally, the CIA denied that it had exerted any pressure on agents.[118] Meanwhile, in September 2013, one year after the initial attacks, CBS News reporter Sharyl Attkisson reported that the State Department had decided not to "honor the request to make Benghazi survivors available for questioning."[119]

In July 2013, Senator Lindsey Graham (R-SC) told CBS News that officials within the military and intelligence echelons had been barred from taking action on pursuing leads in the Benghazi case.[120] Meanwhile, Hicks was barred for months from speaking with Congress or the media. "I was instructed to allow the RSO [Regional Security Officer], the acting Deputy Chief of Mission, and myself to be interviewed by Congressman [Jason] Chaffetz [of the House Oversight Committee]," Hicks testified. Hicks said that he had never experienced a higher-up telling him not to speak with Congress. Hicks also testified that a State Department lawyer attempted to enter a classified briefing Hicks attended with the congresspeople visiting Libya; Hicks tried to bar the lawyer because the lawyer didn't have the proper security clearance. That prompted a screaming phone call from Hillary Clinton's right-hand woman, Cheryl Mills. Hicks said Mills was "very upset" about the lawyers being excluded," and "demanded a report on the visit." Hicks wryly concluded, "A phone call from that near a person is generally not considered to be good news."[121] Hicks was called back from Libya. As of September 2013—a year after the attacks—he had not been reassigned to a post in the State Department. "I don't know why I was punished," Hicks told ABC News. "I don't know why I was shunted aside, put in a closet if you will."[122]

The administration also attempted to throw White House counsel Kathryn Ruemmler under the bus, suggesting to Obama-favored outlet BuzzFeed that Ruemmler had told "senior Obama officials to keep quiet about the attack in Benghazi during the two weeks preceding last year's November presidential election."[123]

Reporters who asked serious questions about Benghazi were castigated by the administration. Hillary henchman Philippe Reines told BuzzFeed reporter Michael Hastings to "f— off" and called him an "unmitigated a—hole" after Hastings emailed him asking about the administration's angry reaction to release of details about Ambassador Stevens's diary.[124] The rest of the media quickly got the hint. CBS News, which has a habit of reading the Obama administration's tea leaves (see Steve Kroft's cut to the Obama interview about Benghazi above), began signaling that intrepid reporter Sharyl Attkisson had sinned against the Obama administration by asking questions about Benghazi. Politico, another favored Obama outlet, reported that CBS News execs had "grown increasingly frustrated with Attkisson's Benghazi campaign. CBS News executives see Attkisson wading dangerously close to advocacy on the issue." Politico reported that Attkisson's increasing marginalization was one reason she might leave before her contract expired.[125] Overall, the media's coverage of Benghazi was so scanty before the election that it can only be labeled shilling for a campaign. Even the *New York Times'* public editor, Margaret Sullivan, later recognized the problem: "I agree that *The Times* seemed to play down the story originally, placing it inside the paper and emphasizing the second-day angle of the [embassy] apology rather than the misconduct itself. . . . Many on the right—as noted last week in my blog posts about Benghazi—do not think they can get a fair shake from *The Times*. This coverage won't do anything to dispel that belief."[126]

The media allowed the Obama administration to bury Benghazi as an issue for months. By the time it came up again in mid-2013, the Obama administration simply declared it a distraction. White House spokesman Dan Pfeiffer informed *Fox News Sunday* in May 2013 that it was "irrelevant" where Obama was the night of the attacks. He blamed "a series of conspiracy theories Republicans have been spinning about it since the time it happened. . . . The question here is *not* what happened that night."[127] A few days later, Obama reiterated that "the core of al Qaeda in Afghanistan and Pakistan is on the path to defeat. . . . They did not direct the attacks in Benghazi." He called Benghazi a "localized threat."[128]

With President Obama safely reelected, the entire Democratic establishment came to the aid of their New Great White Hope 2016, Hillary Clinton. Despite the fact that State Department regulations clearly place responsibility for employee security on the secretary of state, it now turned out that Hillary was clean as a whistle, a wronged woman desperately pursued by a Vast Right-Wing Conspiracy. Senator Dianne Feinstein (D-CA) admitted that the "talking points were wrong," but called Rand Paul's attacks on Clinton "nonsense." Senator Dick Durbin (D-IL) suggested that Benghazi hearings in Congress were a "political show" and said that Republicans were going "after Hillary Clinton" to stop her nomination in 2016. He said that the investigation was a "witch hunt." Former Obama secretary of defense Robert Gates said he didn't think there was any cover-up at all, defending Ambassador Susan Rice in the process.[129] Pfeiffer said that Republicans owed Rice "an apology . . . for accusing her of misleading the country."[130]

The media took its cues perfectly. Stephen Colbert of Comedy Central, who plays a parodic right-winger, suggested that the Benghazi scandal was just old news, and right-wing paranoia at that: "Since last September, Fox News has been pursuing this story doggedly. To uncover how the administration blew it, when they blew it, why they blew [it], and how they will continue to have blown it. And, most importantly, how is this car still burning? I mean, it's been eight months? . . .Well, buckle up, folks, click click, because this story is about to take off like a rocket ship to Planet Scandaltown."[131] The night of May 8, after Hicks and two other whistle-blowers testified before Congress, CNN spent four hours and nine minutes covering the Jodi Arias trial and the Cleveland abduction story. They spent eight minutes on Benghazi. Anderson Cooper ignored the story for two hours. So did Piers Morgan.[132] On May 10, just to ensure that the media continued to perform lapdog duty, White House press secretary Jay Carney held a "deep background" briefing for fourteen invited press outlets. Deep background, explained White House spokesman Josh Earnest, meant "that the info presented by the briefers can be used in reporting but the briefers can't be quoted." And so the propaganda machine rolled on.[133]

THE AFTERMATH

Throughout the Benghazi events and cover-up, Obama administration officials consistently echoed the same refrain: let's not focus on what happened, let's focus on solving the problem. In the immediate aftermath of the attacks, on October 12, 2012, Carney said that President Obama was *committed to finding out what happened. He is committed to making sure that those who killed four Americans are brought to justice, and he is committed to ensuring that actions are taken after the Accountability Review Board thoroughly assesses this matter, to make sure that what happened in Benghazi never happens again.*"[134] Hillary Clinton concluded her disgusting "What difference does it make" routine with a call to fix the issues: "It is our job to figure out what happened and do everything we can to prevent it from ever happening again."[135]

So, what happened to those involved?

To begin, not a single person was fired from the administration over Benghazi. Eric Boswell, head of the Diplomatic Security Bureau, supposedly resigned in December 2012; Charlene Lamb, deputy assistant secretary responsible for embassy security, was reportedly disciplined, as was Raymond Maxwell, a deputy assistant secretary in the Bureau of Near Eastern Affairs. An unnamed fourth person in the Diplomatic Security Bureau was also supposedly disciplined. But a spokeswoman for Senator Paul's office said that "our staff has confirmed with Legislative Affairs at State that all four individuals called out by the ARB are still on administrative leave, getting paid, and expected to return to work." The media initially denied those reports.[136] But in August 2013, just eight months after the supposed resignations, new secretary of state John Kerry cleared all four State Department employees. They were all placed back in regular duty and all disciplinary action was revoked. According to a State Department official, "[Secretary Kerry] studied their careers and studied the facts. In order to implement the ARB and to continue to turn the page and shift the paradigm inside the Department, the four employees who were put on administrative leave last December pending further review, will be reassigned inside the State Department."[137]

Here's what happened to everyone else involved:

State Department spokeswoman Victoria Nuland: Nuland, who helped manipulate the Benghazi talking points, was promoted to assistant secretary of state for European and Eurasian affairs.[138] Republican senators John McCain of Arizona and Lindsey Graham lauded her as "knowledgeable and well-versed on the major foreign policy issues as well as respected by foreign policy experts in both parties."[139]

UN Ambassador Susan Rice: Rice, who actually trotted out those talking points, was originally considered for secretary of state when Clinton stepped down. After Republicans suggested that her involvement in the Benghazi scandal made her a poor choice, President Obama's congressional allies suggested that Republicans were racists and sexists.[140] President Obama eventually appointed Rice his national security advisor, but only after stating that Republicans should stop picking on Rice, since she was an "easy target."[141]

State Department staffer G. Kathleen Hill: Hill, who objected by email to Eric Nordstrom's requests for more security, was awarded the State Department James Clement Dunn Award for Excellence. The award is given for "leadership, intellectual skills, managerial ability, and personal qualities that most fully exemplify the standards of excellence desired of employees at the mid-career level. The winner of the award receives a certificate signed by the Secretary of State."[142] *State* magazine lauded her for her "courage and vision during the establishment of a new base of operations in Libya and the opening of Embassy Tripoli."[143]

Undersecretary of State for Management Patrick Kennedy: Kennedy, who turned down requests for security and reportedly killed requests for the quick-response FEST team during the attacks, has retained his position. He is currently under investigation by an independent inspector general for allegedly covering up former ambassador to Belgium Howard Gutman's alleged involvement with prostitutes and child sex solicitation.[144]

CIA director David Petraeus: Petraeus took over the CIA only five days before Benghazi. Petraeus's CIA drafted the original Benghazi talking points. The CIA ran the annex in Benghazi. The CIA helped run the alleged gunrunning operation. Petraeus was dropped like a hot potato by the administration as soon as the election was over, supposedly over his affair with biographer Paula Broadwell. He quickly told Congress that the events in Benghazi had nothing to do with a YouTube video.[145]

CIA Director Michael Morell: Morell, who had a chief role in editing the Benghazi talking points, was interim head of the CIA before Petraeus's appointment and was reappointed interim head of the CIA after Petraeus left. He would eventually leave the administration in June 2013.[146]

Secretary of Defense and former CIA director Leon Panetta: Panetta, who served as CIA director during the Libya war and during the period in which gunrunning operations allegedly took place, served until February 2013 as secretary of defense. He said he wanted to return to his "walnut farm." In announcing his resignation, he echoed Obama: "We have . . . decimated al Qaeda's leadership and weakened their effort to attack this country."[147]

Chairman of the Joint Chiefs of Staff Martin Dempsey: Dempsey, who oversaw the military response to Benghazi, is still in place.

Secretary of State Hillary Clinton: Clinton left office as the 2016 Democratic presidential frontrunner, and perhaps the most celebrated secretary of state in American history, despite her dramatic failures including Benghazi. Former Florida governor Jeb Bush presented Hillary Clinton with the Liberty Medal from the National Constitution Center in September 2013. "Former Secretary Clinton has dedicated her life to serving and engaging people across the world in democracy," Bush stated.[148] In her resignation letter, Clinton stated, "I am more convinced than ever in the strength and staying power of America's global leadership and our capacity to be a force for good in the world." The day before her resignation, she told the Associated Press, "I was so unhappy with the way that some people refused to accept the facts, refused to accept the findings of an independent Accountability Review Board, politicized everything about this terrible attack. . . . There are some people in politics and in the press who can't be confused by the facts. They just will not live in an evidence-based world. And that's regrettable. It's regrettable for our political system and for the people who serve our government in very dangerous, difficult circumstances."[149]

President Obama: Barack Obama continues to downplay the events in Benghazi. When asked in August 2013 why nobody had been arrested in the Benghazi attacks, Obama sneered, "I also said that we'd get bin Laden, and I didn't get him in 11 months." He then added, "Anybody who attacks Americans, anybody who kills, tragically, four Americans who were serving us in a very dangerous place, we're going to do everything we can to get those who carried out those attacks."[150]

Unless, of course, we're funding them, handing them guns, and then ensuring that our security is too low to protect sovereign U.S. territory overseas.

In August 2013, the week before President Obama made those statements, the United States received word of heightened terror threats from al-Qaeda. The Obama administration promptly shut down twenty-two embassies around the world.

Bin Laden was still dead. But al-Qaeda was very much alive, thanks in no small part to the Obama administration.

CLOSING ARGUMENT

In 1951, Julius and Ethel Rosenberg were put on trial for smuggling nuclear secrets to the Russians. Technically, the United States and the Soviet Union were not at war, so they could not be tried for treason.

Nonetheless, in 1953, they were executed under the Espionage Act of 1917, which prohibited transferring to a foreign government any information "relating to the national defense." Judge Irving Kaufman said, upon giving sentence:

> *I consider your crime worse than murder. . . . I believe your conduct in putting into the hands of the Russians the A-Bomb years before our best scientists predicted Russia would perfect the bomb has already caused, in my opinion, the Communist aggression in Korea, with the resultant casualties exceeding 50,000 and who knows but that millions more of innocent people may pay the price of your treason. Indeed, by your betrayal you undoubtedly have altered the course of history to the disadvantage of our country.*[151]

On September 14, 2001, three days after the devastating terrorist attacks of September 11, 2001, the Congress of the United States passed by a House vote of 420–1 and a Senate vote of 98–0 the Authorization for Use of Military Force. It authorized the use of force against America's enemies: "nations, organizations, or persons he [the president] determines planned, authorized, or aided the terrorist attacks that occurred on September 11, 2001, or harbored such organizations or persons." The goal: "*to take action to deter and prevent acts of international terrorism against the United States.*"[152]

Ethel and Julius Rosenberg did not hand over an atomic bomb to the Soviet Union. The Obama administration has authorized a foreign policy of handing over *weapons themselves* to the very group of people who perpetrated September 11, as well as their Islamist associates. There is little or no evidence that the Obama administration has complied with its duty to receive congressional authorization for such covert acts. By funneling weapons to Libyan terrorists openly associated with al-Qaeda and pushing weapons through Libya to Syrian terrorists openly associated with al-Qaeda, the Obama administration was playing with treasonous fire.

That treasonous fire burned four Americans to death in Benghazi on the eleventh anniversary of September 11. The feckless foreign policy of the Obama administration did not just embolden America's enemies, it handed guns to them. And then, when our American-funded al-Qaeda enemies turned on us, that feckless foreign policy recommended that we keep security low so as not to offend the terrorists openly working with those who flew planes into the World Trade Center and the Pentagon.

Any charges associated with gun smuggling to terrorist groups in violation of American law would not require separate RICO charges. Such charges could spring from the Arms Control Export Act (AECA), which explicitly provides that the United States cannot provide guns or credit to countries supporting terrorism. There is no question that President Obama's administration did this, and did it repeatedly. In fact, President Obama essentially admitted as much when, in September 2013, he attempted to retroactively justify that gun smuggling by waiving the applicable provision under the AECA.[153]

But the crimes didn't stop there.

When it became obvious that revelations about what really happened in Benghazi could undermine President Obama's bid for reelection, deputies throughout his administration began covering up the evidence: silencing witnesses, threatening agents, and lying to the American people. Then those same lackeys had the temerity to label the entire debacle a distraction from the real issues of the day, and to blame those who wanted the truth for supposed conspiracy-mongering.

This is where RICO comes in. The RICO Act explicitly lists among its predicate crimes obstruction of justice (certainly the highly flawed Accountability Review Board would fall under this provision, as would the Obama administration's repeated attempts to silence witnesses to the Benghazi events);[154] tampering with a witness, victim, or informant; and terrorism-related offenses, among others.

There is no question who designed the strategy of attempting to ingratiate the United States to its enemies overseas—and there is little question that President Obama and Hillary Clinton had an inkling of just what was happening in Benghazi. There is no doubt that Clinton in particular had direct contact with Gregory Hicks, a witness involved in the event, and that her direct operatives tampered with witnesses. Meanwhile, the Obama administration is still staffed by the same men and women who made the despicable decisions that led to Benghazi in the first place.

By their betrayal, the Obama administration has undoubtedly altered the course of history to the disadvantage of our country and is guilty of espionage.

COUNT 2

★

INVOLUNTARY MANSLAUGHTER

A person commits manslaughter by recklessly causing the death of another person. . . . Manslaughter is a class 2 felony. . . . "Recklessly" means, with respect to a result or to a circumstance described by a statute defining an offense, that a person is aware of and consciously disregards a substantial and unjustifiable risk that the result will occur or that the circumstance exists. The risk must be of such nature and degree that disregard of such risk constitutes a gross deviation from the standard of conduct that a reasonable person would observe in the situation.

—ARIZONA REVISED STATUTES, TITLE 13, CRIMINAL CODE

OPENING ARGUMENT

The air was dry and cool on the evening of December 14, 2010, in the Peck Canyon area of the southern Arizona desert. The area was well-known as a looting zone for Mexican bandits hoping to rob incoming illegal immigrants of drugs being carried across the border; such *bajadores* were known to bear heavy weaponry and wear ski masks to carry out their crimes, including but not limited to robbery and rape. In the prior few months, there had been several ambushes in the area.

The groups responsible for stopping such activity were known as Border Patrol Tactical Units (BORTACs). "Any time an agent encounters a known suspect who has weapons," said Brandon Judd, president of the Local 2544 agents' union, "we call BORTAC." And that happened often in Peck Canyon. Just three months before, in September, Border Patrol agents had encountered such criminals at Bellota Canyon nearby, and a firefight ensued. "Anywhere that we know that bandit activity is taking place, that's where BORTAC goes," said Judd. "If BORTAC's out there patrolling that area, it's a bad area." It was the feds' job to keep the border secure. It was the feds' job to keep the Border Patrol agents safe. "It's a federal responsibility," explained Sheriff Antonio Estrada. "The Border Patrol, they have the numbers, they have the technology, they have the resources to do that."[1]

One of those border patrol agents was a forty-year-old nicknamed "Superman": Brian Terry. As he and his compatriots patrolled the area, they suddenly came under fire from five gunmen from the Mexican side of the border. While Terry and company fired beanbag guns in an attempt to neutralize the threat without serious injury, the suspects began firing AK-47s and other heavy-duty rifles.

Terry was hit in the aorta. "I can't feel my legs," Terry said as he lay dying. "I think I'm paralyzed." He bled out in his friend's arms as the patrol agents waited for a helicopter.[2]

That was just the beginning of the story. Two of the rifles found at the scene matched the serial numbers of guns bought a year earlier—not in Mexico, but in Arizona.[3] They came from Lone Wolf gun store, owned by Andre Howard.

THE CHARGES

The shipping of guns south of the border to drug cartels should theoretically constitute its own crime under the Arms Control Export Act. The act prohibits the United States government from arming terrorist organizations absent a presidential waiver. But, unbelievably enough, Mexican drug cartels have never been designated as foreign terrorist organizations, despite the fact that State Department officials have admitted that their activities are "consistent with what we would call either terrorism or insurgency in other countries."[4]

That acknowledgment by the State Department demonstrates the reckless disregard inherent in the act of arming the Mexican drug cartels. And that reckless disregard is a key element of involuntary manslaughter.

Involuntary manslaughter is charged at the state level, and typically contains three elements. First, someone had to be killed as a result of action by the defendant. As we'll see, that clearly happened here, given that the Obama administration armed the dangerous quasi-terrorist entity that later used those arms to murder Americans. In the same way that bar owners have been charged for giving visibly intoxicated patrons drinks, then allowing them to drive,[5] the Obama administration gave some of the worst people on earth guns, then allowed them to run free.

The second element of involuntary manslaughter is that the predicate act had to be undertaken with reckless disregard of the consequences, or had to be inherently dangerous. Handing guns to Mexican drug cartels would certainly qualify as dangerous and reckless; as we'll see, no safeguards for Operation Fast and Furious were ever undertaken.

The third element of involuntary manslaughter is that the defendant knew his or her action threatened life. As the reaction of the agents involved in Fast and Furious demonstrates, they knew full well the risks of the operation—which is why they reacted with CYA panic when Brian Terry was killed.

That CYA panic carried all the way up the food chain, given the level of complicity in the cover-up that followed the revelation of Fast and Furious. As we'll see, that cover-up included witness tampering, intimidation, and retaliation against whistle-blowers. All of those are federal crimes chargeable under the RICO Act, implicating the Obama administration as a whole.

"LET THE GUNS GO"

When Vin Diesel and Paul Walker starred in *Fast & Furious*, they had no clue that their popular B-flick would provide the inspiration for a federal operation designed to smuggle guns *to the Mexican drug cartels*. Responsible for at least sixty thousand deaths in Mexico from 2006 to 2013—many of high-ranking public officials, who are often found, heads hacked off, on the sides of roads—the drug cartels are the greatest threat to stability in Mexico. The U.S. government's idea: hand American-marked guns over to "straw purchasers"—middlemen—for the cartels. Track them by serial number. This was the so-called Operation Fast and Furious "gunwalking" operation.

Officials from the FBI, Drug Enforcement Administration, Bureau of Alcohol, Tobacco, Firearms and Explosives (ATF), and Justice Department came up with the plan at a meeting on October 26, 2009, in Washington, D.C. The agenda for the meeting was "discussion, and, if possible, adoption of the Department's Strategy for Combating the Mexican Cartels." Attendees at the initial meeting included Ken Melson, director of the ATF; Michele Leonhart, administrator at the DEA; Robert Mueller, director of the FBI; Dennis Burke, U.S. attorney for the District of Arizona (by telephone); and various other high-ranking officials.

As the *Washington Post* reported, one of the great motivators behind Fast and Furious was to generate enough anecdotal evidence of guns moving across the border via straw buyers—people with no criminal records who acted as middlemen for the cartels—to change the law: "Agents along the border had long been frustrated by what one ATF supervisor later called 'toothless' laws that made it difficult to attack gun-trafficking networks." Thanks to those "toothless" laws, agents had little leverage in pressuring Mexican drug cartel agents to turn against their former bosses.

By October 27, 2009, the Justice Department was circulating its new strategy among its top officers. The strategy stated that its attempts to stem Mexican drug cartel violence would be operated "under the supervision of the newly created Southwest Border Strategy Group."

The department proposed, based on its experiences fighting "the Mafia, international terrorist groups, and domestic and transnational gangs," that the strategy be implemented via "intelligence-based, prosecutor-led, multi-agency task forces." In other words, everybody would be involved.[6]

This was merely the framework. ATF would be tasked with coming up with a specific plan. By January 2010, ATF had come up with the plan, which was then green-lit by Dennis Burke, as well as a task force at the Justice Department. The specific plan, which would become Fast and Furious, focused on tracking the pipelines of weapons into Mexico. The heavily redacted documents show that the department determined initial attempts to prosecute those running guns hadn't met with success. "[T]herefore," the ATF concluded, "additional firearms purchases should be monitored and additional evidence continued to be gathered." The ATF continued, "Currently our strategy is to allow the transfer of firearms to continue to take place in order to further the investigation and allow for the identification of additional coconspirators who would continue to operate and illegally traffic firearms to Mexican [drug organizations] which are perpetrating armed violence along the Southwest Border." The goal was to "identify and prosecute all co-conspirators," from straw purchasers to cartel members.[7]

The plan was called Fast and Furious because the chief pipeline ran out of a chop shop, and those involved liked to race cars as in the film.

The higher-ups throughout the chain of command couldn't have been more excited about the newly dubbed Operation Fast and Furious. Obama appointee Kenneth Melson, acting ATF director, visited Phoenix in March and apparently watched straw purchases live from his offices via a secret IP address. He also received weekly briefings. Attorney General Eric Holder's chief of staff, Gary Grindler, also visited the Phoenix Field Division, where he was briefed on Fast and Furious. Assistant Attorney General Lanny Breuer personally signed off on wiretaps for Fast and Furious.[8]

There was only one problem. There was no way to track the guns. As a congressional report stated, "ATF could have used trackers on a larger scale to interdict more suspicious purchases in conjunction with the contemporaneous knowledge of the purchases that ATF received from cooperating [Federal Firearms License holders]."[9] Another congressional report on Fast and Furious explained, "The Department's leadership allowed the ATF to implement this flawed strategy, fully aware of what was taking place on the ground. . . . This hapless plan allowed the guns in question to disappear out of the agency's view. As a result, this chain of events inevitably placed the guns in the hands of violent criminals. ATF would only see these guns again after they turned up at a crime scene. Tragically, many of these recoveries involved loss of life."[10]

AFT agent John Dodson saw it coming. During his first day on the job, he watched with Agent Olindo Casa from a Chevy Impala as a gun trafficking suspect walked out of a local Phoenix gun shop with ten rifles, and drove to meet another trafficking suspect. When Dodson called it in, ATF told him to let the guns go. The goal, as the *Washington Post* later reported: "follow the paths of guns from illegal buyers known as 'straw purchasers' through middlemen and into the hierarchy of the powerful Sinaloa drug cartel." The gunwalking continued for well over a year.[11] Dodson later said it would have been "impossible" to believe that the guns weren't headed for the cartels. That observation, in and of itself, demonstrates the reckless disregard with which the ATF and its Justice Department overlords acted in allowing Fast and Furious to take place.

"The day I started, there were 240 guns they had let . . . out of Fast and Furious," Dodson told the *Los Angeles Times*. "Guns they were purchasing were showing up on both sides of the border already. . . . I mean . . . guy comes in and purchases 10 AK-47s, and four of them he purchased last time have already shown up on the other side of the border? And you keep going?"[12]

Dodson wasn't the only one objecting. Special Agent William Newell, who ran "Group 7," the subgroup in Phoenix responsible for implementing Fast and Furious, received heavy kickback from multiple agents. So did group supervisor Agent David Voth; so did the agent running the case, Hope MacAllister. The criticism became extraordinarily heated. Casa testified, "We were all sick to death when we realized . . . what was going on."[13] He said, "What I found concerning and alarming was more times than not, no law enforcement activity was planned to stop these suspected straw purchasers from purchasing firearms. The only law enforcement activity that was occasionally taken was to conduct a surveillance of the transaction, and nothing more. On several occasions I personally requested to interdict or seize firearms in such a manner that would only further the investigation, but I was always ordered to stand down and not to seize the firearms."[14]

Yelling broke out at the office. ATF agents in Mexico worried about the flow of guns into that country as well. ATF attaché to Mexico Darren Gil screamed at his superior, "Hey, when are they going to shut this, to put it bluntly, damn investigation down? We're getting hurt down here." The Mexican government apparently had no idea the operation was going on. Dodson asked his superiors in May 2010 if they "were prepared to attend the funeral of a slain agent or officer after he or she was killed with one of those straw-purchased firearms."[15] The actions of the ATF were, as everyone knew, inherently dangerous. Should someone die, involuntary manslaughter would result.

Voth, in particular, would hear none of it. According to Dodson, Voth responded to his complaints: "If you are going to make an omelet, you need to scramble some eggs."[16] On March 12, 2010, Voth wrote to Group 7: "It has been brought to my attention that there may be a schism developing amongst the group. This is the time we all need to pull together not drift apart. We are all entitled to our respective (albeit different) opinions however we all need to get along and realize that we have a mission to accomplish. . . . Whether you care or not *people of rank and authority at HQ are paying close attention to this case* and they also believe we (Phoenix Group VII) are doing what they envisioned the Southwest Border Groups doing" (emphasis added). He added, "If you don't think this is fun you're in the wrong line of work—period! . . . This can be the most fun you have with ATF, the only one limiting the amount of fun we have is you!"[17]

In an email in early April to U.S. attorney Emory Hurley and Phoenix second-in-command George Gillett, and copying Phoenix Group VII, Voth noted that there had been 958 people killed in March 2010 in Mexico, the most violent month in Mexico in five years. He encouraged "a sense of urgency with regards to this investigation," and said that the ATF was "righteous in our plan to dismantle this entire organization and to rush in to arrest any one person without taking into account the entire scope of the conspiracy would be ill advised to the overall good of the mission."[18]

That righteous plan was about to collapse. And on December 14, with Brian Terry's death, it did.

The first person openly involved with Fast and Furious to receive news of Agent Terry's death was Justice Department attorney Dennis Burke. At 2:31 in the morning, someone sent "OIOC" and "SITROOM"—likely the Office of Intelligence and Operations Coordination, a subsection of the Department of Homeland Security that monitors border crime—notice that "a BORTAC agent working in the Nogales, AZ AOR [area of responsibility] was shot." At 3:31 a.m., Burke was notified, "Our agent has passed away." The email came from someone in "HQ." Burke wrote back, "Horrible." He then notified Monty Wilkinson at the Office of the Attorney General—that would be Eric Holder's deputy chief of staff—writing, "Not good. 18 miles w/in [the border]." Wilkinson immediately wrote back, "Tragic. I've alerted the AG, the Acting DAG, Lisa [Monaco], etc." The AG would be Eric Holder. He then asked Burke for "any additional details as they become available to you."

That day, Burke was notified by another assistant attorney that the guns in the Terry murder had been tied to "an on-going Phoenix ATF inv. You will probably get a call from Bill Newell." Burke then let Wilkinson know that "[t]he guns found in the desert near the murdered BP officer connect back to the investigation we were going to talk about—they were AK-47s purchased at a Phoenix gun store." Wilkinson wrote back within minutes: "I'll call tomorrow."[19]

Meanwhile, as news broke of Terry's death, Voth wrote to MacAllister with the subject header: "no more rose colored glasses." "If you have not heard," he wrote, "a Border Patrol agent was shot and killed here in Arizona. The trace came back to Fast and Furious, Jamie Avila, January 2010, LWTC [Lone Wolf]. . . . Ugh! . . . Call as soon as you can, things will most likely get ugly!"[20]

Worried about the scandal likely to ensue, officials rushed to the Terry family's side, including Burke and Secretary of Homeland Security Janet Napolitano, who came to the funeral, where she said she was "carrying a personal note to you from the President of the United States to your family. He, like I, honors Border Patrol agent Brian Terry." Terry's stepmother told local news, "Now she can get on the news and say how she called the family of agent Brian Terry. We didn't get one answer from her. She talked around everything just like the president does."[21]

It soon got worse.

In January 2011, Senator Charles Grassley (R-IA) sent a letter to the ATF demanding answers. "As you may be aware, obstructing a Congressional investigation is a crime," he wrote. "Additionally, denying or interfering with employees' rights to furnish information to Congress is also against the law. Federal officials who deny or interfere with employees' rights to furnish information to Congress are not entitled to have their salaries paid by taxpayers' dollars."[22] On February 4, 2011, Ronald Weich, assistant attorney general, sent a letter to Senator Grassley bluntly denying that the Justice Department and ATF had ever signed off on a gunwalking program. "[T]he allegation," Weich wrote, "that ATF 'sanctioned' or otherwise knowingly allowed the sale of assault weapons to a straw purchaser who then transported them into Mexico—is false. ATF makes every effort to interdict weapons that have been purchased illegally and prevent their transportation to Mexico." Weich added that Congress should not "contact law enforcement personnel seeking information about pending criminal investigations, including the investigation into the death of Customs and Border Patrol Agent Brian Terry. Like you, we are deeply concerned by his murder, and we are actively investigating the matter." In other words, sit down and shut up while we lie to you.[23]

A few weeks later, Immigration and Customs Enforcement agent Jaime Zapata was murdered using a gun that had been trafficked into Mexico by smugglers who were being watched by ATF at the time. Grassley promptly fired off a letter to ATF demanding an answer: "After the delivery of the illegal weapons, the three men were stopped by local police. Why were these traffickers not thereafter arrested in November?"[24]

THE REAL BAD GUYS: GUN SHOPS

Meanwhile, the search for scapegoats was on.

The gun shop owners who had been working with the ATF were convenient patsies for all of this. According to Howard, owner of the Lone Wolf gun store in Glendale, Arizona, which sold the guns used in Terry's murder, he was told by federal agents to sell guns to all of the straw purchasers who made their way to his cash register. The ATF planted a phone line and cameras in the infrastructure to monitor the activity.

For more than a year, Howard did what the ATF told him to do, handing criminals handguns, rifles, revolvers. The ATF told him they were tracking the guns and would stop the guns before they did any harm. Howard says he followed up with ATF when he heard nothing about arrests, and was told to continue funneling arms south of the border. "Every passing week, I worried," he said. "I felt horrible and sick. . . . Every passing week I was more stunned." Howard is a former Army pilot, and felt ill that his actions could result in the death of Americans. He registered his complaints with Emory Hurley, assistant district attorney at the Department of Justice. Nothing happened.

Meanwhile, as Katie Pavlich of Townhall.com has reported, the Obama administration was focused heavily on gun control—and apparently, on demonizing gun shops, even as ATF worked with them. An email from Assistant Director in Charge of Field Operations Mark Chait on July 14, 2010, to Group 7 leader William Newell—five months before Terry's killing—read: "Bill—can you see if these guns were all purchased from the same FFL [Federal Firearms Licensee] and at one time. We are looking at anecdotal cases to support a demand letter on long gun multiple sales."[25] The day before Terry came under fire, the *Washington Post* ran a lengthy story reporting on "U.S. gun dealers with the most firearms traced over the past four years." The *Post* spilled "the names of the dealers, all from border states, with the most traces from guns recovered in Mexico over the past two years." The gun dealers were the bad guys.[26]

Sharyl Attkisson of CBS News reported: "ATF officials didn't intend to publicly disclose their own role in letting Mexican cartels obtain the weapons, but emails show they discussed using the sales, including sales encouraged by ATF, to justify a new gun regulation called 'Demand Letter 3.' That would require some U.S. gun shops to report the sale of multiple rifles or 'long guns.' Demand Letter 3 was so named because it would be the third ATF program demanding gun dealers report tracing information." On January 4, 2011, Newell sent an email about a press conference on arrests in Fast and Furious, which he said could be used "to address Multiple Sale on Long Guns issue." The next day, Chait emailed Newell back: "Bill—well done yesterday . . . in light of our request for Demand [L]etter 3, this case could be a strong supporting factor if we can determine how many multiple sales of long guns occurred during the course of this case."

There was an agenda here. As Senator Grassley stated, "There's plenty of evidence showing that this administration planned to use the tragedies of Fast and Furious as rationale to further their goals of a long gun reporting requirement." In July 2011, Grassley and House Oversight Committee chair Representative Darrell Issa (R-CA) asked Eric Holder whether the Justice Department had talked about how "Fast and Furious could be used to justify additional regulatory authorities." The department never responded. Issa told Attkisson, "In light of the evidence, the Justice Department's refusal to answer questions about the role Operation Fast and Furious was supposed to play in advancing new firearms regulations is simply unacceptable."[27]

Overall, the feds lost control of 1,400 of the 2,000 weapons smuggled across the border in Fast and Furious,[28] from handguns to .50-caliber sniper rifles.[29] The weapons were used in at least three murders, four kidnappings, an attempted murder, and eleven other crime scenes.[30] One hundred ninety-five firearms found at Mexican crime scenes were linked to Operation Fast and Furious. Humberto Benitez Treviño, who chairs the justice committee in Mexico's Chamber of Deputies, said, "we have 150 cases of injuries and homicides with arms that were smuggled and passed illegally into our country. . . . This was an undercover program that wasn't properly controlled."[31] By September 2011, Issa put that number at two hundred murders.[32]

"I DID NOT AUTHORIZE IT"

Just as with a typical mob operation gone wrong, nobody knew anything. That ignorance started at the very top. President Obama told Univision in March 2011, "There have been problems." But as he says so often about scandals stemming from his administration—like Lieutenant Renault in *Casablanca*—he's "shocked, shocked!" to learn about them. "I heard on the news about this story—Fast and Furious—where, allegedly, guns were run into Mexico," he said. "First of all, I did not authorize it. Eric Holder, the Attorney General, did not authorize it. He's been very clear that our policy is to catch gunrunners and put them into jail. So what he's done is he's assigned an inspector general to investigate exactly what happened." Obama then played his second-favorite card: it was a big government, and he didn't know anything that happened in it. "This is a pretty big government," Obama scoffed. "The United States government. I've got a lot of moving parts."[33]

In October 2011, Obama reiterated this stance to then–ABC News White House correspondent Jake Tapper: "People who have screwed up will be held accountable." He continued, "It's very upsetting to me to think that somebody showed such bad judgment that they would allow something like that to happen. And we will find out who and what happened in this situation and make sure it gets corrected." Then Obama shifted attention back to Holder; he said he had "complete confidence" in the man who ran the Justice Department—the same department that oversaw the operation in the first place. Holder, Obama stated, would "figure out who, in fact, was responsible for that decision and how it got made."[34]

President Obama wasn't the only one shifting attention to Holder. In March 2011, Napolitano told the Senate Judiciary Committee that she had not been informed about the operation, and suggested that Holder "had asked his inspector general to look at the operation." Napolitano said that it would be "premature and inappropriate for me to comment" on Fast and Furious before Holder finished his investigation. In September, Napolitano said she'd never spoken to Burke, her former chief of staff, about Fast and Furious, and said she hadn't spoken with Holder about Fast and Furious, either. Katie Pavlich's sources told her that Napolitano's statements were "a lie," and that Holder and Napolitano coordinated on Fast and Furious shortly after Terry's death. "Janet will be lucky not to go to prison," a source told Pavlich.[35]

What, then, of the administration's top hit man, Holder, whose department had overseen Fast and Furious?

On March 2, 2011, Assistant Attorney General Weich informed Senator Grassley that Attorney General Holder had asked the acting inspector general to investigate Fast and Furious.[36] On May 2, Holder, Napolitano, and Obama met at the White House in preparation for Holder's testimony on the hill. The next day, May 3, 2011, Holder told the Judiciary Committee that he had only heard of Fast and Furious "for the first time over the last few weeks."[37] But internal Department of Justice memos showed that Holder had known about Fast and Furious since months before Terry's murder. A memo from Michael F. Walther, director of the National Drug Intelligence Center, hit Holder's desk on July 5, 2010—and it explicitly mentioned Fast and Furious.[38] Another memo from Assistant Attorney General Lanny Breuer to Holder on November 1, 2010, mentions Fast and Furious as well.[39] And did Justice know that Fast and Furious was a gunwalking program? You bet: an email exchange between two high-ranking department officials on October 18, 2010, shows them agonizing about "how much grief we get for 'guns walking' " if the program were to be revealed.[40]

The situation was getting ugly for Holder. In October 2011, Issa subpoenaed Holder for documents on Fast and Furious. "Top Justice Department officials, including Attorney General Holder," Issa said, "know more about Operation Fast and Furious than they have publicly acknowledged. The documents this subpoena demands will provide answers to questions that Justice officials have tried to avoid since this investigation began eight months ago. It's time we know the whole truth." Holder said that the Justice Department would "undoubtedly comply" with the demands. Tracy Schmaler, spokeswoman for the department, said, "We've made clear from the beginning that the Department intends to work with the committee to answer legitimate questions. However, this subpoena shows that Chairman Issa is more interested in generating headlines than in real oversight important to the American people."[41] Jay Carney, White House press secretary, came to Holder's defense as well: "The bottom line is the Attorney General's testimony to both the House and the Senate was consistent and truthful." Obama stated, "I have complete confidence in Attorney General Holder, in how he handles his office."

Issa was less generous. "The President has said he has full confidence in this attorney general. I have no confidence in a president who has confidence in an attorney general who has in fact not terminated or dealt with the individuals, including key lieutenants who from the very beginning had some knowledge and long before Brian Terry was gunned down, knew enough to stop this program."[42]

The promise of compliance with the subpoena was another Holder lie. For months, the Justice Department failed to comply with the subpoena. Finally, in June 2012—eight months after Issa originally issued the subpoena—Issa was prepared to move forward with a contempt vote against Holder in the House Oversight Committee.

Holder would finally be held to the fire.

That's when Obama stepped in to save his legal consigliere: Obama invoked executive privilege to avoid production of documents concerning Fast and Furious. "We regret that we have arrived at this point," said Deputy Attorney General James Cole in a letter. He said that document production "would have significant, damaging consequences." As the *Los Angeles Times* reported, Cole "did not disclose whether Obama has been briefed or had another supervisory role in Fast and Furious."

Holder, it turns out, had written Obama a letter requesting that he invoke executive privilege: "you may properly assert executive privilege over the documents at issue, and I respectfully request you do so." And despite Obama's protestations in 2007 about President Bush's "tendency . . . to hide behind executive privilege every time there's something a little shaky that's taking place," Obama went along with the plan. Grassley immediately fired back, questioning how the White House could invoke executive privilege "if there is no White House involvement?" And Speaker of the House John Boehner's office added that the invocation "implies that White House officials were either involved in the 'Fast and Furious' operation or the cover-up that followed."[43]

The final Department of Justice inspector general report was released on September 19, 2012. It put the blame on everybody around Eric Holder, while leaving Holder unscathed. The people to blame, the report said, were Deputy Chief of Staff Wilkinson, Assistant Attorney General Lanny Breuer, Deputy Assistant Attorney General Jason Weinstein, and former acting Deputy Attorney General Gary Grindler. Those four men "failed to alert the attorney general to significant information about or flaws in those investigations," the report stated.

As soon as the report was released, the Justice Department helpfully let the public know that Melson and Weinstein had stepped down. Holder then blamed Issa, Grassley, and Republicans for politicizing the Fast and Furious operation—a familiar tactic the Obama administration utilizes over and over. "It is unfortunate that some were so quick to make baseless accusations before they possessed the facts about these operations—accusations that turned out to be without foundation and that have caused a great deal of unnecessary harm and confusion," Holder said. "I hope today's report acts as a reminder of the dangers of adopting as fact unsubstantiated conclusions before an investigation of the circumstances is completed." Naturally, fellow Democrats in Congress like Representative Elijah Cummings (D-MD) played the report as a full exculpation of Holder and the Obama administration: "Neither the attorney general nor senior DOJ officials authorized or approved of gun-walking in Fast and Furious . . . gun-walking started under the Bush administration in 2006, and . . . ATF agents in Phoenix and the U.S. Attorney's Office in Arizona share responsibility for misguided operations spanning five years."[44]

The day after the Justice Department report was released, the department's inspector general, Michael E. Horowitz, told the House that the White House had stonewalled on Fast and Furious. According to Horowitz, the White House national security assistant at the time, Kevin O'Reilly, refused to speak with the Justice Department. O'Reilly had been copied on some of the emails from Newell discussing Fast and Furious in detail. "O'Reilly's unwillingness to speak to us made it impossible" for the department to track down who in the White House knew what, Horowitz said. The White House claimed, with no evidence, that Newell and O'Reilly were merely friends, and that the emails were not professionally related. In other words, there was no White House involvement, and no way to force O'Reilly to testify. The White House maintained that the *only* emails it had concerning Fast and Furious were the exchanges between Newell and O'Reilly. Horowitz said, "the White House is beyond the purview of the inspector general's office."[45] O'Reilly was transferred to Baghdad shortly after Newell testified before Congress.[46] He returned to the United States only in October 2012, and was quickly handed a State Department job.[47]

But the favor for the Obama administration had already been done. The same day Horowitz testified that the White House had stonewalled its requests on Fast and Furious, President Obama appeared on Univision and denied once again that there was any cover-up at all. He said, quite to the contrary, that everything was aboveboard and transparent on Fast and Furious. When asked by a Univision interviewer whether Holder should have known about Fast and Furious, and whether Holder should be fired, Obama stated:

> *When Eric Holder found out about it, he discontinued it. We assigned an inspector general to do a thorough report that was just issued, confirming that, in fact, Eric Holder did not know about this, that he took prompt action and the people who did initiate this were held accountable. But what I think is most important is recognizing that we've got a challenge in terms of weapons flowing south. And the strategy that was pursued, obviously, out of Arizona, was completely wrongheaded. Those folks who were responsible have been held accountable. . . . I will tell you that Eric Holder has my complete confidence because he has shown himself to be willing to hold accountable those who took these actions and is passionate about making sure that we're preventing guns from getting into the wrong hands.*

When the questioner followed up by asking why he was not releasing all available documents, Obama said "we've released almost all of them."[48]

That was a lie. As Judicial Watch, an organization dedicated to government transparency, reported, "We've sued the Justice Department and the ATF to obtain Fast and Furious records. They already refused to answer our very request for documents—we haven't received one document from Justice or the ATF regarding Fast and Furious—which is unusual, even for the secretive Obama administration. Given their dissembling, Justice and the ATF are apparently in cover-up mode."[49]

Nonetheless, the only documents that remained filed away, Obama stated, were "internal communications that were not related to the actual Fast and Furious operation." Of course, all we had to go on was his word. But that was good enough for him. Obama also stated that no independent investigation was necessary. Then he fibbed, "we are happy to continue to provide the information that is relevant to this." But, he added, all of it was a "political distraction" anyway from "us actually solving the problems that we need to solve." Those problems, presumably, did not include corrupt gunrunning operations designed to curb Americans' Second Amendment rights.

Obama finally brushed off Fast and Furious as "people who do dumb things." An approved multiagency operation that got hundreds of people killed, including Americans, was now just a "dumb thing." Then, after claiming no responsibility and blaming "political circuses" for making an issue of Fast and Furious, Obama finally disingenuously stated, "ultimately, I'm responsible, and my key managers, including the Attorney General, are responsible, for holding those people accountable, for making sure they are fired if they do dumb things, and then fixing the system to ensure that it doesn't happen again."[50] Only, as we'll see, he didn't.

SNITCHES GET STITCHES

Brave CBS News reporter Sharyl Attkisson—one of the few watchdogs rather than lapdogs in the Obama-loving media—was reamed by the administration for her reporting on Fast and Furious. "The Justice Department's communications director Tracy Schmaler yelled at her over the phone," Katie Pavlich relates. "A White House spokesman, Eric Schultz, reportedly directed a barrage of expletives toward her." Attkisson told radio host Laura Ingraham, "The White House and Justice Department will tell you that I'm the only reporter—as they told me—that is not reasonable. They say the *Washington Post* is reasonable, I'm the only one who thinks this is a story, and they think I'm unfair and biased by pursuing it."[51]

It was worse than that. In June 2013, as other reporters announced having been targeted by the Obama administration, Attkisson revealed that her computer had been hacked during her investigations of Fast and Furious and Benghazi. At first, the media greeted her claim with skepticism. Then CBS News confirmed that she'd been hacked by "an unauthorized, external, unknown party on multiple occasions in late 2012." CBS News said they'd hired a cybersecurity firm to check Attkisson's story: "Evidence suggests this party performed all access remotely using Attkisson's accounts. While no malicious code was found, forensic analysis revealed an intruder had executed commands that appeared to involve search and exfiltration of data. This party also used sophisticated methods to remove all possible indications of unauthorized activity, and alter system times to cause further confusion. CBS News is taking steps to identify the responsible party and their method of access."[52]

As for whistle-blowers within the ATF and Justice Department, they ended up with their heads on platters, in violation of federal law preventing witness tampering and retaliation against whistle-blowers. Dodson, the first ATF agent to testify behind closed doors to Senator Grassley, was granted whistle-blower protection. That didn't help him much—Dodson says Newell and Gillett asked him to recant his testimony in writing. He said no. He says the ATF took away his weapons and reassigned him. Melson called him a "disgruntled" employee. Burke leaked memos to the press attempting to smear Dodson. Dodson was handed over to ATF public affairs chief Scott Thomasson, who allegedly said, "All of these whistleblowers have axes to grind. ATF needs to f—k these guys," and added, "we need to get whatever dirt we can on these guys and take them down." After Melson's ouster, new acting ATF director B. Todd Jones warned whistle-blowers that there would be "consequences." Somebody leaked Dodson's confidential file to *Forbes* magazine for a hit piece; Justice Department public affairs chief Tracy Schmaler was widely suspected.[53]

Other whistle-blowers received similar treatment. ATF investigator Vince Cefalu, who started CleanUpATF.org in an attempt to keep eyes on perceived corruption within the agency, was relieved of his job in

June 2011. The Justice Department tried to shut down the website. ATF agent Peter Forcelli, who testified before Congress that the operation "endangered the American public" and "was orchestrated in conjunction with Assistant U.S. Attorney Emory Hurley" and Dennis Burke, met with similar treatment: in Arizona the Justice Department opened up an old case against him, and Forcelli was transferred to a desk job in ATF headquarters.[54] Overall, three out of four whistle-blowers were reassigned to positions outside Arizona by the end of August 2011.[55]

THE AFTERMATH

Like any good Don, Obama allowed low-level flunkies to take the hits, elevated middlemen, and protected his top agents. In the end, nobody would see any real consequences. Except, of course, Brian Terry, who remained dead.

Here are the fates of those in the ATF involved with Fast and Furious:

ATF agent William Newell, head of Group 7 in Phoenix: In August 2011, Group 7 head Newell became a special assistant to the assistant director of the ATF's Office of Management. The ATF called it a transfer.[56] Newell's lawyer, former Justice Department attorney Paul E. Pelletier, said, "We need more, not less, public servants like Special Agent Newell and the men and women who, despite the challenges imposed by our nation's gun laws and the legal system in which they operated, strove to make a difference and tried their level best to put an end to the illegal gun trafficking the plagues the Southwest Border." He claimed that investigators from the offices of Issa and Grassley were politically motivated: "I have learned that the ultimate success and legitimacy of any investigation depends upon the capacity of investigators to blindly follow the evidence where it leads and to neutrally and dispassionately evaluate that evidence before reaching a conclusion. Given your staff's tortured factual conclusions, your staff's utter disregard of any evidence that contravened or rebutted the preordained and misdirected conclusions of misconduct, speculation to motive is unnecessary."[57] Despite Sharyl Attkisson's report in December 2012 that Newell was likely to be fired,[58] Newell is still working for the ATF in a low-level position in Utah, riding out the rest of his career. Calls to the ATF for comment were not returned.

ATF agent David Voth, Fast and Furious team leader: In August 2011, Voth became a branch chief for the ATF's tobacco division. Again, ATF called it a transfer.[59] Despite Attkisson's report in December 2012 that Voth, like Newell, was likely to be fired,[60] Voth is reportedly still working for ATF. Calls to the ATF for comment were not returned.

ATF agent George Gillett, former assistant special agent in charge, of ATF Phoenix: Gillett ended up at the ATF headquarters in Washington as a liaison to the federal Bureau of Prisons. In January 2013, the *Wall Street Journal* reported that he was under investigation because his gun, an FN Five-seven semiautomatic pistol, ended up at a crime scene in Mexico—a November 23, 2012, shoot-out between the Sinaloa Cartel and the Mexican military. At that shoot-out, Mexican beauty queen Maria Susana Gamez was killed.[61]

ATF agent Mark Chait, assistant director for field operations: Retired with full benefits. ATF did not return request for comment.

ATF agent Hope MacAllister, lead agent: MacAllister is reportedly still an agent in Phoenix, despite reports of upcoming disciplinary action by ATF.[62] Request for ATF comment has not been returned.

ATF agent Tonya English: She's reportedly still in Phoenix as well, despite similar reports of upcoming disciplinary action.[63] Request for ATF comment has not been returned.

ATF deputy director William Hoover: Hoover resigned with benefits.[64]

ATF acting director Ken Melson: After Holder denied knowledge of Fast and Furious, Melson, who also said he knew nothing about Fast and Furious—an untenable position, given the documentary evidence—ended up telling the Department of Justice that their position was simply wrong.[65] Almost immediately, rumors began to swirl that Melson would be fired. Meanwhile, the administration was already tapping anti-gun ATF Chicago head Andrew Traver for Melson's replacement.[66] Melson, worried that he might be fired, told Senator Grassley's chief investigator that he wanted to talk. On July 4, 2011, he sat down with congressional staffers and explained that Justice had barred him from talking to Congress and that, according to the *Washington Post*,

"Justice officials seemed to be more concerned about protecting the political appointees at the top of the department." Issa followed up with Holder after the meeting, warning him not to retaliate against Melson for talking.[67] In August 2011, Melson was reassigned anyway . . . within Eric Holder's Justice Department.[68] He retired with full benefits, and now is a lecturer in law at George Washington University. His biography, of course, contains no mention of Fast and Furious.[69]

And what of Eric Holder's Justice Department? Nothing happened to anyone there, either:

Gary Grindler, Attorney General Eric Holder's chief of staff: Grindler resigned from the Justice Department in December 2012 after the inspector general's report labeled it "significant and troubling" that he supposedly didn't inform Holder about Fast and Furious. Holder obviously didn't see it that way—when Grindler left, Holder said that he had "demonstrated time and again his good judgment and an ability to make the tough—and correct—decisions."[70] He is currently a partner with the international law firm King & Spalding's Special Matters/ Government Investigations Practice Group—precisely his job before he left to join the Obama administration.[71]

Lanny Breuer, assistant attorney general: In January 2013, Breuer resigned with benefits. The Justice Department investigator general's report blamed Breuer in part for failing to notify his higher-ups about Fast and Furious: "we believe that Breuer should have promptly informed the deputy attorney general or the attorney general about the matter in April 2010. Breuer failed to do so." Eric Holder praised him to the skies, even going so far as to thank Breuer for what he had done in "the fight against violent crime along the southwest border and across the country."[72] Breuer is currently vice chair for Covington & Burlington.[73]

Ronald Weich, assistant attorney general for legislative affairs: In July 2012, Weich stepped down from Justice to become dean of University of Baltimore School of Law. He took his benefits with him. He left office still insisting that the ATF "doesn't sanction or approve of the transfer of weapons to Mexico."[74]

Emory Hurley, assistant U.S. attorney in Phoenix: Hurley was reassigned from the criminal to the civil division in August 2011.[75]

Dennis Burke, U.S. attorney for the District of Arizona: Burke resigned his position in August 2011, keeping his benefits. "I am very proud of the dedication and success of the employees in this office," he wrote in his resignation letter to President Obama. "It has really been an extreme pleasure to serve you in this administration and I am confident this office will continue in its immense success and impact."[76] Upon his exit, Holder praised Burke for his "dedication and service to the Department of Justice over these many years and commend[ed] his decision to place the interests of the U.S. Attorney's Office above all else." There was no mention of Fast and Furious.[77] Almost a year later, the Justice Department's inspector general criticized Burke for leaking a document to Fox News attempting to discredit a whistle-blower. The inspector general called Burke's actions "particularly egregious" and "wholly unbefitting a U.S. attorney." Before that leak, Burke had leaked another document to the *New York Times*.[78]

Attorney General Eric Holder: He's still attorney general.

In December 2012, the Terry family launched a lawsuit against the Justice Department and ATF seeking $25 million for wrongful death. The Terry family also sued the gun shops involved in the operation; many of the gun shop owners claim that they felt roped into the scheme, knowing that the ATF regulated their livelihoods.[79] The complaint was directed against agents and officers with the ATF, as well as Emory Hurley, attorney with the department. Lone Wolf Trading Company Inc. and Andre Howard, who were responsible for the gun sales, were also named in the lawsuit.

Those parties, the lawsuit claimed, "conceived Operation Fast and Furious and throughout the conduct of that operation acted to ensure that dangerous firearms were distributed to the Mexican drug cartels, the most violent criminal organizations in North America." Their plan, the lawsuit claimed, was formed "despite the foreseeable certainty that the Mexican drug cartels who Defendant Lone Wolf sold firearms to and who the ATF Defendants and Defendant Hurley intended to receive the firearms would then use those weapons to cause the injury and death to members of the public, including and especially other law enforcement officers like Brian Terry."[80]

As of December 2012, just twenty people had been charged in the gunrunning case, and fifteen of them had pleaded guilty. With regard to

Terry's death, just two of the five men involved have been caught; three others remain on the lam.[81]

CLOSING ARGUMENT

The three elements to involuntary manslaughter are certainly present in Fast and Furious. First, the prosecution must prove that someone was killed as a result of an act by the defendant. That element requires little argument to prove: beyond Border Patrol agent Brian Terry and Immigration and Customs Enforcement agent Jamie Zapata, Fast and Furious guns have been used in the deaths of hundreds of Mexicans.

The second element of involuntary manslaughter is that the act must have been inherently dangerous or reckless. Under Arizona law, the risk must be "of such a nature and degree that disregard of such risk constitutes a gross deviation from the standard of conduct that a reasonable person would observe in the situation." It is difficult to think of a more reckless plan than handing over guns without tracking devices to the Mexican drug cartels, knowing that they will not be identified until they are found at the scene of a crime. Recklessness doesn't go far enough in describing such a plan. As Comedy Central's Jon Stewart put it when he covered Fast and Furious in June 2011, "If this was the plan that they went with, what plan did we reject?"[82] (Naturally, Stewart went back to doing the bidding of his Obama masters; within a year he was mocking Republicans for comparing Fast and Furious to Watergate.[83] He's right. Nobody died during Watergate.)

The third element of involuntary manslaughter is that the defendant knew or should have figured out that his or her action was a threat to life. Not only should the relevant players in Fast and Furious have known that their actions were a threat to life, they *did* know it—they were being told it day in and day out by the gun shop owners involved, as well as perturbed agents on the ground.

And yet nothing was done.

And so the question becomes: how high did this go?

We will likely never know the answer to that question, thanks to the Obama administration's dramatic lack of transparency. Suffice it to say that were the Obama administration a private organization without executive privilege, prosecutions would surely be in order. As Tom Fitton of Judicial Watch put it, "Getting beyond the Obama administration's smokescreen, this lawsuit is about a very simple principle: the public's right to know the full truth about an egregious political scandal that led to the death of at least one American and countless others in Mexico."[84]

Fast and Furious was, simply put, another Obama administration mafia-style operation. Gun trafficking south of the border is under the control of the president under the Arms Control Export Act, but it was certainly never designed to allow the executive branch to become complicit in the murder of Americans—and, in fact, the Arms Export Control Act bars the U.S. government from handing guns to terrorist entities. And that's exactly what happened.

Relying on low-level enforcers anxious to impress the bosses, the administration's political appointees at the Justice Department created Fast and Furious at least partially in order to stump for stricter gun laws. Those political appointees allegedly *celebrated* increased violence in Mexico. Those political appointees allegedly recognized that omelets required broken eggs. Eric Holder lied to Congress. Janet Napolitano, according to reports, lied to Congress. And President Obama sat above it all, smiling it away as something "dumb" while declaring that he, the Big Man, couldn't know about *everything* going on in his administration.

It's only dumb if you get caught. President Obama never was. And even those involved didn't pay the price. Those who were hurt the most by Fast and Furious were the whistle-blowers involved. All of Obama's top cabinet officials emerged unscathed, and continued to serve in his administration. Of the fourteen lower-level officials involved, six are still working in government; the other eight took the Frank Pentangeli option, and left their jobs for cushy jobs elsewhere, their government benefits intact. No one was ever prosecuted—even the guy whose personal firearm ended up at a Fast and Furious crime scene.

But one thing is certain: the president's men were involved. Three years after Brian Terry was murdered in cold blood using American-produced, Justice- and ATF-approved firearms, they're all still on the loose. That's where RICO comes in. While RICO leaves state charges like involuntary manslaughter to the states, the obstruction of justice, retaliation against witnesses and informants, and tampering with witnesses and informants all fall under RICO.

Fast and Furious was a crime that stretched all the way to the top levels of the administration. And that administration must be held responsible in order for the deaths of Brian Terry and hundreds of other to have any meaning.

COUNT 3

★

VIOLATION OF INTERNAL
REVENUE LAWS

Whoever corruptly or by force or threats of force (including any threatening letter or communication) endeavors to intimidate or impede any officer or employee of the United States acting in an official capacity under this title . . . shall, upon conviction thereof, be fined not more than $5,000, or imprisoned not more than 3 years, or both. . . .

—26 U.S. CODE § 7212

★ ★ ★

[A]n employee may take an active part in political management or in political campaigns, except an employee may not use his official authority or influence for the purpose of interfering with or affecting the result of an election . . . [or] knowingly solicit or discourage the participation in any political activity of any person who has an application for any compensation, grant, contract, ruling, license, permit, or certificate pending before the employing office of such employee. . . .

—5 U.S. CODE § 7323

OPENING ARGUMENT

His name was Luis Tascón, and he was just trying to help. Elected to the national legislature, the young left-wing radical was loyal to the president, and deeply committed to rooting out corruption. He knew that this president would do so if given the chance. That's why, after his president's opposition launched a massive campaign against Obama, Tascón began compiling the names of those opponents and publishing them online. He said he was trying to stop fraud.[1]

The president's higher-level officials duly praised Tascón.[2] The president appeared on television and joked with Tascón, asking him whether he was on Tascón's list. Officers across the government used the list to purge opponents of the president's rule, firing state employees, quashing job offers, killing contracts, destroying loans, bankrupting enemies.

Finally, after public attention to the list embarrassed the president, he suggested that it be "archived and buried." He stated, "I say that because I keep receiving some letters . . . that make me think that in some places they still have the Tascón list to determine if somebody is going to get a job or not. Surely it had an important role at one time, but not now." By the same token, when Tascón died, the president said, "I will always remember this great comrade with the deepest affection and acknowledge his integrity and strength."[3]

The president was President Hugo Chávez; the country was Venezuela. But the theme crosses all borders. Every government is filled with Luis Tascóns, eager bureaucrats looking to get ahead. After all, the easiest way to get the attention of the higher-ups is to do them a service. Tascón himself was reelected to the National Assembly, and only found himself on the outs with Chávez after he accused a high-ranking official within the administration of corruption. When it comes to the workings of bureaucracies, there is little difference between tin-pot dictatorships and other forms of administrative government: everyone wants to get ahead, everyone wants to read the tea leaves, and everyone understands that the slightest signal from the top can mean a change in policy. Chávez supporters in Venezuela learned to wear red because the Comandante liked it; when one day he wore a yellow shirt, they considered whether to change the color of theirs.[4]

The enemies list has always been a fundamental tool for would-be banana republic–style leaders. And it's not out of use in the United States.

Shortly after his accession to the Oval Office, President Obama took a trip to Arizona State University to speak at their commencement. Noting that ASU had not given him an honorary degree, based on the fact that he hadn't done anything yet, Obama casually joked, "I really thought this was much ado about nothing, but I do think we all learned an important lesson. I learned never to pick another team over the Sun Devils in my NCAA brackets. . . . President [Michael] Crowe and the Board of Regents will soon learn all about being audited by the IRS." Professor Paul Caron of Pepperdine University rightly pointed out that Internal Revenue Service agents who threaten such audits are immediately terminated. Obama, however, grinned and moved on.[5]

Except that his administration didn't.

THE CHARGES

The Hatch Act of 1939 was passed to prevent the executive branch from using its power to abuse its enemies. In the aftermath of Democratic Party politicians allegedly using the Roosevelt-era Works Progress Administration to pressure political enemies, Senator Carl Hatch pushed through his signature legislation. The original legislation actually included a provision that would have prohibited anyone in the executive branch from taking "any active part in political management or in political campaigns." The Roosevelt administration worked to strip out the language.[6]

Over the past several years, there have been dozens of cases of Hatch Act violations, including Secretary of Health and Human Services Kathleen Sebelius, who gave a political speech during a government event. But there is no question that the Obama administration, in utilizing its power over taxation to hold up the applications of political opponents for the Obama reelection campaign's electoral gain, violated the Hatch Act.

As for violations of the Internal Revenue Code itself, the U.S.

Department of Justice's Tax Division states of the so-called omnibus clause of 26 U.S. Code § 7212, "this charge might also be appropriate when directed at parties who engage in large-scale obstructive conduct involving actual or potential tax returns of third parties." That is a perfect description of the use of the IRS as a political entity, barring entire classes of Obama political enemies from receiving the review and clearance to which they were entitled by law. To prove violation of the "omnibus clause," we must prove that the defendant "(1) in any way corruptly (2) endeavored (3) to obstruct or impede the due administration of the Internal Revenue Code."[7] As we will see, that is precisely what happened from 2010 to 2012.

A SHORT HISTORY OF ENEMIES LISTS

President Obama's administration isn't rare in this respect. Since the rise of administrative government in the United States, targeting of political opposition has become more and more common. It truly began with Franklin Delano Roosevelt, the greatest friend the IRS ever had. During his tenure, FDR sicced the tax authorities on millionaire former Treasury secretary Andrew Mellon. FDR's Treasury secretary Henry Morgenthau Jr. ordered Elmer Irey, head of the criminal division of the Treasury's tax enforcement branch in Washington, to trump up phony tax charges on Mellon. In 1934, despite a Justice Department memo showing that there was nothing legitimate to prosecute Mellon over, the Roosevelt administration announced prosecution against Mellon. Working with the Bureau of Internal Revenue, the FDR administration somehow ginned up fines worth more than $3 million against Mellon. When the original charges were thrown out by a federal grand jury, the supposedly independent Board of Tax Appeals came up with charges worth just under $500,000.[8]

FDR used the IRS to target Senator Huey Long of Louisiana, a fellow Democrat who threatened FDR's hegemony over his populist base; Long ended up speaking against the IRS from the floor of the Senate. FDR also targeted William Randolph Hearst, Father Coughlin, and Representative Hamilton Fish (R-NY), who represented Hyde Park, where FDR lived. For years the IRS dogged Fish, who ended up winning his case against the agency, winning a small tax refund.[9] FDR especially hated Moe Annenberg, the owner of the *Philadelphia Inquirer*; he launched an IRS investigation into him, and refused when Annenberg offered to pay all back taxes. "I want Moe Annenberg for dinner," Roosevelt told Morgenthau. "You're going to have him for breakfast—fried," replied Morgenthau.[10]

FDR wasn't above using the IRS to help his friends, either. In 1942, FDR intervened to save Brown & Root, a Texas defense contractor, on behalf of a young congressman named Lyndon Baines Johnson.[11]

As FDR's son, Elliott, later wrote, "other men's tax returns fascinated Father in the 1930s."[12] He added, "My father may have been the originator of the concept of employing the IRS as a weapon of political retribution."[13]

In the 1950s, the IRS audited Dr. Martin Luther King Jr., resulting in prosecution by the state of Alabama; King was the first person ever prosecuted by the state of Alabama.[14] J. Edgar Hoover, head of the FBI, gave regular intelligence reports on groups ranging from the John Birch Society and the NAACP to President Truman's administration; the program, which was called COINTELPRO, had "unlimited access to tax returns," freely handed out by the IRS. A congressional report found that the IRS "never attempted to find out" why the administration needed that information.[15]

John F. Kennedy used the IRS to target political opposition, according to author John A. Andrew III. Andrew writes that JFK created a "covert effort to discredit the right and undercut its sources of support" by wielding the IRS as a club. It was called the Ideological Organizations Project. The IRS was getting ready to go after ten thousand organizations before JFK was shot.

JFK's good friends Victor and Walter Reuther, both radical left union leaders, sent a twenty-four-page memo to JFK suggesting that the IRS target political enemies. The proposed targets: the "far right." Three-quarters of those audited were enemies of the JFK administration.[16] JFK's IRS even used bugs to monitor its enemies.[17]

The audits continued up to JFK's death. According to former representative John Shadegg (R-AZ), the IRS audited his father, a top political adviser to Senator Barry Goldwater (R-AZ) in 1963. The first audit meeting took place on November 22, 1963. That day, Lee Harvey Oswald assassinated Kennedy. After the news broke, the lead auditor shut his notebook and said, "Well, I guess that ends this discussion, doesn't it?"[18]

JFK's legacy of IRS audits carried forward to the Johnson administration.[19] Under LBJ, Hoover took the lead in utilizing the IRS for political intimidation.[20] When Senator Edward Long (D-MO) tried to investigate the IRS, the IRS promptly leaked information about his ties to union honcho Jimmy Hoffa, leading Long to lose his seat.

Nixon's IRS followed the pattern set by JFK. Nixon himself said he wanted a hit man for the IRS commissioner's job: "I want to be sure he is a ruthless son of a bitch, that he will do what he's told, that every income-tax return I want to see I see, that he will go after our enemies and not our friends. Now, it's as simple as that. If he isn't, he doesn't get the job."[21]

The Nixon administration infamously composed its own enemies list. George T. Bell, special assistant to Nixon, created the list, labeled "the list of opponents." It included figures ranging from Alexander Barkan, national director of the AFL-CIO's Committee on Political Education, to Ed Guthman, managing editor of the *Los Angeles Times* ("It is time to give him the message"), to Michigan Democratic congressman John Conyers ("Has known weakness for white females").[22]

When Congress considered impeaching Nixon before his resignation, one of the charges included use of the IRS to target opponents.[23]

Bill Clinton, one of modern history's worst administrative thugs, used his IRS to target political opposition as well. Between 1992 and 1997, the Clinton administration went light on IRS audits for states he wanted to win, and went heavy in states he knew he'd lose. During Travelgate, the Hillary Clinton–led effort to stack the Bill Clinton White House travel office with friends, an investigation found that an associate White House counsel had sought IRS help in going after current employees.[24]

When Judicial Watch was formed in the 1990s and began suing for President Bill Clinton's records, it quickly found itself on the wrong end of an IRS audit. "What do you expect when you sue the president?"

said senior IRS official Paul Breslan.[25] Judicial Watch's audit began one month after the White House received an email asking "how can this obviously partisan organization be classified as tax exempt." As Judicial Watch reported in its book *The Corruption Chronicles,* "Several democratic politicians, including Representatives Charlie Rangel (D-NY), Martin Frost (D-TX), Jim Moran (D-VA), Tom Harkin (D-IA), John Lewis (D-GA), and Richard Neal (D-MA), were linked to requests that the IRS check out our nonprofit status." The former commissioner of the IRS Donald Alexander stated, "the circumstances surrounding the IRS's audit of Judicial Watch are unusual and deviate from the procedures and practices normally followed by the IRS when investigating and auditing 501(c)(3) tax-exempt organizations."

Other conservative groups, including the National Rifle Association and the Heritage Foundation, also complained of targeting, as did Concerned Women for America, *National Review,* and Joseph Farah's Western Center for Journalism.

President Clinton's alleged sexual misconduct victims fell victim to another sort of targeting from the IRS. After Juanita Broaddrick accused Clinton of rape, her nursing home business was audited. Gennifer Flowers was audited shortly after she sued James Carville, George Stephanopoulos, Little, Brown & Company, and Hillary Rodham Clinton for defamation. Clinton girlfriend Elizabeth Ward Gracen was audited. Even Katherine Prudhomme, a citizen who had the temerity to ask Vice President Al Gore about Broaddrick, was audited.[26] When Paula Jones filed a sexual misconduct suit against Clinton and then refused to settle, the IRS launched an audit against her the very next day. "I find the timing very peculiar," said a spokesperson for the Jones family. "They're a family with two little children. They have one car, they rent a little apartment. How many people renting and making under $40,000 a year get audited?"[27]

OBAMA'S EARLY ENEMIES

President Obama is just as cutthroat a politician as any of his presidential predecessors. That willingness to use dirt against political opponents began early—and Obama has always been careful to avoid getting his hands dirty in the process. Illinois state senator Obama polled as an underdog to Democrat primary opponent Blair Hull in 2004. Hull, a magnificently wealthy former securities trader, had Obama on the ropes when the *Chicago Tribune* suddenly released information about Hull's sealed divorce records, which showed that his second ex-wife filed for an order of protection against him. Where did the *Tribune* get that information? The *Tribune* itself later reported that Obama's "campaign worked aggressively behind the scenes to fuel controversy about Hull's filings."[28] The *New York Times* reported that David Axelrod may have released the story originally, especially given the fact that both parties in the Hull divorce wanted to keep the records under wraps. As Ann Coulter relates, "Both Hull and his ex-wife opposed releasing their sealed divorce records, but they finally relented in response to the media's hysteria—eighteen days before the primary. Hull was forced to spend four minutes of a debate detailing the abuse allegation in his divorce papers, explaining that his ex-wife 'kicked me in the leg and I hit her shin to try to get her to not continue to kick me.'" Hull ended up finishing third in the primary.

Obama trailed Republican opponent Jack Ryan in the general election polling as well. Ryan was a well-regarded former Goldman Sachs partner, a Harvard Law School and Harvard Business School graduate who spent his time after making millions teaching at an inner-city school in the poor South Side of Chicago. Fortunately, the *Tribune* was available to help out again. This time, they filed for release of Ryan's custody records from Hollywood actress Jeri Lynn Ryan. Amid those filings were allegations by Jeri that Jack had taken her to "sex clubs" overseas, as well as in New York and New Orleans. Jack denied her claims—after all, this was a divorce case, when spouses make ridiculous claims on a regular basis—but the media was all over it. Ryan dropped out of the race. Alan Keyes stepped in, and was quickly blown away by Obama.[29]

Obama's team carried forward those tactics in 2008, this time with the help of would-be do-gooders within the government. Samuel Joseph Wurzelbacher, better known as Joe the Plumber, was confronted by then-senator Obama in his driveway on October 12, 2008. He had the temerity to ask Obama questions about his economic plans: "I'm getting ready to buy a company that makes $250,000 to $280,000 a

year. Your new tax plan's going to tax me more, isn't it?" Obama un-
wisely answered, "I think when you spread the wealth around, it's good
for everybody." That answer catapulted Wurzelbacher—aka Joe the
Plumber—to the national spotlight. During the third presidential debate between Republican nominee John McCain and Obama, McCain
brought up Wurzelbacher multiple times. Wurzelbacher then told Katie
Couric of *CBS Evening News* that Obama's tax plan was a slippery slope
toward socialism. In Ohio, McCain told a crowd that they were "all Joe
the Plumber."

With Joe the Plumber becoming a rallying cry for Republicans, the
media began digging into this new obstacle to their favored candidate.
On October 16, four days after the initial encounter, ABC News reported that Wurzelbacher had an outstanding tax lien of approximately
$1,200.[30]

Wurzelbacher quickly paid what he owed. But while the media dug
into Wurzelbacher's past, state employees in Ohio did the same with his
government records. Three separate times, accounts assigned variously
to the offices of Ohio attorney general Nancy H. Rogers, the Cuyahoga
County Child Support Enforcement Agency, and the Toledo Police Department were used to search confidential government information on
Wurzelbacher.[31]

That wasn't Obama's fault. But he certainly didn't speak out too stri-
dently about the digging. His Ohio spokesman, Isaac Baker, said, "Invasions of privacy should not be tolerated. If these records were accessed
inappropriately, it had nothing to do with our campaign and should
be investigated fully." That was the extent of the campaign's response.[32]
New York mayor Rudy Giuliani also called for a full-scale investigation,
but was slightly less tepid in his rationale: "The answer to this should
not be given three to four weeks after election day. . . . If this is the
way an Obama administration is going to conduct itself, the American
people have a right to know this before the fact."[33]

Unfortunately, the investigation didn't conclude until substantially
after the election. On November 20, 2008, the Ohio inspector general reported that Wurzelbacher's records had indeed been improperly
searched. It turned out that Helen E. Jones-Kelley, head of the Ohio
Department of Jobs and Family Services, authorized the searches on

child support payments, temporary aid to families, and unemployment benefits. The report concluded that even though the searches "were done in the midst of a political campaign," it's not clear the information was released "in an effort to support any political activity or agenda."[34] Later, it turned out, Jones-Kelley had been sending fund-raising information to the Obama campaign, and using state email accounts to do so. She also donated $2,500 to Obama's campaign. She resigned from her post on December 17, 2008. So did two other members of her staff. Democratic governor Ted Strickland announced that he "values Helen Jones-Kelley's years of public service as a dedicated advocate for the most vulnerable among us."[35] Wurzelbacher's lawsuit, with the help of Judicial Watch, was dismissed on the grounds that Jones-Kelley's violation of his privacy didn't violate his privacy rights under the Constitution. Tom Fitton of Judicial Watch commented, "The implications of this court decision are frightening. Essentially, the court has said that government officials can feel free to rifle through the private files of citizens without fear of being held accountable in court."[36]

TEA PARTY "TERRORISTS"

Americans celebrated President Obama's inauguration as though it were a coronation. Anchors openly wept on television. Even some conservative commentators wrongly hailed his election as the culmination of the civil rights movement, as though the election of an unqualified black man to the nation's highest office were anything but a perverse form of reverse racism. In the early days of his tenure, Obama had few opponents. His approval rating clocked in at a stellar 68 percent, with just 12 percent disapproving.[37]

But instead of focusing laserlike on the economy, as he had repeatedly promised during his presidential campaign, Obama began crusading for a nationalized health-care program. The push for Obamacare, as it came to be called, launched on March 5, 2009, with Obama holding a conference to discuss health-care reform. Bills began moving through the House in July, and then moved to the Senate in September. Obama's approval ratings sank from 68 percent to 56 percent.[38]

That sinking approval rating came thanks to a new movement in American politics: the Tea Party. Launched shortly after Obama's inauguration in response to his financial proposals, the Tea Party gained prominence as a national movement. Rick Santelli of CNBC, from the floor of the Chicago Mercantile Exchange, stated that the Obama plan to change mortgage standards was "promoting bad behavior." He said that traders should throw derivatives into the Chicago River on July 1, 2009. The idea quickly took off.

The Tea Party's grassroots philosophy of small government alienated and frightened the Obama administration, skyrocketing to the top of the Obama hit list. Marking his hundredth day in office, Obama bashed the Tea Party: "Those of you who are watching certain news channels on which I'm not very popular, and you see folks waving tea bags around," Obama said, "let me just remind them that I am happy to have a serious conversation about how we are going to cut our health care costs down over the long term, how we are going to stabilize Social Security. But let's not play games and pretend that the reason [for the deficit] is because of the Recovery Act."[39] In November 2009, Obama again termed Tea Partiers "tea-baggers," a fringe sexual slang term popularized by Tea Party opponents to degrade the movement.[40]

Obama's rhetoric permeated the media; Rachel Maddow and Bill Maher both began using the term *tea-bagger* as well. The NAACP suggested that the Tea Partiers were closet racists. So did Morgan Freeman, Sean Penn, Alan Cumming, and Janeane Garofalo. Obama himself played the race card with regard to the Tea Party, according to journalist Kenneth T. Walsh: "Obama, in his most candid moments, acknowledged that race was still a problem. In May 2010, he told guests at a private White House dinner that race was probably a key component in the rising opposition to his presidency from conservatives, especially right-wing activists in the anti-incumbent 'Tea Party' movement that was then surging across the country."[41]

In the minds of the Obama higher-ups, the Tea Party wasn't merely racist, it was terrorist. When Tea Partiers urged Congress to use the debt limit as a lever to limit federal spending, former Obama car czar Steven Rattner told MSNBC's audience that Tea Partiers wanted to use a "form of economic terrorism." They were, he said, strapping themselves "with dynamite standing in the middle of Times Square at rush hour, and say-ing 'either you do it my way, or we're going to blow you up.'"[42] Joe Klein of *Time* said, "Osama bin Laden, if he were still alive, could not have come up with a more clever strategy for strangling our nation."[43]

There were early indicators that the Obama administration did not limit its Tea Party opposition to rhetoric. The Department of Homeland Security's first major report on terrorism targeted "rightwing extrem-ism." DHS suggested, "Rightwing extremists have capitalized on the election of the first African American president." DHS continued, "Many rightwing extremists are antagonistic toward the new presiden-tial administration and its perceived stance on a range of issues, includ-ing immigration and citizenship, the expansion of social programs to minorities, and restrictions on firearms ownership and use." Those "rightwing extremists" included those who were "mainly antigovern-ment, rejecting federal authority in favor of state or local authority, or rejecting government authority entirely. It may include groups and in-dividuals that are dedicated to a single issue, such as opposition to abor-tion or immigration."[44] The Obama IRS would later use many of these same descriptors in targeting its enemies.

The IRS got into the act early, too. Unearthed emails between Lois Lerner, the director of the exempt-organizations division, and a Federal Elections Commission lawyer demonstrated nefarious connections be-tween the two organizations in pursuit of Obama-friendly objectives. The FEC lawyer wrote to Lerner in February 2009: "Several months ago . . . I spoke with you about the American Future Fund, a 501(c)(4) organization that had submitted an exemption application the IRS [*sic*]. . . .When we spoke last July, you had told us that the American Future Fund had not received an exemption letter from the IRS." Such correspondence appeared to break the law, since the FEC was not sup-posed to have confidential IRS information. The FEC was, at the time, investigating the American Future Fund based on a complaint from the Minnesota Democratic Farmer Labor Party. Based on the IRS informa-tion, the FEC recommended prosecution. Nonetheless, the FEC com-missioners recommended unanimously that the case be dropped.

That was not the last time the FEC attorney contacted the IRS. He also asked about the American Issues Project: "I was also wondering if you could tell me whether the IRS had issued an exemption letter to a group called the American Issues Project? The group also appears to be the successor of two other organizations, Citizens for the Republic and Avenger, Inc."[45]

The correspondence between the FEC and the IRS represented the tip of the iceberg. Things were about to get much worse for conservative nonprofit applicants.

CLIMATE OF RETALIATION

With the 2010 congressional elections approaching, the Obama administration recognized trouble for Democrats. Polling data showed that Republicans were headed for historic victories in Congress, and historic momentum leading into the presidential election of 2012. Democrats were especially worried about the input of conservative social welfare 501(c)(4) groups on the election cycle in the aftermath of the 2010 Supreme Court decision *Citizens United v. Federal Election Commission*. President Obama hated the decision so much that he lied about it in front of the Supreme Court justices in his 2010 State of the Union address. "Last week, the Supreme Court reversed a century of law to open the floodgates for special interests—including foreign companies—to spend without limit in our elections," Obama said as Justice Samuel Alito quietly shook his head at the lie. "Well, I don't think American elections should be bankrolled by America's most powerful interests, and worse, by foreign entities. They should be decided by the American people, and that's why I'm urging Democrats and Republicans to pass a bill that helps to right this wrong."[46]

Hatred for conservative nonprofits became a central part of the Obama administration's 2010 and 2012 electoral efforts. That hatred seeped down to the IRS, which, as we'll see, soon picked up the Obama administration's signal and began targeting just those entities the Obama campaign wanted to see targeted.

In August 2010, an Obama administration official, Austan Goolsbee, told reporters in a background briefing that Koch Industries—the company owned by the conservative Koch brothers, long a bugaboo of the Obama team—was one of many "multibillion-dollar businesses that are structured as partnerships in ways that allow them to avoid paying sizable corporate taxes." Senator Charles Grassley (R-IA) immediately fired back, pointing out that such revelations violated tax confidentiality. The White House then said that it was all a big mistake: "The official's statement was not based on any review of tax filings and we will not use this example in the future."[47]

The Treasury Department launched an investigation. But the results of that investigation have never been released. Unless the Treasury Department tosses the prosecution to the Department of Justice, it will remain secret.[48]

But that wasn't the end of the story. In October, Republican congressmen warned that the IRS could be auditing conservative groups for political purposes. Senator Max Baucus (D-MT) actually requested an IRS review into political activities of particular tax-exempt groups, "chill[ing] the legitimate exercise of First Amendment rights," according to Senators Orrin Hatch (R-UT) and Jon Kyl (R-AZ). Baucus's requested IRS review would have targeted "major" tax-exempt organizations, which he said were used as "political pawns" by "political campaigns and powerful individuals."

The *New York Times* reported that despite that chilling effect, Democrats were intent on shutting down political opposition from the nonprofit world: "As the November elections approach, Democrats have complained that well-financed conservative groups, including the Chamber of Commerce, Crossroads GPS, Americans for Prosperity, and Americans for Job Security—have improperly exploited gaps in federal tax and campaign finance law to finance attacks on Democratic candidates."[49]

Complaints were filed against the Chamber of Congress; members of the Obama administration, pressed forward by groups like ThinkProgress, began implying that foreign funding stood behind the Chamber. "Just this week, we learned that one of the largest groups paying for these ads regularly takes in money from foreign corporations," Obama said. He continued, "[G]roups that receive foreign money are spending huge sums to influence American elections, and they won't tell you where the money for their ads come from." There was no evidence of any such foreign funding. Nonetheless, Obama directly attacked several conservative nonprofits, claiming they violated tax law: "the American people deserve to know who's trying to sway their elections. . . . It could be the oil industry, the insurance industry, Wall Street—you'll never know. Their lips are sealed, but the floodgates are open. And almost every one of them is run by Republican operatives, even though they're posing as nonprofit, nonpolitical groups, with names like Americans for Prosperity, or the Committee for Truth in Politics."[50]

The IRS heard about all of this. In October 2010, Lois Lerner, the head of the tax-exempt section of the IRS, told Duke University's Sanford School of Public Policy that "everyone is up in arms because they don't like" the rise of 501(c)(4)s. She said, "[E]verybody is screaming at us right now, 'Fix it now before the election. Can't you see how much these people are spending.'" She vowed to look at the tax forms of specified groups the following year.[51] In November 2011, IRS commissioner Douglas H. Shulman said the IRS would focus on "tax-return preparers who have been identified as high risk."[52]

That was just the beginning of the assault. In March 2012, seven senators—Chuck Schumer (D-NY), Michael Bennet (D-CO), Sheldon Whitehouse (D-RI), Jeff Merkley (D-OR), Tom Udall (D-NM), Jeanne Shaheen (D-NH), and Al Franken (D-MN)—wrote a letter to the IRS urging political scrutiny for nonprofit groups, particularly 501(c)(4) "social welfare" organizations. "We urge the IRS to take these steps immediately to prevent abuse of the tax code by political groups focused on federal election activities. But if the IRS is unable to issue administrative guidance in this area then we plan to introduce legislation to accomplish these important changes," the letter said. It was sent to IRS commissioner Shulman.[53]

"The shadowy attack ads we see every day should be brought into the light," said Bennet. "The largest contributors should stand by the ads they've paid for, the voters should know who's behind these ads, and these super PACs should not be allowed to abuse our tax code by masquerading as nonprofit charities." Jay Sekulow of the American Center for Law and Justice shot back, "This is obviously a coordinated effort by the IRS to stifle these Tea Party and Tea Party–affiliated groups, and to stifle free speech activities. It's as onerous as what they did to the NAACP in the 1950s, and I plan to make that point." The *New York Times* commented, "Into that charged atmosphere, the I.R.S. is heightening its own push to ensure that nonprofits are sticking to their primary role as social welfare groups, an effort that began gingerly in 2011." The IRS eventually answered the Democrats, saying it would "review organizations to ensure that they have classified themselves correctly and that they are complying with applicable rules." The *Times* reported one group, specifically, as claiming discrimination: the Kentucky 9/12 Project, originally founded after Glenn Beck launched his 9/12 project.[54] The complaints, however, came from across the country.

As Democrats pushed forward with their IRS pressure, Shulman visited the White House, again and again and again. Between January 2009 and November 2012, he visited the White House 157 times.[55] During the period 132 different congresspeople contacted Shulman about problems with tax exemptions; there were forty-two news stories about it. Shulman later testified that he had not researched the issue at all at the time;[56] he also said that his only truly memorable visit was the White House Easter Egg Roll, although he believed that a huge number of the visits centered on the implementation of Obamacare.[57] Called in March 2012 before Congress to discuss the complaints about IRS scrutiny, Shulman was grilled by Representative Charles Boustany (R-LA), who asked about letters he'd received from constituents about the IRS. "Can you give us assurances that the IRS is not targeting particular groups based on political leanings?" Boustany asked. Shulman answered unequivocally: *"First, let me start by saying, yes, I can give you assurances. As you know, we pride ourselves on being a non-political, non-partisan organization. . . . There is absolutely no targeting. This is the kind of back-and-forth that happens when people apply for 501(c)(4) status."*[58]

THE TARGETING THAT WASN'T

The same month Shulman denied political targeting of Obama's political adversaries, IRS employees in Cincinnati suddenly began focusing with laser eyes on nonprofit groups—conservative nonprofit groups in particular. One Cincinnati IRS employee told the House Oversight

Committee that in March 2010 he or she became aware of applications referencing the Tea Party or conservatism. Early that month, said the witness, an IRS supervisor mandated extra checks with regard to similar applications. "He told me that Washington, D.C., wanted some cases," the witness told the committee. Seven cases were referred to Washington, D.C. "As an agent," the witness stated, "we are controlled by many, many people. We have to submit many, many reports. So the chance of two agents being rogue and doing things like that could never happen." Tea Party application requests, the witness stated, came from the top. Another witness said that the IRS deliberately "was not processing these applications fairly and timely."[59] That alone would be enough to violate Internal Revenue Code regulations against political targeting.

But that was just the beginning. In May 2010, the Determinations Unit came up with what it called the "Be on the Look Out" (BOLO) list. By June 2010, IRS agents entered training on Tea Party cases. In July 2010, Determinations Unit management had told its specialists to single out Tea Party applications. The first formal BOLO listing circulated through the IRS in August 2010. The criteria: "Tea Party organizations applying for IRC § 501(c)(3) or IRC § 501(c)(4) status."[60] In February 2011, despite her later protestations to the contrary, Lerner knew about targeting of the Tea Party, and insisted that such cases be sent to Washington, D.C., rather than left in the outlying Cincinnati office. "Tea Party Matter very dangerous," she wrote in an email. "Counsel and [IRS senior technical adviser] Judy Kindell need to be in on this one. . . . Cincy should probably NOT have these cases."[61]

By July 2011, the BOLO list had expanded to include "Tea Party," "Patriots," "9/12 Project," any organizations concerned about issues like "government spending, government debt or taxes," organizations looking to "make America a better place to live," or using any statements in the application criticizing how "the country is being run." In the understatement of the century, the inspector general of the IRS, J. Russell George, found that the BOLO "gives the appearance that the IRS is not impartial in conducting its mission."[62] Internal IRS documents later showed that during this time, the IRS lawyers in Washington targeted 162 groups by name, specifically worrying about "anti-Obama rhetoric" emanating from some of them. More than 80 percent of the

162 groups were conservative. The IRS suggested they were engaging in "propaganda"—a word that never appears in 501(c)(4) law, and would constitute a subjective characterization by partisan hacks. Patriots of Charleston, for example, found itself singled out by the IRS for "negative Obama commentary."[63]

After the director of exempt organizations, Lois Lerner, found out about the BOLO, the inspector general reported that she "immediately directed the criteria be changed." A month later, they were indeed changed to focus on more general factors. But in January 2012, the standards were changed back. In May 2012, the director of rulings and agreements, Holly Paz, changed the standards back to normal. But the IRS agents got the hint. During the period May 2010 through May 2012, the inspector general reported, "all cases with Tea Party, Patriots, or 9/12 in their names were forwarded to the team of specialists." Meanwhile, forty-four cases that should have been flagged were not. Overall, the political cases took "significantly longer than average to process," effectively ruling many such organizations largely ineffective for the entirety of the 2012 cycle. As of December 2012, 81 percent of political cases had been open longer than a year, with an average of 574 calendar days. As for the IRS's intrusive and inappropriate questions for nonprofits, those stopped suddenly as soon as media attention became heavy. Of the 170 organizations to which the IRS sent requests for additional information, 58 percent were asked inappropriate questions.[64]

On July 10, 2012, Lois Lerner's adviser, Sharon Light, sent Lerner a story from National Public Radio complaining about how outside groups were posing a challenge to Democrats seeking to retain their majority in the Senate. In specific, the piece reported that the Democratic Senatorial Campaign Committee was asking the FEC to target Crossroads GPS and Americans for Prosperity. "Perhaps the FEC will save the day," Lerner replied.[65]

Lerner and commissioner of tax-exempt organizations Sarah Hall Ingram also communicated directly with the White House. Much later, in October 2013, documents broke showing that Lerner had communicated confidential IRS information directly to the White House with regard to conservative groups opposing President Obama's contraception mandate under the Affordable Care Act. The emails, which were given to the House Oversight Committee, were redacted with the note "6103," a reference to the Internal Revenue Code prohibiting federal employees from disclosure of "any return or return information obtained by him in any manner in connection with his service as such an officer or an employee."[66] Overall, Ingram visited the White House 165 times, 155 of those meetings to hang out with deputy assistant to the president for health policy, Jeanne Lambrew.[67]

The Obama IRS also began auditing many of Republican presidential candidate Mitt Romney's biggest donors. As Obama ran neck and neck with Romney, the Obama campaign distributed a list of eight "wealthy individuals with less-than-reputable records," suggesting that these Romney backers were dirty capitalists. One of those men was Frank VanderSloot, national cochair of Romney's finance committee, who gave a pro-Romney super PAC $1 million. Within a week and a half of the Obama hit list hitting the Web, a former staffer on the Senate Permanent Subcommittee on Investigations showed up in Idaho Falls, Idaho, to look for legal records about VanderSloot. Two months later, the IRS announced an audit. One week after that, the Department of Labor began an audit of VanderSloot Farms. Two months after that, the IRS audited yet another VanderSloot company. VanderSloot told Breitbart News, "I've been through one audit, maybe, surely not in the last two decades, I'm thinking thirty years ago. Now, to be hit with two IRS audits within a span of two months of each other? And coming right on the heels of the president's list? Those things just look awful suspicious."[68] VanderSloot wasn't the only top Romney supporter to meet the IRS's watchful eye. So did megadonor Sheldon Adelson.[69] The Obama campaign singled Adelson out for especially anti-Semitic treatment, accusing him of using "dirty money" in his political donations.[70]

That wasn't all. The IRS also handed confidential files about conservative groups to liberal allies—a blatant violation of Internal Revenue Code, as well as a violation of the Hatch Act, given the attempt to sink conservative groups during electioneering. John Eastman's National Organization for Marriage (NOM) apparently watched in horror as a full list of the organization's donors leaked to the far-left Human Rights Campaign, which quickly published the list online. The documents revealed that Mitt Romney's political committee had given NOM cash. Eastman later told Congress that his experts had backtraced the documents posted at the HRC website and found "internal IRS stamps . . . [existing only] within the IRS." He added, "If that's inadvertent, the word no longer means anything."[71]

ProPublica, a liberal outlet, received IRS leaks as well. That publication honorably revealed the IRS's activities within days of the IRS's bias revelations. According to ProPublica, the group asked the IRS for sixty-seven nonprofit applications; the Cincinnati office, which reviewed the nonprofit applications, promptly sent over applications and supporting documents for thirty-one groups. The turnaround time: thirteen days. Meanwhile, conservative nonprofit applicants waited for years for a response. Nine of those hadn't been approved, and weren't supposed to be public. ProPublica then published six of them after redacting financial information. Why would the IRS turn over such documents? ProPublica's stated mission in the run-up to the 2012 election gibed perfectly with the Obama administration's: "Before the 2012 election, ProPublica devoted months to showing how dozens of social-welfare nonprofits had misled the IRS about their political activity on their applications and tax returns." Acting IRS commissioner Steven Miller later testified that the agency handed over the files "inadvertent[ly]."[72]

Meanwhile, as the IRS went after conservative nonprofits, it actually offered campaigning *advice* to black churches in the hopes that *those* nonprofits would get out the vote for President Obama. Before the 2012 election, Attorney General Holder and Shulman, as well as senior IRS official Peter Lorenzetti, met with black church leaders, with Lorenzetti stating, "It is important to note . . . that an organization exempt under 501(c)3—in this case the church or a religious organization—can conduct educational election activities." The event was attended by members of the Congressional Black Caucus, all of whom were Democrats. Representative Emanuel Cleaver (D-MO) actually told MSNBC, "We want to let (the pastors) know that there is a theological responsibility to participate in the political process. We're going to encourage them to encourage their people [to get out the vote]."[73]

"THEY HAVE TO BE HELD FULLY ACCOUNTABLE"

On May 9, 2013, with the inspector general's report about to break, Lois Lerner called one Celia Roady, a Washington tax lawyer working across the street from the IRS. She asked Roady to come to an event at the American Bar Association Tax Section's Exempt Organizations Committee Meeting and ask her a question the next day. She then provided Roady with the question: Roady would ask Lerner about the IRS's targeting of conservative nonprofits.

The next day, Friday, May 10, Roady asked Lerner her prewritten question. Lerner answered that the IRS had used the terms "Tea Party" and "patriot" and "9/12" as red flags for giving conservative groups closer scrutiny. "That was wrong. That was absolutely incorrect. It was insensitive and it was inappropriate. That's not how we go about selecting cases for further review. The IRS would like to apologize for that." She then blamed low-level employees for the targeting, and said that no higher-ups knew about it at all: "It's the line people that did it without talking to managers. They're IRS workers, they're revenue agents." According to Lerner, some seventy-five groups were targeted inappropriately. The IRS released a statement suggesting that while "mistakes were made initially," those mistakes "were in no way due to any political or partisan rationale." The situation, the IRS claimed, had been "fixed."[74] When asked why she had chosen that moment to reveal the scandal, Lerner said that someone had asked her a question. "Someone asked me a question today, so I answered it," she said. It only took a full week for the planted question to become public.[75] The incompetence didn't stop there. When asked about one of the statistics she gave during a May 10 phone call, Lerner answered, "I'm not good at math."[76]

Lerner also lied egregiously while talking about the rationale behind the targeting. She blamed the IRS's political targeting on the supposed "big uptick" in 501(c)(4) applications. But the numbers don't bear that out. Applicants saw a minor increase after *Citizens United*, but the real jump didn't begin until after the targeting started. Lerner further explained that she didn't know about IRS targeting until after the press made an issue of it, but Lerner was briefed long before the 2012 complaints became public. Glenn Kessler of the *Washington Post*, no conservative, gave Lerner's statements four Pinocchios and wrote, "In some ways, this is just scratching the surface of Lerner's misstatements and weasely wording when the revelations about the IRS's activities first came to light on May 10."[77]

As soon as the news broke of the IRS's admissions, conservative groups emerged from the woodwork to tell their stories—or, more accurately, the media finally began paying attention to the accusations. The Richmond Tea Party showed a letter from IRS specialist Stephen Seok that asked for "the names of donors, contributors and grantors"—all information that the IRS had no right to ask. The extended inquiry, said Richmond Tea Party president Larry Nordvig, had a "very chilling effect" on the group's fund-raising efforts. Wetumpka Tea Party of Alabama similarly saw a two-year delay in its approval process. Becky Gerritson, president of the group, called it "intimidation." Catherine Engelbrecht, whose anti–voter fraud group True the Vote became an Obama administration favorite target, felt scrutiny not just from the IRS but from other federal agencies, including the Federal Elections Commission. An IRS agent told her, "I'm just doing what Washington is telling me to do. I'm just asking what they want me to ask."[78] Tea Party groups in Ohio, Hawaii, Texas, and the rest of the country reported similar experiences. Americans for Prosperity (AFP), a nonprofit group the left likes to portray as a front for the Koch brothers, met especially heavy scrutiny—groups that worked with AFP were asked to explain their relationship with it. "At the time we thought it was awfully odd for the IRS to be interested in something like that," said AFP president Tim Phillips. "Now we know that it was part of a pattern of abuse. This is large-scale and systematic."[79]

The conservative Leadership Institute also complained of IRS targeting, stating that over the course of 2012, the IRS forced the institute to hand over 23,400 pages of documents. Morton Blackwell, president of the Leadership Institute, said, "The IRS' indefensible behavior is worse than we first thought, as it targeted both new and existing conservative groups in politically motivated attacks. Fortunately my Leadership Institute had the resources to stand up to the government's bullying and intimidation. Other groups, including grassroots and tea party groups we've helped train, did not."[80] Jenny Beth Martin of the Tea Party Patriots called on President Obama to apologize.[81]

Those were just the groups that were talking. Multiple groups said they had kept quiet to avoid even more IRS scrutiny.[82]

The IRS did not limit its discriminatory treatment to conservative groups. Pro-Israel groups, too, became targets as the campaign heated up. The Obama administration saw pro-Israel groups as possible obstacles to Obama's support base in the Jewish community. And so such groups were systematically silenced. I personally experienced this while attempting to found a nonprofit designed to allow impoverished Jews to travel to Israel for religious holidays; the project, "One Light" was held up by the IRS, with Lois Lerner personally mailing inappropriate questions. I wasn't the only one. At least five pro-Israel groups were targeted by the IRS based on their hawkish views on Israeli security after the *Washington Post*'s David Ignatius questioned whether such groups should have tax-exempt status, and the American-Arab Anti-Discrimination Committee sent complaints to the IRS. The chief negotiator for the Palestinian Authority even got involved, asking U.S. consul general Daniel Rubinstein about such nonprofit groups.[83]

While conservative groups experienced IRS delays and bureaucratic persecution, liberal groups connected with President Obama sailed through the nonprofit process. The Barack H. Obama Foundation, a nonprofit designed to raise cash for charity in Kenya, got the IRS gold stamp in a month, even though it had operated as a charitable organization for longer than allotted under federal law without IRS approval.[84] One conservative group experimented with a liberal name to see if the IRS would then clear its application. The group originally applied as "Media Trackers," a research site billing itself as a "non-partisan investigative watchdog dedicated to promoting accountability in the media and government." The IRS held up the application for well over a year. After fourteen months, the group reapplied as "Greenhouse Solutions." The IRS approved the application within three weeks.[85]

As information broke, the administration, clearly worried about the blowback, prepared its response. By the following Monday, President Obama was ready to talk. He said he had "no patience" with targeting, even though he himself had targeted groups as early as 2010. He then added, "If in fact IRS personnel engaged in the kind of practices that have been reported on, and were intentionally targeting conservative groups, then that's outrageous. And there's no place for it. And they have to be held fully accountable."[86]

Obama's faux anger entered full swing. "Americans are right to be angry about it, and I am angry about it," he said. He pled ignorance: "I can assure you that I certainly did not know anything about the (inspector general) report." He did not comment on whether he knew about the IRS's targeting, however. Obama then proceeded to deny the need for a special prosecutor to investigate the IRS, instead charging the Eric Holder–led Justice Department with looking into the scandal.[87]

The same day Obama denied knowledge of the IRS scandal, White House spokesman Jay Carney said that the White House counsel knew as early as April 22 about the upcoming inspector general's report. Many of the same Democrats who had asked the IRS to target conservative nonprofits similarly claimed outrage. "These actions by the IRS are an outrageous abuse of power and a breach of the public's trust," said Senator Baucus. "The IRS will now be the ones put under additional scrutiny."[88] Senator Dick Durbin (D-IL), one of the senators who specifically asked the IRS to target conservative groups, said that there was "no basis for targeting within the IRS," and added that he hadn't meant the IRS should hit *only* conservative institutions. Rather, he said, asking for an investigation into conservative group Crossroads GPS was a way to send a warning shot to *all* political organizations.[89] Senate Majority Leader Harry Reid (D-NV) said the story was "very troubling." Other Democrats were more honest, complaining that the new focus on the IRS might stop the IRS from going after conservative groups, hampering liberal election efforts.[90]

On May 15, Miller sent Obama a resignation letter. "It is with regret that I will be departing from the IRS as my acting assignment ends in early June. This has been an incredibly difficult time for the IRS given the events of the past few days, and there is a strong and immediate need to restore public trust in the nation's tax agency," Miller wrote. The same day, Obama appeared at an unscheduled press conference and said that he had requested the resignation.[91] The IRS's conduct, Obama added, was both "inexcusable" and an "outrage." He also said it was "fixable," and vowed to "do everything in my power to make sure nothing like this happens again." Obama's job, he said, was "making sure that the law is applied as it should be in a fair and impartial way." Senate Minority Leader Mitch McConnell (R-KY) doubted Obama's newfound zeal on the issue. If Obama wants to show his good intentions, McConnell said, "he'll work openly and transparently with Congress to get to the bottom of the scandal—no stonewalling, no half-answers, no withholding of witnesses."[92]

Obama did not follow through.

THE COVER-UP

On May 17, Miller testified before Congress about the IRS targeting. Miller admitted, "Partisanship or even the perception of partisanship has no place at the IRS. It cannot even appear to be a consideration in determining the tax exemption of an organization." He then added that he didn't believe partisanship was the rationale behind the IRS's activity. He blamed it on "foolish mistakes" by "people trying to be more efficient in their workload selection." Who were these people? What would be their consequences? Miller wouldn't say. He then noted, laughably, "The agency is moving forward. It has learned its lesson." After eighty years of IRS intimidation tactics, that seemed unlikely.[93]

The same day, J. Russell George testified that despite the inspector general's recommendations about how to fix the IRS, the agency did not want to "clearly document the reason applications are chosen for further review for potential political campaign intervention." They wanted to keep their standards vague. The IRS also did not want to "develop specific guidance for specialists processing potential political cases and publish the guidance on the Internet." In other words, no transparency or accountability. As George said, "we do not consider the concerns in this report to be solved."[94]

A few days, Lois Lerner, who headed the nonprofit division of the IRS, made her way before Congress. There, she promptly pled the Fifth Amendment, protecting herself against self-incrimination. But in doing so, she made a bizarre statement—she was completely innocent, she said, but was pleading the Fifth anyway. "I have not done anything wrong," she said. "I have not broken any laws. I have not violated any IRS rules and regulations and I have not provided false information to this or any other congressional committees." She paused. Then she said she would not "answer any questions or testify about the subject matter of this committee's meeting." She had arguably waived her right to plead the Fifth Amendment by proclaiming her innocence, but the public relations damage was done. Who, exactly, was Lois Lerner protecting? If she was innocent, who wasn't?[95]

The answer, according to the IRS and the Obama administration: low-level officials. As with Benghazi and Fast and Furious, nobody knew anything in the upper echelons. Lerner claimed that the bad guys were "our line people in Cincinnati who handled the applications." The *New York Times* promptly echoed Lerner, claiming that rogue, "low-level employees in what many in the IRS consider a backwater" had done the dirty deeds. Representative Elijah Cummings (D-MD) blamed one particular Cincinnati employee who called himself a "conservative Republican."[96] An internal IRS report on the scandal found that there was no "involvement in these matters by anyone outside of the IRS."[97]

Some of the "low-level employees" knew where their bread was buttered. When the inspector general quizzed the top IRS officials as to whether the BOLO listing was "influenced by any individual or organization outside the IRS," they demurred. They claimed instead that the Determinations Unit "developed and implemented inappropriate criteria in part due to insufficient oversight provided by management." But this makes no sense. Where would the low-level employees have gotten the idea to target the Tea Party in the first place? Did it spring, like Athena, full-blown from the head of its Zeus-like creators in the dank cubicles of Cincinnati? Or was it employees reading the prevailing political tea leaves, and hoping for advancement?[98]

The problem was not relegated to low-level employees. One IRS witness, who worked in the Cincinnati office, said that administration claims that low-level employees were responsible for targeting were simply false. "They were basically throwing us under the bus," the witness stated.[99]

Elizabeth Hofacre, an agent in Cincinnati, said, "I was essentially a front person, because I had no autonomy or no authority to act on [applications] without Carter Hull's influence or input." Hull was a lawyer in the Washington, D.C., office.[100] Hull testified that he originally told his underlings to quickly approve certain nonprofit applications, but that Lerner held them up. Hull said that he had been at the IRS for forty-eight years, but this marked the first time he had been forced to funnel applications through Lerner's office. The applications sat there for months. When Lerner's office finally got around to them, Hull said, they asked for updates on them. Hull said that the request surprised him, and that he was especially surprised when the IRS chief counsel's office stated that they would need more information about the political activities of the organizations.[101]

Hofacre blasted Lerner: "It looked like Lois Lerner was putting it on us." Hofacre expressed rage that the Washington office had involved itself in the first place. "All I remember saying and thinking is, 'This is ridiculous,'" Hofacre averred. "Because at the same time, you are getting calls from irate taxpayers. And I see their point. Even if a decision isn't favorable, they deserve some kind of treatment and they deserve, you know, timeliness, and . . . these applications and their responses were just being sent up there [to Washington] and I am not sure what was happening."[102] Both Hofacre and Hull, career IRS employees, carefully avoided blaming the political targeting on politics, instead chalking it up to delays from Washington, D.C. They did not explain why the delays occurred.[103]

Another IRS employee, Cindy Thomas, who headed the Cincinnati office, told the House Oversight Committee that she asked Washington for guidance but received none.[104] According to CNN, the IRS informed House investigators that eighty-eight agents were involved in the targeting. Those employees were asked to preserve documentation.[105] Letters from multiple offices of the IRS, including Washington, D.C., evidenced involvement in the scandal.[106]

Holly Paz, the director of rulings and agreements, even told Congress in June 2013 that she personally supervised the scrutiny for Tea Party groups. She said she went over somewhere between twenty and thirty different applications. She also explained that agents in Cincinnati routinely talked about looking at "Tea Party" cases, but that she somehow thought they were talking about all political cases, regardless of political orientation. She likened *Tea Party* to using *Kleenex* as a generic term for tissue—a dubious assertion at best.[107] Furthermore, Paz somehow supervised 36 of the 41 interviews conducted by George for his audit.[108] Even Representative Cummings was stunned by that admission: "It sounded like Ms. Paz felt like she needed to be in the room because she wanted to be able to defend herself—or the agency, I don't know—based on what may have been said or the information gathered in that interview. Usually when you are conducting an investigation . . . you want to keep your witnesses separate because you're in search of the truth and you are trying to make sure there's no advantage of a person hearing what somebody else said."[109]

Nonetheless, allies of the Obama administration came out in force to fight the obvious. Cummings stated, "The Committee has identified no evidence that the IRS discriminated against conservative groups that had been approved for tax exempt status."[110] Cummings launched into a tirade against Inspector General J. Russell George, suggesting that George had purposefully biased his report in order to push the IRS scandal narrative forward.[111] In fact, Cummings tried to falsely claim that progressive groups had been targeted, too—a ridiculous claim to which George responded that his audit "did not find evidence that the IRS used the 'Progressives' identifier as selection criteria for potential political cases between May 2010 and May 2012 and said, in total, 30 percent of the organizations we identified with the words 'progress' or 'progressive' in their names were processed as potential political cases. . . . In comparison, our audit found that 100 percent of the tax-exempt applications with Tea Party, Patriots, or 9/12 in their names were processed as potential political cases during the timeframe of our audit."[112]

Meanwhile, the White House continued to claim that President Obama had remained in the dark about the IRS scandal, despite Jay Carney admitting that the White House had been informed as early as April 2013. "There's been some legitimate criticisms about how we're handling this," Carney said in May 2013. Carney then blamed White House counsel Kathryn Ruemmler for not telling President Obama— the same woman the White House tried to throw under the bus for the administration's failed PR rollout on the Benghazi scandal.[113]

THE AFTERMATH

By August, the White House felt enough time had passed to try to brush the IRS scandal under the rug. President Obama began using a new phrase in his speeches: "phony scandals." He said that the Republicans' focus on such "phony scandals" had prevented him from getting any work done.[114] Carney later clarified: "I think we all remember a few weeks ago when Washington was consumed with a variety of issues that, while in some cases significant, there was an effort under way to turn them into partisan scandals. I don't think anybody here would doubt that . . . when it comes to the IRS, as I said the other morning, the President made very clear that he will—that he wants the new leadership there to take action to correct improper conduct, and that is happening and he expects results. What some in Congress have failed to do despite many attempts is to provide any evidence—because there is none—that that activity was in any way known by, or directed by, the White House, or was even partisan or political."[115]

And poof! Just like that, by utilizing the Old Jedi Mind Trick, the White House expected the entire situation to disappear. A new man, Acting Commissioner Danny Werfel, was on the job. The evidence didn't matter. Obama had done his due diligence. Nothing to see here. These were not the droids America was looking for.

Except nothing changed. The IRS reportedly has never stopped its targeting of conservative groups. In early August, House Ways and Means Committee chairman Representative Dave Camp (R-MI) released testimony from an agent who told the committee that the IRS continued to give special scrutiny to Tea Party groups. According to that agent, Tea Party groups were still being sent to the holding tank of "secondary screening" because the IRS had developed no new guidelines. Here's the conversation between the investigator and the agent:

INVESTIGATOR: "If you saw—I am asking this currently, if today if a Tea Party case, a group—a case from a Tea Party group came in to your desk, you reviewed the file and there was no evidence of political activity, would you potentially approve that case? Is that something you would do?"

AGENT: "At this point I would send it to secondary screening, political advocacy."

INVESTIGATOR: "So you would treat a Tea Party group as a political advocacy case even if there was no evidence of political activity on the application. Is that right?"

AGENT: "Based on my current manager's direction, uh-huh."

That was six weeks after the new acting IRS commissioner, Danny Werfel, told the committee that the criteria for targeting had been stopped.[116] As Representative Aaron Schock (R-IL) told Fox News in August, "After the investigation had already begun, after the illegal behavior had already been exposed, they were asking pro-life groups how much of their time was being spent in prayer, how much of their time was being spent outside of abortion clinics, things that are clearly illegal for the IRS to ask when it's determining the tax-exempt status of any organization." He continued, "despite [President Obama's] promise to the American people that it was going to stop, it hasn't. . . . I would remind you that the only reason the American people are continuing to hear about this, the only reason that we know that the illegal targeting is continuing, is because we have a Republican-controlled House. The Democrats on the committee have already said if they ran the place, the investigation would be complete."[117]

Unbowed by the IRS scandal, Democrats continued to push forward with their persecution of conservative nonprofits. Representative Chris Van Hollen (D-MD) announced in late August 2013 that he would join up with liberal nonprofits Campaign Legal Center, Democracy 21, and Public Citizen to sue the IRS to encourage them to increase scrutiny of nonprofits. Democracy 21 and Public Citizen were two of the groups that petitioned the IRS over conservative nonprofits in 2011.[118]

Treatment of the Tea Party didn't improve, either. In May 2013, Tea Partiers showed up in Orlando, Florida, to protest the local IRS office over the scandal. The Department of Homeland Security—Janet Napolitano's office, which had always worried so much over those crazy Tea Party kooks—showed up to monitor the protests.[119]

It still paid to be an IRS agent, though. On June 5, 2013, the IRS reported that it would pay out $70 million in employee bonuses. Over the previous five years, the IRS paid out $92 million in bonuses.[120] The IRS is slated to be the chief beneficiary of Obamacare; some studies say that 16,500 new employees will have to join the IRS to help with the Obamacare implementation.[121]

So, what happened to the other people involved in the IRS scandal? They're doing quite well, naturally.

Lois Lerner, director for exempt organizations: The day after invoking the Fifth Amendment, Lerner was placed on paid administrative leave— meaning paid vacation. She wrote her colleagues, "Due to the events of recent days, I am on administrative leave starting today. An announcement will be made shortly informing you who will be acting while I am on administrative leave. I know all of you will continue to support EO's mission during these difficult times."[122] Despite a House vote to declare that Lerner's invocation of the Fifth Amendment was improper after she declared her innocence, Lerner will likely not testify again.[123] Her lawyer stated that Lerner would not testify again unless the House gave her immunity from prosecution. "They can obtain her testimony tomorrow by doing it the easy way . . . immunity," said the lawyer.[124] Lerner continued to earn $177,000 per year,[125] until she retired in September 2013.

Holly Paz, director of rulings and agreements: Paz was placed on administrative leave at about the same time Lerner went on her paid vacation. Her lawyer told the *Wall Street Journal*, "Holly Paz did nothing wrong and in fact she was an ideal employee, an ideal public servant."[126]

Sarah Hall Ingram, commissioner for tax-exempt organizations: Ingram ended up heading up the Obamacare IRS office. The unit has been tasked with enforcing Obamacare. And as we'll see, the application of Obamacare is already eminently political. "Now more than ever, we need to prevent the IRS from having any role in Americans' health care," Senator John Cornyn (R-TX) said upon hearing of Ingram's new job.[127] Between January 2011 and June 2013, Ingram visited the White House 165 times. Between 2009 and 2012, she received more than $100,000 in bonuses.[128]

Douglas Shulman, commissioner of the IRS: Shulman presided over the IRS for virtually the entirety of the targeting. He told Congress, "I feel very comfortable with my actions."[129] He retired with full benefits in November 2012.

Steven Miller, acting commissioner of the IRS: Miller earned $100,000 in bonuses in the five years before his resignation.[130] He was preparing to retire anyway—his term was limited by statute. Nonetheless, both the Obama administration and Miller pretended that his decision to retire was some sort of incredible act of sacrifice and strength.

Joseph Grant, former commissioner for tax-exempt and government entities: Grant retired from the IRS on June 3, 2013, just days after receiving a promotion to that role, meaning he had little involvement in the situation at all. He kept his benefits.[131]

Carter Hull, tax specialist in exempt organizations: Hull reportedly retired, keeping his benefits.[132]

CLOSING ARGUMENT

"The IRS!" Jerry Seinfeld once exclaimed. "They're like the mafia, they can take anything they want!"

Seinfeld would have loved President Obama. Presidents have historically used the IRS as a tool of intimidation and oppression. The Obama administration has followed that pattern, all the while ensuring that nobody gets blamed for a basic violation of Americans' rights and blaming conservative paranoia for focus on the IRS's discrimination in the first place. While the left proclaims that the IRS never targeted conservative groups, the statistics simply don't bear that out—just as with JFK, the IRS was careful enough to pick out a few specific liberal groups to check out, just enough to grant plausible deniability.

Except it isn't plausible, and the American people know it. The House Oversight Committee staff report concludes, "As prominent politicians publicly urged the IRS to take action on tax-exempt groups engaged in legal campaign intervention activities, the IRS treated tea party applications differently. Applications filed by tea party groups were identified and grouped due to media attention surrounding the existence of the tea party in general." President Obama and his Democratic allies had created that media attention. And the IRS regulators could read the tea leaves.[133] In the process of reading those tea leaves, the IRS and the

Obama administration violated both the Hatch Act and the "omnibus" provision of the Internal Revenue Code.

The targeting continues. In August 2013, Judicial Watch got hold of a training manual for the Department of Defense on "extremism." The manual labeled "the colonists who sought to free themselves from British rule" extremists. "Nowadays," the department warned, "instead of dressing in sheets or publicly espousing hate messages, many extremists will talk of individual liberties, states' rights, and how to make the world a better place."[134] With such nefarious characters running around, no wonder the IRS targets conservatives. That same month, Tea Party Patriots received a letter from the IRS requesting a "laundry list of requests related to virtually all the group's activities, including its involvement in the 2012 election cycle and its get-out-the-vote efforts, fundraising activities, all radio and TV advertising, and other information," according to the *Washington Times*.[135]

The result of such discrimination will be a general distrust of the government as a whole. In Italy, the population is so sick of corruption within the government that it avoids taxes at an incredible rate, shortchanging the tax funds approximately 18 percent of gross domestic product every single year.[136] In Vladimir Putin's Russia, where enemies of the prime minister are considered enemies of the state and targeted regularly by tax officers, bribery is so lucrative that young people would rather become tax inspectors than engineers or oilmen. Naturally, the Russian people feel by wide margins that the government is corrupt.[137]

Americans are increasingly feeling the same thing. As of late May 2013, 76 percent of Americans wanted a special prosecutor to investigate the IRS scandal. We didn't get it.[138] As of August, 59 percent of Americans thought that the IRS scandal was a serious problem.[139]

The IRS represents the worst of American government: a faceless, vast bureaucratic agency without consistently applied rules, and easily exploitable by the corrupt or the malevolent. The Obama administration is both.

COUNT 4

★

UNAUTHORIZED DISCLOSURE OF INFORMATION

Whoever, lawfully having possession of, access to, control over, or being entrusted with any . . . information relating to the national defense which information the possessor has reason to believe could be used to the injury of the United States or to the advantage of any foreign nation, willfully communicates, delivers, transmits or causes to be communicated, delivered, or transmitted or attempts to communicate, deliver, transmit or cause to be communicated, delivered or transmitted the same to any person not entitled to receive it . . . [s]hall be fined under this title or imprisoned not more than ten years, or both.

—18 U.S. CODE § 793

OPENING ARGUMENT

On May 2, 2011, President Barack Obama swaggered to the podium in the historic Cross Hall of the White House. "Good evening," Obama stated. "Tonight, I can report to the American people and to the world that the United States has conducted an operation that killed Osama bin Laden, the leader of al-Qaeda, and a terrorist who's responsible for the murder of thousands of innocent men, women, and children." It was an incredible moment—a cathartic moment for millions of Americans who had watched in horror as fellow Americans flung themselves from the flaming wreck of the World Trade Center on September 11, 2001, or saw smoke plume from the caved-in wall of the Pentagon, or smelled the ash rising from a hole in Shanksville, Pennsylvania. Bin Laden was dead. President Obama had made the right call to go after him.

And President Obama didn't let anyone forget who had made the call. In his speech to the nation, Obama focused on his central role in the bin Laden killing. "[S]hortly after taking office, I directed Leon Panetta, the director of the CIA, to make the killing or capture of bin Laden the top priority of our war against al Qaeda, even as we continued our broader efforts to disrupt, dismantle, and defeat his network," he said. "Then, last August, after years of painstaking work by our intelligence community, I was briefed on a possible lead to bin Laden. . . . I met repeatedly with my national security team. . . . I determined that we had enough intelligence to take action. . . . Today, at my direction, the United States launched a targeted operation against that compound in Abbottabad, Pakistan."[1]

President Obama's credit-taking was graceless, but not criminal.

The same could not be said for his vice president. Speaking on May 4, 2011, at the Ritz-Carlton hotel in Washington, D.C., Joe Biden—Uncle Joe, as he is termed by members of the media as a way of writing off his numerous gaffes—dropped crucial information to terrorists. "Let me briefly acknowledge tonight's distinguished honorees," he said. "Admiral Jim Stavridis is a—is the real deal; he could tell more about and understands the incredible, the phenomenal, the just almost unbelievable capacity of his Navy SEALS and what they did last—last Sunday," he blurted. "Folks, I'd be remiss also if I didn't say an extra word about the incredible events, extraordinary events of this past Sunday. As vice president of the United States, as an American, I was in absolute awe of the capacity and dedication of the entire team, both the intelligence community, the CIA, the SEALs. It just was extraordinary."

Then he dropped the other shoe: "And what was even more extraordinary was—and I'm sure former administration officials will appreciate this more than anyone—there was such an absolute, overwhelming desire to accomplish this mission that although for over several months we were in the process of planning it, and there were as many as sixteen members of Congress who were briefed on it, not a single, solitary thing leaked. I find that absolutely amazing."[2]

Biden apparently believed that leaking information about the perpetrators of the bin Laden killing now had no consequences. He couldn't have been more wrong.

The family members of SEAL Team Six realized the problem immediately. According to the *Washington Times*' Jeffrey Kuhner, Aaron Vaughn, one of the SEALs, "told his mother, Karen Vaughn, to delete every reference to SEAL Team 6 from her Facebook and Twitter accounts." Karen said, "I never heard Aaron this concerned and worried in his entire life. He called me and said, 'Mom, you and Dad have to take everything down. Biden has just put a huge target on everybody.'"[3] SEAL Team Six member Michael Strange told his father he had put together a will, just in case.[4]

On August 6, 2011, just over two months after bin Laden's killing, terrorists in eastern Afghanistan shot down a U.S. military helicopter, a twin-rotor Chinook, carrying members of SEAL Team Six—the team whose identity Biden had leaked, and who had taken out bin Laden. Thirty Americans were killed, twenty-five of them from SEAL Team Six, including Vaughn. It was the single worst loss America had experienced in Afghanistan. "We don't believe that any of the special operators who were killed were involved in the bin Laden operation," said a senior U.S. military official. President Obama immediately released a statement mourning the "extraordinary sacrifices" made by the military.[5] The Pentagon stated that SEAL Team Six had not been specifically targeted. The Defense Department said there was no "established ambush," instead calling the attack "a lucky shot of a low-level fighter that happened to be living [in the area]. He heard all the activity and he happened to be in the right spot." But insurgents apparently began bragging about the helicopter takedown immediately afterward, naming SEAL Team Six. The Defense Department further claimed that all of the bodies had been so badly charred that they had to be cremated—but Representative Jason

Chaffetz (R-UT) said he had seen pictures of the bodies, and at least one deceased SEAL did not need to be cremated. The black box of the helicopter was never found, a coincidence Chaffetz called "awfully odd."

At Dover Air Force Base, greeting the bodies of those killed in the attack, Charles Strange, Michael's father, asked President Obama to investigate. After Obama began praising Michael, Charles responded, "I don't need to know about my son. I need to know what happened to my son." According to Charles, Obama never followed up on his promise to investigate.[6] Billy Vaughn, Aaron Vaughn's father, told Fox News, "The media has let [Biden] get away with saying 'Uncle Joe's gaffes.' This is not Uncle Joe and he's not some senile old grandfather. He is the second in command of the most powerful country in the world and he needs to take responsibility for the comments he makes and quit being given a pass."[7]

THE CHARGES

The Obama administration violated the Espionage Act in its gunrunning activities in Libya and Syria, which resulted in the deaths of Americans. But it has repeatedly and undoubtedly violated the Espionage Act, which includes 18 U.S. Code § 793, in its leaks of information. The relevant provision of the Espionage Act was edited in 1950 to remove intent as an element of the crime—even retention of classified information could be a crime.

But even had the act not been altered, the Obama administration would be guilty of repeatedly and routinely violating it. Never has there been a more selectively leaky administration. And by the same token, never has an administration been so aggressive in targeting leakers of information that make it look bad.

TARGETING THE "ENEMY" LEAKERS: JAMES ROSEN

The Obama administration is quite brutal with leakers that it believes harm its political interests. Aside from targeting Fast and Furious whistle-blowers, silencing would-be Benghazi witnesses, and attempting to delegitimize the reporters who cover them, the Obama administration aggressively monitors and prosecutes anyone it suspects of working with the press to undermine its preferred policies. So even as Joe Biden was shooting his mouth off and putting Navy SEALs squarely in the crosshairs, the Obama administration launched the greatest crackdown on leaks in American history.

In 2009, the Justice Department started investigating reports from Fox News' James Rosen about North Korea. Rosen reported in June 2009 that North Korea would likely respond to UN action against it by speeding up nuclear testing. Rosen attributed that information to sources within the CIA. Soon the Obama administration tracked down the man they believed was the source of the leak: Stephen Jin-Woo Kim, a State Department security adviser. But the administration didn't stop there: it obtained phone records for Rosen, used his security badge to track his ins and outs at the State Department, backtracked his calls with Kim, and got a secret warrant to check out Rosen's personal emails. Kim's lawyer accused the Obama administration of using "20 [telephone] lines and months of records with no obvious attempt to be targeted or narrow."

The lawyer spoke truthfully. FBI investigators' evidence against Kim included specific information about Rosen's movements. Rosen used his Google email account, and asked that his source send code to pass along information: "One asterisk means to contact them, or that previously suggested plans for communication are to proceed as agreed," the FBI reported; "two asterisks means the opposite." The *Washington Post*, which broke the story about the administration's targeting of Rosen, pointed out the outrageous nature of such monitoring: "No reporter, including Rosen, has been prosecuted [for soliciting information]."[8]

So how exactly did the surveillance get cleared by a court? The Justice Department labeled a potential "co-conspirator" in its filings. That's right: a journalist doing his job ended up as a possible co-conspirator in espionage, according to the Obama administration.

Meanwhile, the Obama administration lied about its blatant violation of First Amendment principles. Attorney General Eric Holder, testifying before Congress in May 2013, stated, "With regard to potential prosecution of the press for the disclosure of material: that is not something I've ever been involved in, heard of, or would think would be wise policy."[9] Only one problem: Holder personally signed off on the warrant request for Rosen's information. According to a Justice Department official leaking to NBC News, "After extensive deliberations, and after following all applicable laws, regulations and policies, the Department sought an appropriately tailored search warrant under the Privacy Protection Act. And a federal magistrate judge made an independent finding that probable cause existed to approve the warrant."[10] Not just that: the department even went so far as to request that the warrant against Rosen be kept a secret so it could monitor him more completely.[11] Bret Baier of Fox News reported that Rosen's *parents'* phone records were pulled by the Justice Department as well.[12]

Holder gave a pricelessly Clintonian response to his perjury: "I do not agree that characterizations establishing probable cause for a search warrant for materials from a member of the news media during an ongoing investigation constitute an intent to prosecute that member of the news media," he wrote to Congress. "I do believe that a thorough investigation of the disclosure of classified information that threatened national security was necessary and appropriate." In other words, the department could claim someone might be prosecuted, but that didn't mean they might be prosecuted. Or something.[13]

This was clearly an act of perjury. And it was perjury required by the Obama administration in order to cover up its targeting of journalists who didn't parrot the party line.

TARGETING THE "ENEMY" LEAKERS: ASSOCIATED PRESS

The Obama administration didn't merely target Rosen. It went after the entire Associated Press after the AP's May 7, 2012, report about a barely foiled terror plot based in Yemen to blow up a U.S.-bound airplane. The report noted the attack came close to fruition, even though White House officials told the American public that terrorist organizations were not threatening activity at the time. In the midst of the president's reelection campaign, the last thing the Obama White House wanted was a story about al-Qaeda's continuing threat to the security of the country. After all, al-Qaeda was supposed to be on the run. As Carney said, "We have no credible information that terrorist organizations, including al-Qaeda, are plotting attacks in the U.S. to coincide with the anniversary of bin Laden's death."[14]

The AP piece blew that lie wide open. That angered the Obama White House. CIA director John Brennan called the report an "unauthorized and dangerous disclosure of classified information."[15]

But was it? As it turns out, the Obama administration knew full well that the AP planned to publish information on the thwarted Yemen plot. Actually, the Obama administration *worked with the AP* in planning release of the story. The White House wanted to put some spin on the Yemen story, and asked the Associated Press to delay publication of its story for several days. The AP agreed, on the condition that they would have a one-hour exclusive. But when the White House refused to allow that, the AP ran with the story.

Immediately, *truly* crucial leaks began—from the White House itself. Reuters reported that Brennan briefed members of the press about the Yemen plot early on the evening of May 7. He said that the plot didn't threaten American safety because the Obama administration had "inside control" of the plot. That information was crucial, and Brennan leaked it directly to the press. As Reuters reported, "Brennan's comment appears unintentionally to have helped lead to disclosure of the secret at the heart of a joint U.S.-British-Saudi undercover counter-terrorism operation." The leak killed the undercover operation. But it didn't kill White House ire at the AP. The White House quickly released a statement blaming AP rather than Brennan for the leak: "The egregious leak here was to the Associated Press. The White House fought to prevent this information from being reported and ultimately worked to delay its publication for operational security reasons. No one is more upset than us about this disclosure, and we support efforts to prevent leaks like this which harm our national security." But as Reuters pointed out, the AP report didn't have any information of an undercover informant or Washington control over the operation.[16] Brennan's own lame explanation for how his leaks didn't matter, but the AP's did: "Once someone leaked information about interdiction of the IED and that the IED was actually in our possession, it was imperative to inform the American people consistent with government policy that there was never any danger to the American people associated with this al-Qaida plot."[17]

That didn't stop the Obama administration from going full bore in its attempt to crack down on those rogue reporters at the AP. One year later, AP reported that the Justice Department had "secretly obtained two months of telephone records of reporters and editors for The Associated Press in what the news cooperative's top executive called a 'massive and unprecedented intrusion' into how news organizations gather the news." Among other information grabbed by the department: outgoing calls for work and personal phone numbers of reporters, and records of more than twenty telephone lines used by more than one hundred reporters. AP president and CEO Gary Pruitt sent a letter to Holder blasting the Justice Department's violations of the First Amendment: "There can be no possible justification for such an overbroad collection of the telephone communications of The Associated Press and its reporters. These records potentially reveal communications with confidential sources across all of the newsgathering activities undertaken by the AP during a two-month period, provide a road map to AP's newsgathering operations and disclose information about AP's activities and operations that the government has no conceivable right to know."

The Justice Department gave no reason for the seizure of records in notifying the AP that it had grabbed the information. AP noted, "The Obama administration has aggressively investigated disclosures of classified information to the media and has brought six cases against people suspected of providing classified information, more than under all previous presidents combined."

The Obama administration violated federal law in grabbing AP's records in such heavy-handed fashion. As Nate Cardozo of the Electronic Frontier Foundation stated, "The DOJ's regulations prohibit subpoenas of this breadth and require that notice be given to the affected people within 90 days at the absolute outside." Other reporters said that sources had been chilled by the reports of the department's targeting.[18]

As usual, the White House claimed it had no clue what its right hand was doing at Justice. "We are not involved in decisions made in connection with criminal investigations, as those matters are handled independently by the Justice Department," said Jay Carney.[19] President Obama himself claimed ignorance, as per the usual arrangement, in which the head of the executive branch knew nothing about the internal workings of the executive branch. The president, said Carney, "found out about the news reports yesterday on the road."[20]

SOME LEAKERS ARE MORE EQUAL THAN OTHERS

But not all leakers are created equal for the Obama administration. Some leaks that obviously violate America's national security interests receive no blowback whatsoever from the White House—so long as those leaks help the political interests of one Barack Obama.

On August 3, 2013, President Obama ordered that twenty-two U.S. embassies and consulates throughout the world close in anticipation of potential terrorist activity from al-Qaeda.[21] The blowback came quickly, with Republicans demanding an explanation from the Obama administration as to why, if al-Qaeda had been largely defanged, as the Obama administration claimed, America had cut and run with regard to sovereign United States territory. Some Republicans also suggested that the Obama administration had played up the global threat in an attempt to justify unprecedented government spying on American citizens via the National Security Agency.

None of that sat right with the image-conscious Obama White House. And thus, on August 7, 2013, Eli Lake and Josh Rogin of the *Daily Beast* reported that the embassy closures had been provoked not by vague threats by al-Qaeda, but by a highly specific piece of intelligence information: a tapped conference call between al-Qaeda leaders. "The intercept provided the U.S. intelligence community with a rare glimpse into how al Qaeda's leader, Ayman al-Zawahiri, manages a global organization that includes affiliates in Africa, the Middle East, and southwest and southeast Asia," the reporters wrote. "[T]he conference call provided a new sense of urgency for the U.S. government, the sources said."

Wasn't this a crucial national security leak? According to the reporters, of course not—original reports suggesting that communications had been intercepted had already blown the administration's cover.[22] But when CNN reported the initial "intercepted message among senior al Qaeda operatives," it added that "CNN has agreed to a request from an Obama administration official not to publish or broadcast additional details because of the sensitivity of the information." The *Daily Beast*'s big scoop went far beyond the details exposed by CNN.[23]

And the leaks continued. On August 14, the Associated Press, citing three "intelligence officials," broke the news that the administration had been charting chat rooms and Internet message boards for al-Qaeda communications. The AP report explicitly linked the al-Qaeda communications to the Obama administration's call for even broader Internet surveillance powers: "Exactly how U.S. spy systems picked up the latest threat is classified. . . . Intelligence officials have suggested that the plot was detected, in part at least, through NSA surveillance programs that have been under harsh worldwide criticism for privacy intrusions in the name of national security."[24]

Vital American security information was breaking across the country every single day. Yet, oddly, CNN, the *Daily Beast*, and AP received zero harsh words from the Obama administration over these leaks.

How odd. How convenient.

And how perfectly consistent with past Obama administration orchestrated leaks. On May 29, 2012, the *New York Times* reported that the Obama White House had a "kill list" designed to allow the president to determine whom among al-Qaeda suspects to take out.[25] As Greg McNeal of *Forbes* pointed out, the story clearly sprang from the White House, given that the *Times* sourced it to "three dozen" current and former Obama administration officials. Obama gave a quote to the *Times* on this critical national security information. So did Thomas Donilon, the national security advisor; Bill Daley, the former chief of staff; Dennis Blair, former director of national intelligence; and Brennan. All of the quotes from administration officials make Obama look like a tough cowboy, just in time for the 2012 election. "He is determined that he will make these decisions about how far and wide these operations will go," Donilon told the *Times*. "His view is that he's responsible for the position of the United States in the world."[26]

These leaks were so bad that even Senator Dianne Feinstein (D-CA), a quasi-hawkish Obama administration ally, blasted them: "It's dismayed our allies. It puts American lives in jeopardy. It puts our nation's security in jeopardy."[27] But, more important, it helped Obama look tough—which, to Obama, was all that mattered.

When confronted about the leak of the kill list, Obama put on his righteous-indignation face. "The notion that my White House would purposely release classified national security information is offensive," he blustered during a press conference. "It's wrong, and people I think need to have a better sense of how I approach this office and how people around here approach this office."[28]

The problem for Obama is that the American people were quite aware of how he approached his office: as a public relations full-time spin zone. And in violation of law designed to protect American classified information.

While Obama has deployed his leak machine to great effect in an attempt to bolster his national security credentials, he has saved his greatest leaks to target America's only true ally in the Middle East: Israel.

THE ISRAEL LEAKS

President Obama's relationship with Israel began in ugly fashion. After years of associating with anti-Semites like Jeremiah Wright ("Them Jews ain't going to let him talk to me," Wright said of the likelihood of speaking to Obama after his election),[29] Bill Ayers ("The Zionist state is clearly the aggressor, the source of violence and war in the Mideast, the occupier of stolen lands. . . . It is racist and expansionist—the enemy of the Palestinians, the Arab people, and the Jewish people"),[30] Rashid Khalidi (former Palestine Liberation Organization spokesman), and Derrick Bell ("Jewish neoconservative racists . . . are undermining blacks in every way they can"),[31] President Obama attempted to mend fences with the American Jewish community by placating them at the 2008 American-Israel Public Affairs Committee annual conference. The day after winning the Democratic presidential nomination, Obama took to the podium at AIPAC, where he stated, "Jerusalem will remain the capital of Israel, and it must remain undivided." The crowd duly applauded. The next day, Obama walked it back.[32]

Obama's actions spoke louder than his words. He quickly staffed up his campaign with a notorious bunch of anti-Israel career politicians, including:

- Samantha Power, who once suggested that America place troops on the ground in Israel to prevent "human rights abuses" by the Israelis against the Palestinians;
- Zbigniew Brzezinski, former Jimmy Carter national security advisor who defended Carter's anti-Semitic diatribe *Peace, Not Apartheid*;
- General Merrill McPeak, Obama's campaign cochair, who said that the Jewish lobby based in "New York City, Miami," controlled American foreign policy;
- Robert Malley, who served on the Obama campaign until the media discovered his secret meetings with Hamas.[33]

Nonetheless, Obama was elected with 78 percent of the Jewish vote.

Once elected, Obama proceeded to use his power to stifle Israel's ability to defend itself against the imminent nuclear development of the Iranian regime. Obama had stated during the campaign of 2008 that he would negotiate with Iran without preconditions. Now he made it clear that he would not support any Israeli action against Iran. In July 2009, within weeks of the Iranians shooting protesters in the streets, Obama told CNN that the United States was "absolutely not" giving Israel the green light to strike Iran's nuclear facilities. "We have said directly to the Israelis that it is important to try and resolve this in an international setting in a way that does not create major conflict in the Middle East," Obama said.[34] Israeli prime minister Benjamin Netanyahu continued to maintain that Iran was a threat to Israeli existence, and reserved the right to defend his country.

In June 2010, as concerns rose from the Obama administration over the possibility of an Israeli strike on Iran, an unnamed "U.S. defense source" told the *Times of London* that Israel had cut a deal with Saudi Arabia to use Saudi airspace to launch a strike against Iran's nuclear facilities. "To ensure the Israeli bombers pass without hindrance," the *Times* said, "Riyadh has carried out tests to make certain its own jets are not scrambled and missile defense systems not activated. Once the Israelis are through, the kingdom's air defenses will return to full alert."[35]

The conflict between Israel and the anti-Israel Obama administration continued to simmer. In May 2011, Obama said in a high-profile speech at the State Department that the pre-1967 borders—also known as the Auschwitz borders by those in Israel—should be the starting point for negotiations between the Israelis and the Palestinians. Netanyahu reportedly tried to pressure Secretary of State Hillary Clinton to cut that reference in Obama's speech. Obama refused.[36] The Saudis quickly backed out of any possible deal.[37]

Netanyahu responded by visiting Congress and spoke directly to a joint session. To standing ovations, Netanyahu slyly laid out his message to Obama: "Now, as for Israel, if history has taught the Jewish people anything, it is that we must take calls for our destruction seriously. We are a nation that rose from the ashes of the Holocaust. When we say never again, we mean never again. Israel always reserves the right to defend itself."[38]

Leading up to the presidential election, the Obama administration ramped up its efforts to forestall any Israeli action against Iran. As the election neared, Netanyahu and the Israeli government worried about the possibility of Barack Obama's reelection, knowing that his anti-Israel record would certainly not get any better were he freed from the burden of answerability to the largely pro-Israel public. Concurrently, Netanyahu knew that Obama's rival for the presidency, Mitt Romney, was not only pro-Israel but an old Netanyahu friend from their university days. Given Romney's successful attacks on the Obama administration's anti-Israel foreign policy, and given pressure on Obama to do something to stop Romney from cutting into Obama's share of the Jewish vote, the chances of U.S. support for Israeli action against Iran were far greater pre-election than post-election.[39]

But Obama didn't want to take action. Furthermore, he didn't want Israel to take action. Were Israel to do so, the Obama administration could be dragged into a controversial foreign engagement; oil prices could rise; Obama's own left-wing base could turn on him. And so the Obama administration began to leak at record rates.

In February 2012, Secretary of Defense Leon Panetta told favored Obama administration outlet David Ignatius at the *Washington Post* that his greatest worry was preventing an Israeli strike on Iran. "Panetta believes there is a strong likelihood that Israel will strike Iran in April, May or June—before Iran enters what Israelis described as a 'zone of immunity' to commence building a nuclear bomb," Ignatius reported.[40] The goal of the leak: to push the possibility of an Israeli strike beyond the election.

In March 2012, NBC News somehow got information that Israel had worked with the Iranian opposition to kill several Iranian nuclear scientists. Two "senior Obama Administration officials" confirmed that the Iranian opposition group Mujahideen-e-Khalq (MEK) had been financed and trained by the Israeli secret service, Mossad. The Obama administration unnamed sources further leaked that the Americans had nothing to do with the hits on the Iranian scientists. But Seymour Hersh of the *New Yorker* had sources outside the administration who said that the Americans did in fact have a hand in working with and building up the MEK, and that even under the Obama administration, "the United States is now providing the intelligence" for operations.[41] The leak exposed the link between Israel and the MEK, allowed American hands to remain clean, and delayed further Israeli action against the Iranian nuclear program.

Later that same month, on March 29, 2012, the Obama administration leaked to *Foreign Policy* that Israel had attempted to broker a deal with Azerbaijan to use air bases in that country to stage attacks on Iranian sites. "In particular," *Foreign Policy* reported, "four senior diplomats and military intelligence officers say that the United States has concluded that Israel has recently been granted access on Iran's northern border." The publication quoted a "senior administration official" as stating, "The Israelis have bought an airfield, and the airfield is Azerbaijan." The intent of the leak was absolutely clear. *Foreign Policy* spat it right out: "Senior U.S. intelligence officials are increasingly concerned that Israel's military expansion into Azerbaijan complicates U.S. efforts to dampen Israeli-Iranian tensions, according to the sources."[42] The

Azerbaijan deal never came to fruition, obviously. Former UN ambassador John Bolton fumed, "Clearly, this is an administration-orchestrated leak. It's just unprecedented to reveal this kind of information about one of your own allies."[43]

The same day the *Foreign Policy* leak broke, another leak came via Bloomberg. This one concerned a Congressional Research Service report, which posited that Iran's nuclear development couldn't be stopped by Israel in any case. The report stated that it was "unclear what the ultimate effect of a strike would be on the likelihood of Iran acquiring nuclear weapons."[44] ABC News quoted Yoel Guzansky at the Institute for National Security Studies stating that the leak was orchestrated as part of a "big campaign to prevent Israel from attacking." Columnist Ron Ben-Yishai of the popular Israeli newspaper *Yedioth Ahronoth* wrote, "In recent weeks the administration shifted from persuasion efforts vis-à-vis decision-makers and Israel's public opinion to a practical, targeted assassination of potential Israeli operations in Iran. The campaign's aims are fully operational: To make it more difficult for Israeli decision-makers to order the IDF [Israeli Defense Forces] to carry out a strike, and what's even graver, to erode the IDF's capacity to launch such strike with minimal casualties."[45]

Obama, however, had to retain the impression that he was pro-Israel, even as his administration repeatedly leaked information designed to help Iran escape Israeli defense strikes. Thus, on June 1, 2012, David Sanger of the *New York Times* reported about a mysterious cyberattack on Iran's nuclear facilities. Shockingly, it turned out that the Obama administration and the Israeli government had worked hand in hand for years on the project. "From his first months in office," Sanger reported, "President Obama ordered increasingly sophisticated attacks on the computer systems that run Iran's main nuclear enrichment facilities, significantly expanding America's first sustained use of cyberweapons, according to participants in the program. Mr. Obama decided to accelerate the attacks—begun in the Bush administration and code-named Olympic Games—even after an element of the program accidentally became public in the summer of 2010 because of a programming error that allowed it to escape Iran's Natanz plant and sent it around the world on the Internet. Computer security experts who began studying the worm, which had been developed by the United States and Israel, gave it a name: Stuxnet."

President Obama was, after all, a hawkish Likudnik on Iran, rather than a spineless panderer to the mullahs. The *Times* breathlessly reported, again citing "members of the president's national security team who were in the room," that Obama took charge and ordered a ramp-up in cyberattacks against Iran. The piece quoted Obama, Vice President Joe Biden, and CIA director Leon Panetta. The *Times* reported that no source would go on the record because "the effort remains highly classified."[46]

Until this time, it had been widely suspected, but never confirmed, that Israel had been behind the technological masterpiece that was Stuxnet. The program subtly ruined Iran's nuclear progress by sabotaging the rotations of the centrifuges, meanwhile reading out normal results to the watching scientists. But now the cat was out of the bag.

Did the Obama administration respond with ire? Of course not. Instead, White House deputy press secretary Josh Earnest refused to comment on the leak, and instead talked up Obama's supposed muscularity against Iran: "I've read the story that you're referring to . . . and I'm not able to comment on any of the specifics or details that are included in that story. I can tell you more, though, about what this president's approach to Iran has been in terms of dealing with the threat." Tellingly, Earnest refused to deny that the White House authorized the leak in the first place, and refused to say whether there would be an investigation into the leak. It took three days for Jay Carney to answer the question. "No," Carney said. "Look, our interest is always in protecting sensitive information, protecting classified information, because it's important for our national security."[47] When Senator John McCain (R-AZ) blasted the leaks, Carney fired back: "Any suggestion that this administration has authorized intentional leaks of classified information for political gain is grossly irresponsible." Sanger, too, awkwardly denied that the White House leaked information. "All that you read about this being deliberate leaks out of the White House wasn't my experience," he said.

Carney and Sanger were apparently lying. Long after the 2012 election was over, in August 2013, the State Department released emails showing that the Obama White House gave Sanger special access to national security officials. Sanger spoke with Secretary of State Hillary Rodham Clinton, Deputy Secretary of State William Burns, Deputy Chief of Staff Jake Sullivan, and National Security Advisor Thomas Donilon, among others. One senior State Department public affairs official, Michael Hammer, corresponded frequently with Sanger, including sending articles to Sanger on Stuxnet.[48]

And thus the image of Obama, friend to Israel, was preserved—at the cost of America's and Israel's national security.

After Obama won reelection—and successfully stalled an Israeli strike on Iran—Obama came fully out of the closet on his anti-Israel positions. He appointed known anti-Semite Chuck Hagel secretary of defense. He appointed Samantha Power the UN ambassador. And his administration kept leaking—this time, in an attempt to provoke Israel into taking action in Syria, an outcome the dithering Obama would have preferred to taking direct U.S. military action. In May 2013, members of the Obama Pentagon leaked information that Israel had attacked the Damascus airport in an attempt to stop shipment of weapons to terrorist groups. Obama officials had to apologize to Israel for this leak, since it directly put Israeli lives in danger. Naturally, they blamed "low-level" employees.[49]

Yet just weeks later, in June, the administration somehow leaked information with specific Israeli Arrow 3 antiballistic missile sites. The information went public via the U.S. Federal Business Opportunities website while inviting bids from U.S. defense contractors to help build the installation.[50]

And then again, just weeks after that, U.S. sources told CNN that Israel had attacked Latakia, an installation in Syria chock-full of Russian-provided missiles. Forced to respond, Israeli defense minister Moshe Ya'alon stated, "We have set red lines in regards to our own interests, and we keep them. There is an attack here, an explosion there, various versions—in any event, in the Middle East it is usually we who are blamed for most."[51]

That same month, U.S. "officials" and "American intelligence analysts" told the *New York Times* that Israeli strikes in the past targeting terrorist weapons caches had not been fully successful. All the information revealed was classified.[52] "It is hard to avoid the conclusion that this story is either the work of anti-Israel figures working in the Pentagon or has been orchestrated by the administration in order to deter Israel from continuing its efforts to prevent weapon transfers to terrorists," Jonathan Tobin of *Commentary* magazine wrote.[53]

The Obama campaign falsely claimed to be pro-Israel. Its history of leaks detrimental to Israel's national security—none of the leakers were ever found or prosecuted—demonstrates just how false those claims were. Now Israel is under assault from all sides. America's interests in the Middle East remain in the direst jeopardy since the fall of the Soviet Union.

But at least Barack Obama got reelected.

THE AFTERMATH

In October 2011, President Obama authorized a new program designed to crack down on potential leakers. News service McClatchy reported, "The order covers virtually every federal department and agency, including the Peace Corps, the Department of Education and others not directly involved in national security." The new system uses "indicators of insider threat behavior," with coworkers reporting on one another, as well as "suspicious user behavior." Employees have been asked to look at the "lifestyles, attitudes and behaviors" of their fellow employees. The entire federal apparatus refused comment to McClatchy on what such "lifestyles, attitudes and behaviors" looked like. But the FBI's version of the program suggests giving a close eye to anyone with "a desire to help the 'underdog' or a particular cause."[54]

No administration in the history of the country has been quite as interested in prosecuting leakers as the Obama administration . . . or at least, a certain *type* of leaker. The leakers who help the Obama administration are rewarded; those who hurt the Obama administration are punished to the fullest extent of the law, or monitored in violation of it.

In May 2010, FBI linguist Shamai Leibowitz received a twenty-month sentence to federal prison after leaking classified information about Israel, giving information to a blogger about activity he believed violated the law by the FBI. Even the judge did not know what exactly Leibowitz had leaked. "The court is in the dark," said the judge. "I'm not a part and parcel of the intricacies of [the alleged national security threat]. . . . I don't know what was divulged, other than some documents." Leibowitz's sentence was one of the longest ever given for a crime like his.[55]

In August 2010, federal law enforcement slapped an indictment on State Department employee Stephen Kim for allegedly leaking information about North Korea to James Rosen. "The willful disclosure of classified information to those not entitled to it is a serious crime," Assistant Attorney General David Kris stated. "Today's indictment should serve as a warning to anyone who is entrusted with sensitive national security information and would consider compromising it."[56]

That same year, the government prosecuted Thomas Drake, a fifty-three-year-old intelligence officer for the National Security Agency, after he allegedly leaked classified information to members of the press regarding the NSA's warrantless surveillance. His crimes were eventually dropped to a misdemeanor.[57]

In January 2011, the administration brought charges against former CIA officer Jeffrey A. Sterling for leaking information about America's Iran policies to James Risen for the latter's 2006 book, *State of War*. The information leaked showed that the CIA had no clue how to actually derail the Iranian nuclear program, and had actually implemented plans that would have *accelerated* it.[58]

In the midst of all of this, Director of National Intelligence James Clapper sent a memo to members of the intelligence community telling employees to cease "blabbing secrets." He wrote, "We have established procedures for authorized officers to interact with the media. For everyone else, unauthorized disclosure of our work is both a serious matter and a diversion from the critical tasks we face. In other words, blabbing secrets to the media is not 'in' as far as I'm concerned."

The memo leaked to administration-friendly sources—and those sources praised Clapper, the man responsible for keeping national security secrets behind lock and key, as "plainspoken, not given to nonsense or ornamental language."[59] Some leaks are better than others.

CLOSING ARGUMENT

The Obama administration has repeatedly violated the Espionage Act's prohibitions on release of classified information in order to benefit President Obama himself. Dead Navy SEALs? At least Obama made a "gutsy call" on bin Laden. Compromised terrorism procedures? At least Obama's not a wimp. Destruction of American alliances? At least Obama got himself past the 2012 election without having to face the specter of open warfare in the Middle East.

Meanwhile, the Obama administration's focus on possible leakers who might hurt the administration has led the administration into murky legal waters, violating the Department of Justice's own procedures in order to monitor journalists—and putting the First Amendment in deep freeze in the process.

It's all about Obama. That's why nobody in the Obama administration has been fired for any of these leaks, or for the malicious persecution of journalists who print information the administration doesn't like. In truth, a wide variety of Obama officials should be headed to prison for the same traitorous behavior for which they have charged leakers over and over again.

COUNT 5

★

DEPRIVATION OF RIGHTS UNDER COLOR OF LAW

★ ★ ★

If two or more persons conspire to injure, oppress, threaten, or intimidate any person in any State, Territory, Commonwealth, Possession, or District in the free exercise or enjoyment of any right or privilege secured to him by the Constitution or laws of the United States, or because of his having so exercised the same . . . [t]hey shall be fined under this title or imprisoned not more than ten years, or both. . . .

—18 U.S. CODE § 241

★ ★ ★

A person is guilty of an offense if he intentionally—(1) engages in electronic surveillance under color of law except as authorized by this chapter, chapter 119, 121, or 206 of title 18, or any express statutory authorization that is an additional exclusive means for conducting electronic surveillance under section 1812 of this title. . . .

—18 U.S. CODE § 1809

OPENING ARGUMENT

Americans are being watched. That's nothing new—the Obama administration follows in the footsteps of a dozen other administrations. But there *are* two new facts: first, the unprecedented extent of the Obama administration's targeting of American citizens for surveillance; second, the Obama administration's unprecedented surveillance despite the administration's own insistence that the war on terror has been ended.

The rationalization for an increase in surveillance began with George W. Bush, after the horrific attacks of September 11, 2001. In the days after al-Qaeda terrorists flew passenger airliners into the World Trade Center towers and the Pentagon, and passengers aboard United Airlines flight 93 crashed their airplane into a field in Shanksville, Pennsylvania, President Bush declared a war on terror: "Our war on terror begins with al Qaeda, but it does not end there. It will not end until every terrorist group of global reach has been found, stopped, and defeated."[1]

Six weeks later, President Bush signed into law the so-called Patriot Act, which allowed for increased security measures, including surveillance of Americans under certain conditions. He stated, "With my signature, this law will give intelligence and law enforcement officials important new tools to fight a present danger. . . . As of today, we're changing the laws governing information-sharing. And as importantly, we're changing the culture of our various agencies that fight terrorism. Countering and investigating terrorist activity is the number one priority for both law enforcement and intelligence agencies. Surveillance of communications is another essential tool to pursue and stop terrorists. The existing law was written in the era of rotary telephones. This new law that I sign today will allow surveillance of all communications used by terrorists, including e-mails, the Internet, and cell phones." Bush added that the law "upholds and respects the civil liberties guaranteed by our Constitution."[2]

Barack Obama was a lowly state senator from Illinois at the time. But he opposed the essence of the Bush foreign policy. The day before Bush's speech, Obama stated, "The essence of this tragedy, it seems to me, derives from a fundamental absence of empathy on the part of the attackers: an inability to imagine, or connect with, the humanity and suffering of others. . . . it grows out of a climate of poverty and ignorance, helplessness and despair."[3]

Global redistributionism was the answer, not surveillance or force.

As a senator, Obama worried about the use of the Patriot Act to violate civil liberties; he even sent a letter to the Bush administration asking that the government should be required to convince a judge that the records they are seeking have some connection to a suspected terrorist or spy, as the three-part standard in the Senate bill would mandate. "[T]he government should be required to certify that the person whose records are sought has some connection to a suspected terrorist or spy."[4]

Obama's future vice president, then-senator Joe Biden (D-DE), criticized the Bush White House's use of the Patriot Act to monitor patterns in phone conversations. "I don't have to listen to your phone calls to know what you're doing. If I know every single phone call you made, I'm able to determine every single person you talked to. I can get a pattern about your life that is very, very intrusive. . . . If it's true that 200 million Americans' phone calls were monitored—in terms of not listening to what they said, but to whom they spoke and who spoke to them—I don't know, the Congress should investigative this," Biden said in the aftermath of reports about the Bush NSA getting warrantless records of phone calls within the United States.[5]

Once in office, President Obama doubled down on his perspective: American intransigence had created the war on terror. "All too often," Obama said in his first presidential interview, symbolically granted to *Al Arabiya*, "the United States starts by dictating . . . and we don't always know all the factors that are involved. So let's listen."[6]

Fast-forward four years. Obama was listening . . . to American citizens, Bush-style. That despite the fact that according to Obama, the war on terror had ended. In March 2013, at the National Defense University, a triumphant Obama explained that he had brought the war on terror to a victorious close—and in the process, he explained where that dastardly Bush character had gone wrong: "expanded surveillance . . . raised difficult questions about the balance that we strike between our interests in security and our values of privacy. And in some cases, I believe we compromised our basic values—by using torture to interrogate our enemies, and detaining individuals in a way that ran counter to the rule of law."

Now that Obama had taken over, however, things had changed. "[W]e have to recognize that the threat has shifted and evolved from the one that came to our shores on 9/11," Obama stated.[7]

It was time to go back to the pre-9/11 Clintonian mind-set of anti-terror as law enforcement.

So why, exactly, was the Obama National Security Agency ramping up the most intrusive surveillance of American citizens in the history of the country?

THE CHARGES

Historically, the provisions of 18 U.S. Code § 241 were passed as a portion of the Civil Rights Act of 1964 in order to prevent attacks by private citizens on the rights of blacks. In order to enable it to be effectively used, the Supreme Court declared in *United States v. Price* (1966), "We think that history leaves no doubt that, if we are to give § 241 the scope that its origins dictate, we must accord it a sweep as broad as its language." The Department of Justice notes that unlike other conspiracy laws, the so-called civil rights conspiracy statute does not require that a conspirator "commit an overt act prior to the conspiracy becoming a crime." In most conspiracy cases, one predicate act is necessary to establish an underlying crime; in the case of violating civil rights, organizing to do so is enough. And, as the Justice Department states, "The offense is punishable by a range of imprisonment up to a life term or the death penalty, depending upon the circumstances of the crime, and the resulting injury, if any."[8] As we will see, the Obama administration has repeatedly violated the rights of American citizens in surveilling them in violation of the Fourth Amendment. And unlike prior administrations, the Obama administration cannot even credibly claim that it was doing so for national security purposes, given its public proclamations to the contrary.

Section 1809 of Title 18 of the U.S. Code similarly prohibits violation of privacy rights via electronic surveillance "under color of law"—

meaning with the appearance of authority. That section of the code explicitly provides exceptions under which such information can be gathered. Under the Patriot Act, the attorney general or his subordinates can authorize an application to a judge for an order granting the right to surveil citizens to prevent terrorism. However, authority for blanket surveillance is not granted by the Patriot Act, merely specific surveillance. As we will see, it was precisely that sort of blanket surveillance the Obama administration embraced to the fullest extent of the law.

And when it came time to come clean with the American people, the Obama administration involved itself in a conspiracy of silence that forced some its most prominent members into perjury.

"THEY QUITE LITERALLY CAN WATCH YOUR IDEAS FORM AS YOU TYPE"

On March 12, 2013, Director of National Intelligence James Clapper appeared before the Senate Intelligence Committee. Senator Ron Wyden (D-OR) asked Clapper about the nature of American intelligence gathering on fellow Americans. "This is for you, Director Clapper, again on the surveillance front," he asked. "Last summer, the NSA director was at a conference, and he was asked a question about the NSA surveillance of Americans. He replied, and I quote here, 'The story that we have millions or hundreds of millions of dossiers on people is completely false.' . . . [D]oes the NSA collect any type of data at all on millions or hundreds of millions of Americans?"

Clapper answered: "No, sir." Then he added, "Not wittingly. There are cases where they could inadvertently perhaps collect, but not wittingly."[9]

There was only one problem. That was a lie. But he wasn't the only one twisting the truth. That same week, NSA director general Keith Alexander appeared before the House Emerging Threats and Capabilities Subcommittee of the Armed Services Committee. There, no less than fourteen times, he denied that the NSA had the ability to check Americans' communications.[10] At the Aspen Institute conference just a few months later, Alexander said, "To think we're collecting on every U.S. person . . . that would be against the law. . . . The fact is we're a foreign intelligence agency."[11]

Oops.

On June 5, 2013, leftist journalist Glenn Greenwald at the *Guardian* broke news of a deeply disturbing NSA program designed to collect records of millions of U.S. customers. The court order allowing such "ongoing, daily basis" surveillance suggested, as Greenwald wrote, that "under the Obama administration the communication records of millions of U.S. citizens are being collected indiscriminately and in bulk—regardless of whether they are suspected of any wrongdoing." The numbers of the parties, location data, call duration, and time all calls ended up in the hands of the government. Overall, Greenwald reported, the surveillance represented a massive increase from the Bush years. Two Democratic senators, Wyden and Mark Udall (D-UT), actually wrote the Obama administration to complain that "most Americans would be stunned to learn the details of how these secret court opinions have interpreted" the relevant provisions of the Patriot Act authorized in the aftermath of 9/11.[12]

The Obama administration immediately responded by saying it needed the information for national security reasons—even though Obama had recently declared the war on terror largely over. Leaker and liar par excellence James Clapper told the media, "information collected under this program is among the most important and valuable foreign intelligence information we collect, and is used to protect our nation from a wide variety of threats." He blasted the "unauthorized disclosure of information about this important and entirely legal program," which he called "reprehensible," and he suggested that Americans had been put at risk by being made aware that the government was watching them.

The very next day, the *Washington Post* had a similarly shocking scoop. The NSA and FBI were "tapping directly into the central servers of nine leading U.S. Internet companies, extracting audio and video chats, photographs, e-mails, documents, and connection logs." The program, apparently created in the Bureau of Scary-Sounding Code Names, was called PRISM. The PRISM program bragged in internal documents that it had access directly to "servers of these U.S. Service Providers: Microsoft, Yahoo, Google, Facebook, PalTalk, AOL, Skype, YouTube, Apple."[13] The NSA covered millions of dollars' worth of costs to help grease the skids for the Internet providers. That revelation broke wide open the companies' widespread denials of involvement in surveillance.[14]

And just as Greenwald reported, although the program had started under Bush, it expanded exponentially under Obama. In 2008, the court handling requests for warrants under the Foreign Intelligence Surveillance Act (FISA) banned certain searches of U.S. communications by the NSA; in 2011, the Obama administration even asked the FISA court to throw out limits of NSA spying on phone calls and emails, requesting permission for deliberate searches of such communications. The court complied, allowing the NSA to keep U.S. communications for six years.[15]

The PRISM program, according to the *Post*, made it possible for the NSA to grab virtually "anything it likes." "They quite literally can watch your ideas form as you type," said a career intelligence officer, who leaked the information to the *Post*.[16] A forty-one-slide PowerPoint presentation about PRISM stated openly that the program cost $20 million per year. The slide show further recommended that NSA employees use both Upstream, a collection of communications on fiber cables and infrastructure allowing government employees to grab data as it "flows past," and PRISM. The information, once gathered, is passed on to one of myriad different agencies, including the FBI, CIA, or NSA. As of April 5, 2013, there were 117,675 active surveillance targets in the counterterrorism database.[17]

Later reports revealed that the NSA didn't restrict its information gathering to computers and phone calls—the NSA could tap data held on smartphones, including contact lists, SMS traffic, and locations of cell phone users. The NSA could hack iPhones and BlackBerrys.[18]

The supposed legal basis for all of this information gathering was Patriot Act Section 215, which states that the government can push businesses to turn over information to it based on national security need. But the information sought "must be 'relevant' to an authorized preliminary or full investigation to obtain foreign intelligence information not concerning a U.S. person or to protect against international terrorism or clandestine intelligence activities." The section also required congressional monitoring of such activities.[19] How this information was "relevant" was never explained. And most members of Congress had no knowledge of these programs. So much for congressional monitoring.

The leaker of the information, it turned out, was one Edward Snowden, a former employee of Booz Allen Hamilton, a government contractor with the NSA. Snowden considered himself a whistle-blower. "Everyone everywhere now understands how bad things have gotten— and they're talking about it," Snowden said. "They have the power to decide for themselves whether they are willing to sacrifice their privacy to the surveillance state. . . . My sole motive is to inform the public as to that which is done in their name and that which is done against them."[20]

But the revelations did not end there. Just days later, Greenwald broke the story that the NSA had a datamining tool called Boundless Informant, which had gathered some three billion pieces of intelligence from U.S. computer networks in just one month.[21]

"WE DON'T HAVE A DOMESTIC SPYING PROGRAM"

On June 7, President Obama—the great civil libertarian and victorious luminary in the war on terror—finally spoke up. But instead of taking credit for the program, he blamed Congress and the judiciary. "If people don't trust Congress and the judiciary then I think we are going to have some problems here," he intoned, suggesting that Congress had been fully briefed and that the secret courts making determinations about surveillance were totally trustworthy. In an odd mixture of bellicosity and timidity, Obama said, "I don't welcome leaks, because there's a reason why these programs are classified. . . . I think it's healthy for democracy. I think it's a sign of maturity." He added that he didn't think Americans should buy into the "hype" about surveillance activities.[22] He concluded, "Nobody is listening to your phone calls. . . . They are not looking at people's names, and they're not looking at content. But by sifting through this so-called metadata, they may identify potential leads with respect to folks who might engage in terrorism." In other words they had access to names, calls, and content. But trust Big Brother.

That same day, Obama said that it wasn't his fault that the NSA could spy on anything Americans did: Congress knew about it. "The programs that have been discussed over the last couple days in the press are secret in the sense that they're classified, but they're not secret in the sense that when it comes to telephone calls, every member of Congress has been briefed on this program," Obama stated. "[I]t's important to understand that your duly elected representatives have been consistently informed on exactly what we're doing."[23] On August 9, Obama reiterated that Americans should have felt comfortable about NSA surveillance, since Congress knew about it.[24]

But Congress didn't know about all of the Obama administration's activities. Shortly after Greenwald's revelations, the Obama administration granted a hasty briefing to Congress. Afterward, Representative Loretta Sanchez (D-CA) said, "I can't speak to what we learned in there, and I don't know if there are other leaks, if there's more information somewhere, if somebody else is going to step up, but I will tell you that I believe it's the tip of the iceberg. . . . I think it's just broader than most people even realize, and I think that's, in one way, what astounded most of us, too." She wasn't the only one admitting she hadn't been made fully aware of what went on at the NSA. Senator Jon Tester (D-MT) said that he didn't understand how the Snowden leak "compromises the security of this country whatsoever . . . quite frankly, it helps people like me become aware of a situation that I wasn't aware of because I don't sit on that Intelligence Committee."[25]

Obama later claimed that no innocent American needed to worry about being spied on at all. Appearing on Jay Leno's *Tonight* show on NBC—a safe forum for the president, and the first place Obama took questions about the NSA scandal—Obama blathered, "We don't have a domestic spying program. What we do have is some mechanisms that can track a phone number of an email address that is connected to a terrorist attack. . . . That information is useful." Obama said that the program was "critical."[26]

A few days later, Obama finally confronted the press on the NSA. He opened with a bizarre statement acknowledging the legitimacy of Americans' worries, but simultaneously pooh-poohing them. He said it was "right to ask questions about surveillance . . . it's not enough for me, as president, to have confidence in these programs." As usual, he announced a review board, appointed by him, to review surveillance methods. He called those who "lawfully raised their voices on behalf of privacy and civil liberties . . . patriots who love our country and want it to live up to our highest ideals." But then, swerving, he stated that there was truly no problem at all: "As I've said, this program is an important tool in our effort to disrupt terrorist plots. And it does not allow the government to listen to any phone calls without a warrant." When questioned, Obama said, "the fact that I said that the programs are operating in a way that prevents abuse, that continues to be true, without the reforms. . . . I am comfortable that the program currently is not being abused."[27]

Except, of course, that it was being abused. Repeatedly. In a wide variety of ways.

An internal audit of the NSA done in May 2012 showed 2,776 violations of rules and court orders for surveillance within the United States from April 2011 to March 2012. That number covered only one headquarters and a couple of local units. The actual number is far higher. Some incidents included thousands of files. Infractions largely centered around unauthorized surveillance of Americans or foreign citizens, and included significant legal violations. Furthermore, documents showed that the NSA told employees to use generic language and scrub details of violations before reporting to the Justice Department and the director of national intelligence. In one case, the Foreign Intelligence Surveillance Court wasn't informed of a massive operation with a new collection method for months. When it found out, the court struck it down. The Obama administration covered up the ruling. Even though oversight staff increased dramatically under Obama, so did violations.[28]

Overall, the NSA admitted, staffers could have illegally grabbed 56,000 emails of innocent Americans each year between 2008 and 2011 under the program the FISA court struck down. Each year, in total, the NSA collects 250 million emails, as well as millions of phone calls.[29] In response, Obama remarked on CNN that the government had to "do a better job" of creating confidence in the NSA.[30]

Staffers didn't just make mistakes—a few purposefully violated surveillance law. "Very rare instances of willful violations of the NSA's authorities have been found," the NSA admitted, without giving numbers. One NSA official used the government tools to track an ex-spouse. Senator Dianne Feinstein (D-CA) put the number of such violations at "roughly one case per year," and said that the NSA took disciplinary action.[31]

And all of this represented just the "tip of a larger iceberg," according to Senators Wyden and Udall. "In particular, we believe the public deserves to know more about the violations of the secret court orders that have authorized the bulk collection of Americans' phone and email records under the USA PATRIOT Act. The public should also be told more about why the Foreign Intelligence Surveillance Court has said that the executive branch's implementation of Section 702 of the Foreign Intelligence Surveillance Act has circumvented the spirit of the law, particularly since the executive branch has declined to address this concern," Wyden and Udall wrote.[32]

What of the vaunted FISA court ensuring that Americans' rights were not violated? U.S. District Judge Reggie B. Walton said that the courts are "forced to rely upon the accuracy of the information that is provided to the court. . . . [The court] does not have the capacity to investigate issues of noncompliance, and in that respect the [court] is in the same position as any other court when it comes to enforcing [government] compliance with its orders."[33] Even when the government goes to the FISA courts, it doesn't always tell the truth. In one ruling, Judge John Bates of the FISA court wrote, "The court is troubled that the government's revelations regarding the NSA's acquisition of Internet transactions mark the third instance in less than three years in which the government has disclosed a substantial misrepresentation regarding the scope of a major collection program."[34] Jameel Jaffer, deputy legal director of the American Civil Liberties Union, blasted the NSA over the revealed Bates opinion: "the NSA misrepresented its activities to the court just as it misrepresented them to Congress and the public, and they provide further evidence that current oversight mechanisms are far too feeble."[35]

The NSA didn't just keep the information it gathered in-house, either. It sent out information to other agencies that requested it, including the Drug Enforcement Administration—a law enforcement body designed solely to police *domestic crime*. According to the *New York Times*, "Smaller intelligence units within the Drug Enforcement Administration, the Secret Service, the Pentagon and the Department of Homeland Security have sometimes been given access to the security agency's surveillance tools for particular cases, intelligence officials say."[36] Actually, the DEA had its own version of blanket surveillance: it paid AT&T to put DEA employees in supervisor positions to request information going all the way back to 1987. Four billion call records enter the database each and every day. Training slides on that program contain the logo of the White House Office of National Drug Control Policy.[37]

Good thing that President Obama pledged to create a panel of "outside experts" to get to the bottom of all of this NSA hubbub. Except that like all of Obama's other scandal panels, this one was stacked with Obama insiders: Richard Clarke and Michael Morell. Clarke served as counterterrorism czar for President Bush, where he approved such surveillance; Morell was a career CIA officer. The "outside experts" were actually insiders par excellence. Cass Sunstein, Obama's onetime regulatory czar, also joined the panel. The only true outsider on the panel was one Peter Swire of the Georgia Institute of Technology.[38]

THE TRAITOR

The Obama administration's response to the NSA revelations wasn't to come clean, or to fire those responsible for the massive overreach that allowed Americans' Gchats to be accessed by any one of the thousands of federal employees with clearance. It was to attack Edward Snowden. The administration immediately moved to try Snowden under the Espionage Act—even though the administration itself routinely leaked national security information to the press, and engaged in illegal espionage in the Middle East. Glenn Greenwald said, "I think it's very surprising to accuse somebody of espionage who hasn't worked for a foreign government, who didn't covertly pass information to an adversary-enemy of the United States, who didn't sell any top secret information, who simply went to newspapers, asked newspapers to very carefully vet the information to make sure that the only thing being published are things that inform his fellow citizens but doesn't harm national security. That is not espionage in any real sense of the word."[39]

Meanwhile, the Justice Department revoked Snowden's passport, with Secretary of State John Kerry explaining, "What I see is an individual who threatened his country and put Americans at risk through the acts that he took. People may die as a consequence of what this man did. It is possible the United States will be attacked because terrorists may now know how to protect themselves in some way or another that they didn't know before." He also assured the public that the government didn't "look at people's emails and we don't go inside and just do a random scoop like that."[40] Kerry called Snowden's leaks "despicable and beyond description."[41]

The NSA was a bipartisan scandal, so it made sense that the attacks on Snowden came from both sides of the political aisle. House Speaker John Boehner (R-OH) said Snowden was a "traitor," and explained, "The disclosure of this information puts Americans at risk. It shows our adversaries what our capabilities are. And it's a giant violation of the law."[42] Former vice president Dick Cheney also called Snowden a "traitor" who had done "enormous damage" to American counterterrorism efforts.[43] Senator Feinstein added that she thought Snowden had committed "an act of treason."[44]

Finally, Obama sounded off on Snowden directly. At the same August 9 press conference in which Obama called those concerned about civil liberties violations "patriots," he declined to label Snowden a patriot. "I don't think Mr. Snowden was a patriot," Obama stated. "My preference—and I think the American people's preference—would have been for a lawful, orderly examination of these laws; a thoughtful, fact-based debate that would then lead us to a better place." Presumably, a debate behind closed doors, without the involvement of the public.[45]

The media jumped on the "Snowden: Traitor or Hero?" bandwagon, turning the entire NSA fiasco into a referendum on whether Snowden was a civil libertarian or a traitor looking to harm America's national security. David Brooks of the *New York Times* wrote, "He betrayed the Constitution. The founders did not create the United States so that some solitary 29-year-old could make unilateral decisions about what should be exposed." On the other side of the political aisle, Jeffrey Toobin of CNN said that Snowden "wasn't blowing the whistle on anything illegal; he was exposing something that failed to meet his own standards of propriety."[46]

The attempt to shift the narrative from NSA malfeasance to Snowden didn't stop there. Politicians began targeting Greenwald, the reporter who worked with Snowden on his leaks. Representative Peter King (R-NY) suggested that journalists who printed the leaks should be prosecuted. "[I]f they willingly knew that this was classified information," he said, "I think action should be taken, especially on something of this magnitude." He said there was "an obligation both moral but also legal, I believe, against a reporter disclosing something that would so severely compromise national security."[47] Representative Mike Rogers (R-MI) added that Greenwald "doesn't have a clue" about how the NSA actually worked.[48]

On August 18, 2013, David Miranda, Greenwald's gay partner, found himself detained at Heathrow Airport for nine hours. The authorities questioned him under the Terrorism Act of 2000, which grants officers the right to stop, search, and detain people for questioning. Officers grabbed Miranda's cell phone, laptop, camera, memory stick, and DVDs. "This is a profound attack on press freedoms and the news gathering process," Greenwald lamented. "To detain my partner for a full nine hours while denying him a lawyer, and then seize large amounts of his possessions, is clearly intended to send a message of intimidation to those of us who have been reporting on the NSA and GCHQ [Britain's Government Communications Headquarters]. The actions of the UK pose a serious threat to journalists everywhere."[49] The White House admitted that it knew in advance that Miranda would be stopped, and that it received access to information seized from Miranda—but added that it didn't play a role in that detention.[50]

These were the supposed villains in this morality play created by the White House: Snowden, Greenwald, Miranda.

But Snowden's status didn't really matter, of course. Neither did Greenwald's journalistic activities. Who cared what Snowden's motivation was, or why Greenwald had reported on Snowden's leaks? But the hubbub over Snowden's character obscured two key questions. First, if

Snowden *was* such a traitor, wouldn't it suggest that the government's unfettered access to information created the significant risk of nefarious people gaining access to Americans' private lives? After all, this twenty-nine-year-old "traitor" had taken laptops full of information straight from the NSA. And as of October 2012, approximately 1.7 *million* Americans either had top-secret clearance or approval for it, including nearly 800,000 who didn't even work for the government.[51] There are virtually no checks on people who want to steal information. According to the *Federal Times*, "Nearly half the agencies handling classified data on their networks lack capabilities to thwart damaging information leaks by disgruntled insiders."[52] Who are the people staffing those agencies? According to a document released by Snowden, a full one in five people who applied to the CIA and were red-flagged had ties to Hamas, Hezbollah, or al-Qaeda.[53]

Even more important, there was a second question: were intrusions by the federal government truly justified in order to achieve security?

"IT'S CALLED PROTECTING AMERICA"

While members of the federal government had no answer to the first question, they repeatedly answered the second question in the affirmative. Rogers said, "Within the last few years, this program was used to stop a terrorist attack in the United States. We know that. It's important. It fills in a little seam that we have, and it's used to make sure that there's not an international nexus to any terrorism event that they may believe is ongoing in the United States." White House deputy press secretary Josh Earnest agreed, calling the NSA surveillance a "critical tool" for protecting Americans.[54] Senator Saxby Chambliss (R-GA) added, "To my knowledge, there has not been any citizen who has registered a complaint. It has proved meritorious because we have collected significant information on bad guys, but only on bad guys, over the years." And Feinstein said, "It's called protecting America."[55]

Senator Lindsey Graham (R-SC) actually celebrated the government sifting his phone calls. "I'm a Verizon customer," Graham said. "I don't mind Verizon turning over records to the government if the government is going to make sure that they try to match up a known terrorist phone with somebody in the United States. I don't think you're talking to the terrorists. I know you're not. I know I'm not. So we don't have anything to worry about."[56] A few days later, he went even further: "If I thought censoring the mail was necessary, I would suggest it, but I don't think it is."[57]

But was it? Not one politician provided any evidence that the government's antiterror efforts required the vast scope of surveillance provided for by the NSA programs. Did millions of American emails and calls need to be stored? Or could a more targeted approach have worked?

At 2:49 p.m. EDT on April 15, 2013, Patriots' Day, two pressure-cooker bombs blew up near the finish line of the Boston Marathon. Three were killed, and 264 others were injured. Three days later, law enforcement centered on the culprits: Tamerlan and Dzhokhar Tsarnaev, two brothers from Chechnya involved deeply in Islamism. The federal government's red flags should have been raised full-mast for months before the attacks. In March 2011, the Russians intercepted a phone call between Tamerlan and his mother involving jihadism. The Russians warned the FBI; the FBI went to check on Tsarnaev. Tamerlan and his mother ended up in the American TIDE database, which contained five hundred thousand names at the time. In September 2011, the Russians sent that information to the CIA. The CIA did nothing. The feds closed the case, and didn't consider reopening it even after the Russians warned the feds again that Tamerlan Tsarnaev had traveled to Dagestan, an Islamist training center.[58] "The Russian side warned the American side about the Tsarnaev brothers," said Valentina Matvienko, Speaker of the Russian Senate, "but this information was not taken seriously, which is what led to that tragedy."[59]

The FBI claimed that they simply didn't have enough information, according to the testimony of Director Robert Mueller: "I do believe that when we got the lead on Tamerlan from the Russians, that the agent did an excellent job in investigating, utilizing the tools that are available to him in that kind of investigation. . . . At that point in time, I do not know that there was much else that could be done within the statutes, within the Constitution, to further investigate him."[60]

But there was more that the FBI could have done to monitor the Tsarnaevs. That, of course, was the entire point of the NSA surveillance program. But the Tsarnaevs slipped through the cracks nonetheless. Who, exactly, was the NSA monitoring if *not* the Tsarnaevs?

CLOSING ARGUMENT

Americans' civil rights—our most treasured rights to privacy—were violated on a blanket basis by both the Bush administration and the Obama administration. The difference between the two administrations, however, lay in both the extent of the surveillance activities and in the justification for them. Bush's were more limited and more justified; President Obama has yet to lay out clear justification for blanket surveillance of millions of American citizens.

On June 11, 2013, the American Civil Liberties Union filed a lawsuit against the NSA's phone surveillance program, claiming violation of constitutional rights. Brett Max Kaufman, a legal fellow at the ACLU, pointed out the risks to controversial organizations of having the government monitor broad swaths of private information: "The nature of the ACLU's work—in areas like access to reproductive services, racial discrimination, the rights of immigrants, national security, and more—means that many of the people who call the ACLU wish to keep their contact with the organization confidential. Yet if the government is collecting a vast trove of ACLU phone records—and it has reportedly been doing so for as long as seven years—many people may reasonably think twice before communicating with us."

On September 4, the National Rifle Association joined the ACLU's lawsuit, explaining that the government's collection of information under the surveillance programs effectively created a national gun registry in violation of law. "It would be absurd to think that the Congress would adopt and maintain a web of statutes intended to protect against the creation of a national gun registry, while simultaneously authorizing the FBI and the NSA to gather records that could effectively create just such a registry," the NSA explained.[61]

This is not paranoia. It is the reality of dealing with a massive government staffed by millions of people who may or may not be trustworthy. If Americans have learned nothing else from the IRS scandals, the Obama targeting of whistle-blowers in Benghazi and Fast and Furious, and the unending leaks from the Obama administration, they should know by now that the government does the right thing, up until the point it doesn't. When the IRS targeted Obama's political opponents, it did so on the basis of tax information. When the Obama Justice Department targeted Obama's journalistic opponents, it did so using phone records. What could a politically motivated government do with access to emails, phone records, and virtually all other information about Americans' private lives?

Were a private entity to gather all of the information gathered by the NSA, it would be prosecuted and sued out of existence. But the federal government has done so in the name of national security—even though Obama himself has claimed that the threat of terrorism has decreased markedly, and that effectively, the war on terror is over. Not only that—the federal government is lying about it. When Director of National Intelligence Clapper told Congress that the NSA had not collected data on millions of Americans, he lied. Even Clapper admitted privately to Congress that his statements were "clearly erroneous." But he refused to correct the record publicly.[62]

On June 7, 2013, President Obama explained that he, too, worried about privacy. He said, "I will leave this office at some point, sometime in the last—next three and a half years, and after that, I will be a private citizen. And I suspect that, you know, on—on a list of people who might be targeted, you know, so that somebody could read their emails or—or listen to their phone calls, I'd probably be pretty high on that list. So it's not as if I don't have a personal interest in making sure my privacy is protected."[63]

That is akin to Don Corleone claiming that he had an interest in murder laws. It's true, but it's not the whole story. President Obama and his administration have shown a peculiar addiction to gathering information on Americans. That addiction endangers Americans' most basic protections against government intrusion. It also violates the law. Nothing in the Patriot Act authorizes the sort of blanket surveillance utilized by the Bush administration and exponentially multiplied by the Obama administration.[64]

That's exactly what a federal judge found in December 2013. In *Klayman v. Obama*, U.S. District Court judge Richard Leon ruled that the Obama administration's collection of metadata on millions of Americans could not be justified under law or public policy. In the ruling, Leon wrote, "I cannot imagine a more 'indiscriminate' and 'arbitrary invasion' than this systematic and high tech collection and retention of personal data on virtually every single citizen for purposes of querying and analyzing it without prior judicial record." He added, "Surely, such a program infringes on 'that degree of privacy that the founders enshrined in the Fourth Amendment.' "[65]

Even more stunning: Leon found that the government could not provide one shred of evidence that its surveillance had actually effectuated terror prevention. "[T]he government," Leon wrote, "does not cite a single instance in which analysis of the NSA's bulk metadata collection actually stopped an imminent attack, or otherwise aided the government in achieving any objective that was time-sensitive in nature."[66]

Leon's ruling has already been contradicted by other judicial bodies. The outcome of the NSA surveillance program remains up in the air. Nonetheless, Leon is correct. The Obama administration has violated the civil rights of millions of Americans. And those responsible must pay the price.

COUNT 6

★

BRIBERY

Whoever being a public official or person selected to be a public official, directly or indirectly, corruptly demands, seeks, receives, accepts, or agrees to receive or accept anything of value personally or for any other person or entity, in return for: being influenced in the performance of any official act; being influenced to commit or aid in committing, or to collude in, or allow, any fraud, or make opportunity for the commission of any fraud, on the United States; or being induced to do or omit to do any act in violation of the official duty of such official or person . . . shall be fined under this title or not more than three times the monetary equivalent of the thing of value, whichever is greater, or imprisoned for not more than fifteen years, or both, and may be disqualified from holding any office of honor, trust, or profit under the United States.

—18 U.S. CODE § 201

OPENING ARGUMENT

Barack Obama campaigned as an outsider to Washington, D.C., politics. On October 1, 2008, Obama told a massive crowd in Wisconsin, "Make no mistake: We need to end an era in Washington where accountability has been absent, oversight has been overlooked, your tax dollars have been turned over to wealthy CEOs and the well-connected corporations." He continued, "You need leadership you can trust to work for you, not for the special interests who have had their thumb on the scale. And together, we will tell Washington, and their lobbyists, that their days of setting the agenda are over. They have not funded my campaign. You have. They will not run my White House. You'll help me run my White House."

On his first day in office, Obama signed an executive order purportedly attempting to quash the connection between his administration and those who would seek to corrupt it. The executive order mandated that every appointee in every federal agency sign a pledge: "I will not accept gifts from registered lobbyists or lobbying organizations for the duration of my service as an appointee." The pledge also included provisions requiring an end to the revolving door between lobbying and the executive branch.[1]

That promise lasted a grand total of one day.

The day after signing the executive order, Obama appointed William J. Lynn III to deputy secretary of defense. Lynn made his fame and fortune as a lobbyist for defense contractor Raytheon. White House press secretary Robert Gibbs said that the rules had to go out the window for Lynn: "In the case of Mr. Lynn, he's somebody who obviously is superbly qualified. His experience going back to his Pentagon jobs during the Clinton administration make him uniquely qualified to do this." Defense secretary Robert Gates said he requested a waiver because "he came with the highest recommendations of a number of people that I respect a lot."[2] A few days after that, Obama named former Goldman Sachs lobbyist Mark Patterson chief of staff to the Treasury Department.[3] And a few weeks later, the White House tapped former National Partnership for Women & Families lobbyist Jocelyn Frye to direct policy and projects for Michelle Obama, as well as Cecilia Muñoz, lobbyist for National Council of La Raza, to head up Obama's Hispanic outreach. The White House eventually settled on the position that lobbyists could hold any position they wanted in the administration, so long as they "recused" themselves from conflict of interest.[4]

Not a comforting thought from an administration riddled with corruption and abuse of power.

Sadly, the Obama administration has been the largest purveyor of governmental corruption in American history. The malfeasance of Obama officials makes the Teapot Dome scandal of Warren G. Harding look minor-league. Over and over again, President Obama's minions have used the tools of executive power to extract concessions from those at his political mercy, and to help those who do his political bidding. It helps to be a friend to the Obama regime. And it hurts to be an enemy.

THE CHARGES

There are two main provisions governing bribery and kickbacks under federal law. The first, specifically aimed at bribery, establishes that something of value was "given, offered, or promised to a public official," according to the Supreme Court. Alternatively, the prosecution can establish that something of value was "corruptly demanded, sought, received, accepted, or agreed to be received or accepted by a public official" with intent to influence an official act. This crime requires the intent to influence or be influenced.

The second crime is the acceptance of an "illegal gratuity." That crime, according to the United States Office of Government Ethics, requires only that the thing of value "be given or accepted 'for or because of' an official act." Bribery requires intent; illegal gratuity is a lesser burden of proof.

In the case of the Obama administration, both bribery and acceptance of illegal gratuities are in the mix. Proving bribery is obviously far more difficult than showing acceptance or demanding of illegal gratuities. But in many cases, there is a clear quid pro quo implemented by members of the Obama administration with the direct intent of influencing public acts.

THE BRIBEMASTER

Barack Obama has a long personal history with financial corruption. It began in his adopted hometown of Chicago, shortly after he was elected to the United States Senate. Obama desperately wanted to buy a home that was simply too expensive for him. So he went to a local fixer known as Antoin "Tony" Rezko for "advice." The advice ended with Obama buying the home for $300,000 below asking price, even as Rezko's wife bought the land on which the home was located for more than market value. The Obamas bought the house for $1.65 million. Obama then turned around and bought a part of the Rezko land for $104,500, below market value. During the 2004 campaign, Rezko and his friends gave Obama $120,000. At the time, the FBI was investigating Rezko.[5] Later, Rezko would be sentenced to ten years in jail for corruption; one of his closest political associates, Governor Rod Blagojevich, would head to prison, too.[6] Blagojevich, of course, went to jail because he attempted to sell Obama's vacant Senate seat.

Right around the same time as the Rezko affair, the Obamas became embroiled in another Chicagoland financial snafu. From 2004 to 2007, Michelle Obama worked for the University of Chicago Medical Center. Shortly after her husband became a U.S. senator, Michelle received a massive pay raise, skyrocketing from $121,910 in 2004 to $316,962 in 2005.[7] Her colleagues on the board at the University of Chicago Medical Center included Valerie Jarrett. In 2006, Senator Obama directed a $1 million earmark to the University of Chicago Hospitals.[8]

Michael Riordan, the president of the University of Chicago Medical Center, insisted that Michelle was hired thanks to her own job skills. "She is worth her weight in gold, and she is just terrific," he told the *Chicago Tribune.* That was almost literally true. As to the contention, made by Riordan, that Michelle's position was designed to "evolve into a vice president's post as a way of showing the organization's commitment to community outreach,"[9] the medical center quickly eliminated Michelle's post entirely.[10] Obama did, however, announce that the woman who recruited Michelle to the medical center, Susan Sher, would join the administration to give Michelle legal advice.[11]

The ties between the Obamas and the University of Chicago Medical Center didn't end there. In 2012, President Obama's controversial racist and anti-Semitic former pastor, Jeremiah Wright, decided to spill the beans to author Edward Klein about his less-than-cordial parting with the Obama clan. "Man," he told Klein, "the media ate me alive. After the media went ballistic on me, I received an e-mail offering me money not to preach at all until the November presidential election." According to Wright, the email originated with "one of Barack's closest friends," who sent an offer to another church member, who forwarded it to Wright. When asked how much the Obama associate had offered Wright to shut up, Wright promptly answered, "One hundred and fifty thousand dollars."

That offer was just the first step in an Obama attempt to quiet Wright. Obama met with Wright personally, and said to him, according to Wright, "I really wish you wouldn't do any more public speaking until after the November election. . . . I wish you wouldn't speak. It's gonna hurt the campaign if you do that." Here's how the rest of that conversation went, according to Wright: "Barack said, 'I'm sorry you don't see it the way I do. Do you know what your problem is?' And I said, 'No, what's my problem?' And he said, 'You have to tell the truth.' I said, 'That's a good problem to have. That's a good problem for all preachers to have. That's why I could never be a politician.' "[12]

The man who attempted to bribe Wright, he said, was one Eric Whitaker—one of Obama's closest friends, a man who plays basketball and vacations with the president, and who, according to Wright, "made it comfortable" for Obama to become Christian without discarding his "Islamic background." Whitaker was also a higher-up at the University of Chicago Medical Center when Michelle worked there.[13] Governor Blagojevich appointed Whitaker to his position. In 2012, the U.S. Department of Health and Human Services decided to kick $5.9 million to Whitaker's University of Chicago Medical Center Urban Health Initiative.[14]

"BOSS TWEED ON STEROIDS"

During the 2008 election cycle, unions spent in excess of $200 million to elect Barack Obama president. That included $68 million in direct campaign contributions from unions and union members, $52 million via 527 organizations, and tens of millions more in on-the-ground get-out-the-vote efforts.[15] As Mallory Factor, author of *Shadowbosses: Government Unions Control America and Rob Taxpayers Blind*, describes, that effort continued into the 2012 election cycle. "AFL-CIO volunteers," Factor says, "knocked on almost 14 million doors nationwide." The unions put 400,000 pairs of boots on the ground to work the pavement for their man. In Ohio alone, unions handed over 1,800 offices to Democrats for campaign use. AFL-CIO president Richard Trumka rightly stated of Ohio and Wisconsin, "We did deliver those states. None of those would have been in the president's column." Overall, the unions spent at least $500 million on the 2012 election cycle.[16]

One of the biggest donors to President Obama was the United Auto Workers. Between 2000 and 2008, the UAW handed almost $24 million to Democrats.[17] It also handed $1.14 million to its congressional allies—representatives who would vote UAW cash.[18] The UAW spent $11 million on the 2008 election alone.[19]

For good reason.

In November 2007, Obama spoke at the United Auto Workers Conference in Dubuque, Iowa. There he blasted the Bush administration: "I'm tired of playing defense. I know the UAW is tired of playing defense. We're ready to play some offense." He added, "There are few more important unions in this country than the UAW. You created the auto industry. You secured good-paying jobs for generations of workers. And you built the American middle class—the backbone of our economy. So I know someone once said what's good for GM is good for America. But it's time we also recognized that what's good for the UAW is good for America." He called for making "the UAW's agenda America's agenda."[20]

This was one promise Obama would keep.

On June 1, 2009, General Motors declared bankruptcy. Once America's largest corporation, GM had sunk into the red thanks to rich union contracts guaranteeing massive benefits to retired workers. Union costs *per car* for GM measured up to $1,500.[21] The 2007 contract between GM and the UAW forced GM to hand up to $140,000 in severance to fired workers.[22] UAW workers earned up to $73 per hour, compared to $44 at competitors like Toyota and Honda; workers who had their jobs outsourced were not fired, but instead picked up 95 percent of their paycheck to do nothing until another job could be found; thirty-year employees could retire with full pensions, up to $37,500 per year. By the end of its long decline, GM signed checks to 4.6 retirees for every worker.[23] In 2007, GM lost $40 billion. In 2008, its sales plummeted 45 percent.[24]

Instead of GM going bankrupt, however, the Obama administration got directly involved, cramming down a managed bankruptcy deal to pay off the UAW.[25] The actual deal worked out great for the UAW: bondholders got 10 percent of the new GM, but couldn't sell their stock, meaning that they ended up with ten cents on the dollar. Those bondholders included retired teachers, investors, and victims of GM who had won lawsuits against the company. Chris Crowe, for example, described himself thus: "I'm a retired electrician from Denver, Colorado. I'm not rich and I'm not a Wall Street bank. These bonds finance my son's college tuition and my retirement. I'm actually very concerned about not getting a check on May 15 from my bonds because I need this money to pay my property taxes. When the Administration refuses to meet with the bondholders or chooses to wipe them out, they're wiping me out, and lots of others like me. We are Main Street, not Wall Street. Who is looking out for us and our interests? Mr. President, please protect us."

Crowe had one problem: he hadn't given millions to the Obama election fund.[26] The union, however, received 100 percent of its pensions. The union's health-care trust also received 17.5 percent of the equity in the new company, and an additional $9 billion in preferred stock (the highest level of stock). Altogether, the unions received 93 percent of what they were owed.[27] The taxpayers footed the bill to the tune of $19.1 billion.[28] "Priority one was serving the interests of the UAW," said CreditSights analyst Glenn Reynolds, who likened the deal to "the Putin political asset reallocation and reward system . . . Boss Tweed on steroids."[29]

Chrysler, too, went bankrupt—and again, the Obama administration crammed down a bankruptcy bargain on behalf of the UAW. The

UAW emerged with 55 percent ownership of the company. Investors got 10 percent. Creditors with secured loans—those who should have been paid back first from bankruptcy proceeds—were placed behind unsecured debtors like the UAW. Bondholders got 29 cents on the dollar. The UAW's pension fund got 40 cents on the dollar. Why did the bondholders accept such a rotten deal? Professor Todd Zywicki of George Mason University School of Law explains that many bondholders had picked up cash from the feds through the Troubled Assets Relief Program already, and notes that institutions that hadn't taken federal cash fought back unsuccessfully.[30] President Obama took the opportunity to rip such bondholders as selfish, calling them a "small group of speculators" who "were hoping that everybody else would make sacrifices and they would have to make none." He said, "I don't stand with them. I stand with Chrysler's employees and their families and communities. I stand with Chrysler's management, its dealers and its suppliers. I stand with the millions of Americans who own and want to buy Chrysler cars."[31] One of those "speculators" was Jeremy K. Warriner, who lost his legs in a Jeep Wrangler accident.[32]

In the GM bankruptcy, the unionized employees of Delphi Corporation, which handles auto parts supply, walked away with a sweet deal, too: GM would pick up the full checks. As for nonunionized salaried employees of Delphi? They lost up to 70 percent of their pensions, life insurance, and health insurance. During the bankruptcy, the Obama administration Treasury Department Auto Task Force promised that "all stakeholders [would be] treated fairly and [receive] neither more nor less than they would have simply because the government was involved." The insanity of the deal even prompted former UAW president Ron Gettelfinger to call the bargain a "grave injustice."[33]

The bribery for Democrat allies via GM didn't end there. GM had a deal to buy mineral palladium from Montana; during its bankruptcy, GM tried to shift such purchases to Russia and South Africa. Montana senators Max Baucus and Jon Tester killed the deal so as to keep GM spending taxpayer cash in their state. When GM tried to create cars in India, Capitol Hill killed that as well.[34]

For the Obama administration, the auto bailout bribery was a win-win: the unions got their cash, the taxpayer got the bill, and President

Obama got reelected on the platform that bin Laden was dead and Detroit was alive. This was a textbook case of illegal gratuities, with the unions donating money to Obama's election coffers in exchange for a future promise that Obama would save them from their own bad contracts when the time came.

Unfortunately, Detroit itself went bankrupt. And the American people are still over a barrel with Government Motors. In order for the taxpayers to get their money back, GM's stock would have to triple.[35] Overall, the UAW walked away with more than $26 billion—as much money as the United States spends virtually every year on foreign aid. The factories closed anyway.[36]

"SEIU IS ON THE FIELD, IT'S IN THE WHITE HOUSE"

Senator Obama began his presidential campaign among friends at the Service Employees International Union; in September 2007, he told the Purple People Eaters, "Your agenda's been my agenda. . . . I'm tired of playing defense all the time. . . . I've spent my entire adult life working with the SEIU. . . . The question I ask SEIU members is, not 'Who is talking about your agenda?' but 'Who can change politics in Washington to make that a reality?' Change starts by making sure a Democrat is in the White House. Change doesn't end just because a Democrat is in the White House. It's time to turn the page on the old way of doing business."[37]

The SEIU spent $85 million on the 2008 election. "SEIU is on the field, it's in the White House, it's in the administration," SEIU president Andy Stern told members on the hundred-day mark of the Obama White House. He wasn't kidding: between Obama's inauguration and July 31, 2009, Stern visited the White House twenty-two times, more than any other person. He met personally with Obama seven times.[38] Obama stacked his administration with SEIU bigwigs: former SEIU official Patrick Gaspard joined Obama as the White House political director; Anna Burger, a high officer in the SEIU, ended up on the Obama Economic Recovery Advisory Board.

Most important, though, Obama tapped associated general counsel for the SEIU and AFL-CIO Craig Becker for the all-important National Labor Relations Board.[39] The NLRB is granted power under federal law to fix unfair labor practices—when unions don't like what management does, they take their complaints to the NLRB. For years, Democrats in the Senate had stopped President Bush from appointing members to the NLRB. Upon Obama's accession to the White House, however, he simply crammed his appointees into the NLRB under the auspices of recess appointments. After an attempted filibuster by Republican senators, Obama announced in March 2010 that Becker, along with Mark Gaston Pearce—a labor lawyer—would join the shorthanded NLRB.[40]

The NLRB quickly became a union tool. As the National Right to Work Legal Defense Foundation pointed out, the NLRB launched an Office of Public Affairs to publicize its decisions—and proceeded to cover only decisions beneficial to unions. Its rulings, according to NRTW, came out pro-union in 88.7 percent of cases between October 14, 2009, and August 2013.[41]

The most egregious case of NLRB bias began in April 2011, when the International Association of Machinists and Aerospace Workers tried to file a case with the NLRB against Boeing, on behalf of thirty-one thousand workers for the company. The union objected to Boeing's building a $750 million Dreamliner factory in South Carolina, a right-to-work state, instead of in Washington State. The union said that building outside Washington constituted illegal retaliation against strikers under federal law.

The NLRB agreed, based on the fact that Boeing was being rational: it wanted to locate in a state where it wouldn't have to deal with unions destroying all economic incentives. Acting NLRB general counsel Lafe Solomon said that such sentiments displayed "anti-union animus," and that the Boeing factory was therefore illegal. The NLRB requested that a judge order Boeing to relocate its production from South Carolina to Washington. Representative John Kline (R-MN) called the NLRB's action a "shameless campaign to bully an American employer."[42]

That was accurate. Solomon actually attempted to broker a deal with Boeing whereby Boeing would give extra goodies to the Washington union employees, and the NLRB would then drop the charges. Boeing agreed not to fire Dreamliner employees in Washington State before the end of its union contract—but that wasn't enough for Solomon, who withdrew his proposed settlement and went ahead with the prosecution anyway. As Greg Mourad of the National Right to Work Committee said, "Mr. Solomon did what IAM bosses told him to."[43]

Solomon, for his part, treated the whole sham prosecution of an American company jovially. In one email, he responded to an article criticizing the NLRB's economic impact: "The article gave me a new idea. . . . We screwed up the [U.S.] economy and now we can tackle europe [sic]."[44] He told the press that even if Boeing had made the decision because it wanted to locate in a state with free labor, that could be enough to allow the government to crack down: "Companies can make rational economic decisions that can be in violation of the National Labor Relations Act."[45]

Blackmailed by the NLRB, Boeing caved, announcing a new contract that would give workers in Washington a four-year extension with huge raises, ridiculous job security provisions, and commitment to spend cash building new production facilities in the Puget Sound area. The union promptly asked the NLRB to drop the case, and the NLRB complied. Solomon said, "This case was never about the union or the NLRB telling Boeing where it could put its plants. This was a question for us of retaliation, and that remains the law." He added ominously that if the NLRB saw a similar case, "we might well issue a complaint."[46] The corrupt bargain prompted the *Wall Street Journal* editorial board to fume, "The NLRB is supposed to be a fair-minded referee in labor disputes, making sure neither side breaks the law. But the board put its fist squarely on the union side to make Boeing pay a price for moving one of its 787 assembly lines to a right-to-work state, to make sure Boeing never did that again, and to demonstrate to any other unionized company that its investment is at risk if it makes the same decision. . . . [I]n practice the result is likely to be that more companies simply send jobs overseas where there's no NLRB. Congratulations."[47]

In 2013, Obama renominated Solomon to join the NLRB as permanent counsel.[48]

Solomon, Becker, and Pearce weren't the only union lackeys packed into the NLRB. In January 2012, Obama sought to stack the NLRB further by appointing Sharon Block and Richard Griffin. Block made her bones working for Senator Ted Kennedy (D-MA) and as deputy assistant secretary for congressional affairs at the Department of Labor. Griffin was a lawyer on the board of directors for the AFL-CIO Lawyer Coordinating Committee. Obama had just one problem: Congress wasn't in recess when he tried to appoint the two via "recess appointments." The federal appeals courts of both the Third and Fourth Circuits agreed that the Becker, Griffin, and Block appointments were illegal and in violation of the constitutional rights accorded to the Senate to advise and consent on nominees.[49] Judge David Sentelle wrote that Obama's attempt to stack the NLRB without Congress would amount to "free rein to appoint his desired nominees at any time he pleases, whether that time be a weekend, lunch or even when the Senate is in session and he is merely displeased with its inaction."[50]

As of September 2013, despite the court rulings, biographies of both Griffin and Block state that they were "recess appointments" of the president.[51]

In July 2012, Obama decided to appoint Nancy Schiffer, associate general counsel at the AFL-CIO, and Kent Hirozawa, chief counsel for Pearce.[52] That's horrible news for American business, which remains subject to the whims of the paid-off Obama NLRB. And it's horrible news for fans of anticorruption, given the cozy relationship between the unions and President Obama's labor policies.

STIMULATING THE OBAMA CAMPAIGN

Great spending always comes attendant with great corruption. President Obama has spent more money than any president in American history. And with the administration awash in inflated cash, Obama's cronies have reaped the benefit.

In February 2009, shortly after his election, President Obama made the case that the only way to stimulate the American economy back into life would be to infuse massive amounts of money into the consumer economy. The recession, Obama argued, could "linger for years" unless

America decided to "take dramatic action as soon as possible."[53] The stimulus package included massive subsidies for green energy, "shovel ready" projects, and public welfare programs. Obama also promised that with his proposed $787 billion stimulus package, the unemployment rate would drop below 6 percent quickly.

That obviously has not happened. But even as the economy continued to experience the slowest recovery in American history, Obama's friends got rich. More than $1 billion went to airports in the middle of nowhere, including a $5 billion taxiway in Findlay, Ohio, $2.2 million for a runway extension at Wilbur Airport in Washington State, and $1 million for a runway in Dover, Delaware. Three million dollars went to a turtle crossing in northern Florida, $10 million to an abandoned train station, and millions more to ten thousand corpses still getting Social Security checks, according to Judicial Watch.[54] Democratic states with low unemployment rates received wildly disproportionate checks from the stimulus package. According to Grover Norquist, head of Americans for Tax Reform, and John Lott Jr., "Obama may have claimed that he was motivated to help out those in the toughest shape, but it looks more likely that Democrats were more interested in helping their supporters." No joke. Washington, D.C., received $3,745 per capita, while Florida got just $553 per capita.[55]

Throw Them All Out author Peter Schweizer found that the Obama administration's $20 billion in green technology loans contained $16 billion for companies related to President Obama or his cronies—companies with links to Obama bundlers or people on his campaign finance committee. A full 16 of the 27 companies funded by Al Gore and John Doerr, a major Obama donor, got loans. Ninety percent of applicants for energy loans failed. Gore and Doerr got 59 percent of the loans for which they applied. As Ashton Ellis of the Center for Individual Freedom wrote, "Simply put, without the massive amount of money being spent from the Recovery Act, bundlers-turned-government-cronies would have been unable to funnel billions of dollars to friends and colleagues."[56] This is textbook bribery.

The Center for Public Integrity (CPI) has studied the Obama administration's corruption in depth. During Obama's first three years, campaign bundlers visited the White House more than three thousand times combined. Many of their companies got federal contracts, including one company—Level 3 Communications, whose vice president Donald H. Gips raised over $500,000 for Obama—that pulled down $13.8 million. Thomas McInerney, an Obama bundler, explained, "There was so much money this time, and there were so many people involved in raising the money, the number of people looking for something was exponentially more."

CPI also found that "184 of 556, or about one-third, of Obama bundlers or their spouses joined the administration in some role." That number jumped to 80 percent for those who put together more than half a million for President Transparency. Some of those appointees included Professor Spencer Overton of the George Washington University Law School, who became deputy attorney general in the Justice Department's Office of Legal Policy; Thomas Perrelli, who went to law school with Obama and also ended up at Justice; and Karol Mason, who ended up at the department, too. The Justice Department declined comment.

The Department of Energy also ended up chock full of Obama bundlers. Four people who raised $1.6 million for Obama's election effort ended up working at the department.[57]

No wonder the Department of Energy became a hotbed of kickbacks.

Solyndra was a solar panel maker owned by Argonaut Ventures, which was part of a broader foundation owned by George Kaiser, an Obama fund-raiser. The company was the first to get a loan from the Obama stimulus program. Solyndra received a $535 million federal loan. Two years later, the company collapsed, leaving taxpayers on the hook for the entire amount, and putting out of work some 1,100 employees.

The White House denied any involvement in the loans. But that was a lie. Just as Solyndra sought a second loan, Kaiser met with the White House. He visited the White House on several occasions during 2009–2010. Kaiser and his partners in Argonaut saw the Obama White House's involvement as crucial to the success of the company. "It appears things are headed in the right direction and [Secretary of Energy Steven] Chu is apparently staying involved in Solyndra's application and continues to talk up the company as a success story," wrote Steven R. Mitchell, managing director of Argonaut.[58] Kaiser, meanwhile, was busy dumping $340 million into Tulsa, Oklahoma, Kaiser's hometown. "George saw Solyndra as an investment and as something that could provide jobs in Tulsa," said Tulsa mayor Dewey Bartlett Jr.[59]

Emails from the Obama White House demonstrate that the White House directly pressured the Office of Management and Budget for final sign-off on the Solyndra loan so that Vice President Biden could announce the loan at an event in September 2009. The OMB repeatedly objected, complaining about "the time pressure we are under to sign-off on Solyndra." OMB officials worried, "There isn't time to negotiate." "We have ended up with a situation of having to do rushed approvals on a couple of occasions (and we are worried about Solyndra at the end of the week)," one official wrote to Biden's domestic policy adviser. The White House, which officially suggested that it had no involvement in the loans, responded to the emails by stating that the White House just had *interest* in the loans, but wasn't trying to exert pressure. Which is like saying that Don Corleone had an interest in Johnny Fontaine receiving a movie part.[60]

Secretary of Energy Steven Chu testified before Congress, "As the secretary of Energy, the final decisions on Solyndra were mine, and I made them with the best interest of the taxpayer in mind." Just to emphasize the point, he added, "I want to be clear: over the course of Solyndra's loan guarantee, I did not make any decision based on political considerations."[61] The bankruptcy of Solyndra didn't stop two dozen employees from taking down a total of $368,500 in bonuses.

Solyndra was only the beginning.

The Department of Energy gave BrightSource Energy, a company building solar thermal power plants, a $1.6 billion loan guarantee under the auspices of the stimulus program. The single biggest investor in BrightSource: VantagePoint Capital Partners, headed by Sanjay Wagle. Wagle raised millions for Obama in 2008 and—yes, really—was "renewable energy grants advisor" at Obama's Department of Energy. BrightSource was also a massive supporter of Senate Majority Leader Harry Reid. The company canceled its initial public offering thanks presumably to its inability to show a marketable decent balance sheet.[62]

The Vehicle Production Group, a portfolio company of Perseus—another company affiliated with an Obama bundler—picked up a $50 million loan. The Department of Energy stated that "the decision to provide the Vehicle Production Group a loan was made based on the merits after more than two years of review by officials in the DOE loan program."[63] The company stopped operations in 2013 and dropped its staff. The company didn't file for bankruptcy, but all one hundred employees ended up out of work.[64]

Overall, the *Washington Post* reported "$3.9 billion in federal grants and financing flowed to 21 companies backed by firms with connections to five Obama administration staffers and advisers."[65] The green loans program created fewer than 2,400 jobs between the passage of the stimulus plan and June 2012—a cost of $6.7 million per job, according to Mercatus Center research fellow Veronique De Rugy.[66] One of the biggest companies in the United States, General Electric, got particularly special treatment from President Obama—not surprising, given the fact that GE also owned NBC. GE gave the Obama campaign in excess of $529,000 during the 2008 election cycle;[67] Obama provided GE with extraordinarily generous financial benefits. No wonder GE CEO Jeffrey Immelt told a group of businesspeople in July 2011, "The people who are part of the business sector, the people in this room, have got to stop complaining about government and get some action under way." As Immelt stated in 2008, "We at GE will continue to support and advocate swift passage of [stimulus] legislation that is acceptable to the Senate, the House, and the Administration, and that can be promptly signed into law by the President." According to some estimates, GE received in excess of $3 billion in green loans from the Obama government.[68]

In November 2012, San Francisco–based XP Technology filed a federal claim against the Department of Energy alleging favoritism in its loans. "XP has received information demonstrating that the unprecedented number of failures in the DOE program relative to what DOE officials have claimed to be 'the most expensive and extensive due diligence in history' is explained by manipulated reviews, in the due diligence effort, on behalf of what the United States Government Accountability Office (GAO) investigations found to be 'favoritism' in published investigation reports. A [S] enate ethics investigation states, in published reports, that 'negligence and mismanagement by DOE officials' was a regular occurrence," the lawsuit claimed.[69] No one at the Energy Department has been fired or prosecuted.

SPREADING THE GREEN AROUND

In May 2013, the Competitive Enterprise Institute released a bomb-shell report alleging illegal favoritism at the Environmental Protection Agency. Under Obama administration EPA administrator Lisa Jackson, the agency had become a bulwark of pro-environmentalist corruption, with Jackson utilizing her vast regulatory power to target coal plants, pipelines, and factories across the country. But now the CEI alleged that the EPA had forced conservative groups to pay fees for their Free-dom of Information Act requests, while waiving those same fees for green groups. According to the CEI, "green groups, such as the Natural Resources Defense Council, Sierra Club, Public Employees for Envi-ronmental Responsibility and EarthJustice, had their fees waived in 75 out of 82 cases. Meanwhile, EPA effectively or expressly denied [Chris-topher] Horner's request for fee waivers in 14 of 15 FOIA requests over this same time." That means that green groups got waivers 92 percent of the time, compared with conservative groups' 7 percent.[70]

Each one of those green groups endorsed President Obama. The environmental lobby spent millions pushing forward Obama's reelec-tion campaign. No wonder Obama quickly began stumping for climate change legislation upon reelection.

Meanwhile, Jackson tried to hide her correspondence, using a sec-ondary EPA address labeled "Richard Windsor," and an outside email account as well. Such emails would have been untraceable for purposes of FOIA requests.[71]

OBAMACARE

The stimulus package represented the tip of the iceberg. The Obama crime machine swept into full gear in President Obama's signature legislation: Obamacare. To begin, the bill couldn't have been passed through the Senate without outright bribery. In order to get a Senate cloture vote, Harry Reid loaded up the original Obamacare bill with goodies for his friends, with special provisions applying to Nebraska, Vermont, Massachusetts, Pennsylvania, Florida, Michigan, New York, Louisiana, Hawaii, Connecticut, and Montana. Every vote eventually received for Obamacare was Democratic.[72] Initial Obamacare waivers went directly to the entire state of Nevada—Senate Majority Leader Harry Reid's home state—and to an inordinate number of businesses in House Minority Leader Nancy Pelosi's district in California.[73]

The greatest kickback to lawmakers on both sides of the aisle came in the form of Obamacare waivers applied to congressional staffers. Each staffer would have been forced to spend an extra $5,000 to $11,000 under Obamacare. But thankfully, Obama was there to pay off his congressional supporters: his Office of Personnel Management waived congressional restrictions on federal government cash to help those poor Washington, D.C., insiders.[74]

Obama's allies in the media also received sweeteners. The Labor Department dropped hundreds of thousands of dollars' worth of stimulus cash on MSNBC, the Temple of Obama Worship. Rachel Maddow and Keith Olbermann were the chief beneficiaries of those dollars during 2009, with dozens of commercials running in their time slots to push "green training" jobs. How many such jobs were created overall? Zero. The cost of the commercials? Four hundred and ninety-five thousand dollars. Repaying undying support for the hard left agenda? Priceless.[75]

One of the great puzzles of Obamacare's rollout sprang from the fact that unions largely supported Obamacare. Many of the public sector unions were enthused about Obamacare thanks to the growth of government—government is significantly more unionized than the private sector, and Obamacare would allow government to effectively swallow one-sixth of the private economy. But what about private sector unions? If Obamacare passed, union members were set to lose their Cadillac coverage. Wasn't that a problem?

Not really.

In January 2012, as Obamacare began to kick into place, so did the union bribes to the Obama administration. Obama officials quickly began issuing waiver after waiver for unions, so that they could keep their health insurance plans even as more and more Americans were thrown off their own health insurance plans. Between June 2011 and January 2012, the Obama Department of Health and Human Services granted Obamacare waivers to unions representing 543,812 workers. Private employers received just 69,813 waivers. Just 12 percent of the American workforce is unionized.[76]

Those who helped the Obamacare rollout also ended up with special goodies. Hollywood received a massive payoff for putting up with Obamacare propaganda in prime time. In August 2009, as Obama faced down town halls full of angry Americans raging against the Obamacare machine, he desperately wanted to do a public press conference on all the networks over his beloved health-care overhaul. So he had then White House chief of staff Rahm Emanuel call up all the corporate owners of all the networks: Les Moonves of CBS, Jeff Immelt of GE (NBC), and Bob Iger of Disney (ABC). All the networks made the call to break through the prime-time lineup for a boring news conference. The Obama administration then forced the pharmaceutical industry to spend $150 million on television commercials for Obamacare. That's what the Obama administration calls a win-win![77]

Thanks in part to Hollywood's love affair with President Obama, and thanks in part to Obama's all-too-obvious pandering on same-sex marriage, Tinseltown is one of Obama's chief sources of cash as well as in-kind donations. On one trip to Hollywood in September 2008, Obama raised $11 million.[78] In 2012, Obama similarly cleaned up. Hollywood still backs President Obama to the hilt, of course—and they've reenlisted in the Obamacare Propaganda Army. In July 2013, with President Obama attempting to convince the American people that Obamacare wasn't a disastrous mistake, Hollywoodites ranging from emissaries of Oprah Winfrey to messengers from the website Funny or Die and the YouTube comedy channel came to the White House to offer their aid. So did Amy Poehler, the woman behind *Parks and Recreation*; as well as singer Jennifer Hudson; also a lackey for Alicia Keys; Jon Bon Jovi; and former White House staffer and *House* dead guy Kal Penn.[79] Naturally, the Obama administration has been just as generous in return, with a massive tax incentive—a deduction of up to $15 million for film pro-

176 ★ BEN SHAPIRO

duction, or $20 million in low-income areas—for Hollywood loaded into the fiscal cliff legislation passed at the beginning of 2013.[80]

CLOSING ARGUMENT

Fabulously wealthy industrialist Simon Cameron served as secretary of war under Abraham Lincoln. He served one year before being ousted over corruption charges. He then ended up back in the Senate. "An honest politician," he once remarked, "is one who, when he is bought, will stay bought."

By that measure, the Obama administration is chock-full of honest politicians.

It is admittedly very difficult to determine, in a day and age of behemoth government, where impropriety ends and actual criminality begins. But there is no question that the Obama administration's approach to governance—spreading the wealth around—benefits its friends, and that when donors funnel cash to President Obama, they benefit from it. There is also no question that that approach violates the RICO Act, which explicitly provides for RICO prosecution where bribery is in play. And bribery isn't the only charge available; illegal gratuities do not require the same level of quid pro quo specificity as bribery charges. When we view the Obama administration through the lens of giving out benefits and expecting favors in return, or vice versa, an unshakable pattern of illegality emerges.

In 1921, President Warren G. Harding decided to hand over supervision of naval oil reserve lands—lands held by the U.S. Navy for security purposes—to the Department of the Interior. That department was run by former Senator Albert Bacon Fall, who promptly handed cheap leases on the land to Mammoth Oil, run by one Harry Sinclair, and Pan American Petroleum, run by Edward Doheny. The lease terms made Fall extraordinarily wealthy, since Sinclair and Doheny handed him gifts worth more than $5 million in today's dollars. Sinclair was convicted of bribery in 1929 and served one year in prison.

The members of the Obama administration make Fall look like a piker. Whether it is the unions handing hundreds of millions of dollars over to the Obama 2008 and 2012 campaigns in return for favorable legislation, the secretary of health and human services seizing nonprofit cash under duress, or President Obama's friends getting rich via the stimulus program, this administration is riddled with corruption and bribery.

"In the end, if the people cannot trust their government to do the job for which it exists—to protect them and to promote their common welfare—all else is lost. And this is why the struggle against corruption is one of the great struggles of our time," then-senator Obama said in Kenya in 2006. There is a reason that American confidence in government has sunk to all-time lows, with under 20 percent of Americans trusting government in Washington to do the right thing always or even most of the time.[81] President Obama should have heeded Senator Obama's advice. Unfortunately, Barack Obama was, is, and always will be Barack Obama—and those who surround him will always be crony political hacks looking for the nearest taxpayer wallet to steal.

COUNT 7

★

OBSTRUCTION OF JUSTICE

Whoever corruptly, or by threats or force, or by any threatening letter or communication, endeavors to influence, intimidate, or impede any grand or petit juror, or officer in or of any court of the United States, or officer who may be serving at any examination or other proceeding before any United States magistrate judge or other committing magistrate, in the discharge of his duty . . . or corruptly or by threats or force, or by any threatening letter or communication, influences, obstructs, or impedes, or endeavors to influence, obstruct, or impede, the due administration of justice, shall be punished . . . [with] imprisonment for not more than 10 years, a fine under this title, or both.

—18 U.S. CODE § 1503

OPENING ARGUMENT

On July 13, 2013, twenty-nine-year-old Hispanic neighborhood watch volunteer George Zimmerman of Sanford, Florida, was acquitted of all charges in the killing of seventeen-year-old black suspended student Trayvon Martin. The case never should have gone to trial. The state presented virtually no evidence for its contention that Zimmerman stalked Martin with reckless intent to kill him. Instead, it presented an agglomeration of conjecture and speculation masquerading as a legal case.

An hour after Zimmerman's acquittal, his defense attorney, Mark O'Mara, spoke to the media. "Things would have been different for George Zimmerman if he was black for this reason: he would never have been charged with a crime," he said. "This became a focus for a civil rights event, which again is a wonderful event to have. But they decided that George Zimmerman would be the person who they were to blame and use as a creation of a civil rights violation, none of which was borne out by the facts. If only those who decided to condemn Mr. Zimmerman as quickly and as viciously as they did would have taken just a little bit of time to find out who it was they were condemning, it never would have happened. And it certainly wouldn't have happened if he was black, because those people who decided that they were going to make him the scapegoat would not have."[1]

Who were "those people" who decided to make George Zimmerman a racial scapegoat? And who, exactly, had the power to leverage a prosecution of an innocent man without evidence of wrongdoing?

To answer that question, we only need to take a look at the timeline of events. On February 29, 2012, George Zimmerman got in his car to head to the grocery store when he saw Trayvon Martin in the neighborhood. He called the Sanford Police Department, informed the dispatcher that there had been a series of recent break-ins in Sanford, Florida, and reported that the "guy looks like he's up to no good, or he's on drugs or something." When prompted, Zimmerman said that Martin "looks black," and was wearing "[a] dark hoodie, like a gray hoodie, and either jeans or sweatpants and white tennis shoes." Zimmerman stayed on the phone with dispatch as he followed Martin. Zimmerman's phone then cut out. The next events remain in controversy; the prosecution charged that Zimmerman tracked down Martin, provoked a confrontation, and then shot Martin. Zimmerman claimed, with no evidence to the contrary, that he began walking back to his vehicle when Martin confronted him, initiated a fight, punched him in the face breaking his nose, and put him on his back on the ground. Witness testimony then states that Martin began pounding Zimmerman's head into the pavement. At that point, Zimmerman shot Martin once in the chest.

The police quickly arrived on scene, and took Zimmerman in for questioning. He was released based on self-defense.

For the next week and a half, nothing happened. On March 8, the Associated Press wrongly reported the killing as a racial incident perpetrated by a "white" man against a "young black man." Al Sharpton headed down to Florida to bring his very special brand of race-baiting to the proceedings. The media firestorm grew and grew, with the media painting Zimmerman as a racist, editing his 911 call to make him seem like a closet KKK member, and using dated photos of Trayvon as a twelve-year-old clean-cut kid and a police photo of Zimmerman from 2005 looking swarthy in his orange shirt. The New Black Panthers showed up in Sanford, as did the National Association for the Advancement of Colored People, and the Urban League.

On March 19, 2012, with the media and Obama supporters everywhere baying for Zimmerman's blood, the U.S. Department of Justice announced it would investigate the Martin killing. The Sanford police continued to maintain that there just wasn't evidence to support an arrest. But by now, the story was national. And so Democratic politicians who had a stake in race-baiting ran to the cameras to push for Zimmerman's arrest. Representative Frederica Wilson (D-FL) said on the House floor, "Mr. Speaker, I am tired of burying young black boys. I am tired of watching them suffer at the hands of those who fear them and despise them. I am tired of comforting mothers, fathers, grandparents, sisters and brothers after such unnecessary, heinous crimes of violence," adding, "Trayvon was running for his life. He was screaming for help, fighting for his life, and then he was murdered, shot dead. . . . I am tired of fighting when the evidence is so clear, so transparent." Representative Maxine Waters (D-CA) called the killing a "hate crime." Representative Sheila Jackson Lee (D-TX) called for Zimmerman's arrest. Representative Corrine Brown (D-FL), who represented the area including Sanford, stated, "I don't know whether it's incompetence, or whether it's a cover-up, or all of the above. But we have got to make sure that what has happened in Sanford, with the police department and how they have handled this situation, never happens again in the United States."[2]

On March 22, state attorney Norm Wolfinger recused himself from the case. Sanford police chief Bill Lee said he would "temporarily resign."

On March 23, 2012, Florida governor Rick Scott appointed state attorney Angela Corey to prosecute Zimmerman. He also formed a task force on the Florida "stand your ground" law, a bugaboo of the left, but a law that was never applied in the Zimmerman case.

Just coincidentally, that very same day, President Obama decided to get directly involved. He said that America needed to undergo some "soul searching." Then he inserted himself into the criminal justice process.

"Well, I'm the head of the executive branch, and the attorney general reports to me so I've got to be careful about my statements to make sure that we're not impairing any investigation that's taking place right now," Obama admitted. "But obviously, this is a tragedy," he continued. "I can only imagine what these parents are going through. And when I think about this boy, I think about my own kids. And I think every parent in America should be able to understand why it is absolutely imperative that we investigate every aspect of this, and that everybody pulls together—federal, state, and local—to figure out exactly how this tragedy happened. So I'm glad that not only is the Justice Department looking into it, I understand now that the governor of the state of Florida has formed a task force to investigate what's taking place." This would be violating all applicable law. But Obama had one more point to make, just to ensure that the country turned against Zimmerman: "If I had a son, he'd look like Trayvon. And I think they are right to expect that all of us as Americans are going to take this with the seriousness it deserves, and that we're going to get to the bottom of exactly what happened."[3]

What was Obama's motivation for getting his minions involved? He was in the midst of a tough reelection race with Mitt Romney, and it was important for him to continue to push the notion, especially among his black supporters, that America is an irretrievably racist place—and that he was the cure for such racism.

The price was George Zimmerman's freedom.

Federal involvement quickly ratcheted up—in support of the anti-

Zimmerman lynch mob. The Justice Department's so-called Community Relations Service (CRS) headed down to Sanford, Florida, where it expended thousands of taxpayer dollars helping to facilitate "marches, demonstrations, and rallies." The peacekeepers attended events at which attendees called for Zimmerman's arrest and Lee's firing.[4] Regional director Thomas Battles went to one meeting at which he stated, "We work with communities where there is real or perceived racial tensions. If a community perceives that there's something wrong in the black community, there's something wrong."

This is the height of racial paternalism—instead of objectively assessing the facts, the CRS was there to throw gasoline on the fire. Judicial Watch, which obtained the documentation about the CRS, alleged that CRS "actively worked to foment unrest, spending thousands of taxpayer dollars on travel and hotel rooms to train protestors throughout Florida."[5] Former CRS director Ondray T. Harris said that he "regularly had to warn or take corrective action against career employees for acting as advocates instead of mediators." Those employees, he said, "talked neutrally in public and spoke in the tenor of mediators in public, but behind the scenes, when they talked to the civil rights groups or the perceived aggrieved parties, they'll say, essentially, 'Don't worry. The Department of Justice is here and we're going to get to the bottom of it.'" Harris, who is black, said that Battles was "black, and very pro-black," and accused him of "racial favoritism." He said that Battles pushed his "extremely pro-minority [views] at the expense of the majority views."[6]

On April 3, 2012, the FBI announced it had opened its own investigation.

On April 11, 2012, Corey announced Zimmerman would be charged with second-degree murder.

When Zimmerman was acquitted more than a year later, the Justice Department continued to press forward an investigation into a possible hate crime—a crime for which there was no evidence. They even went so far as to seize the evidence from the incident, depriving Zimmerman of his handgun.[7] The department also set up a special tip line just for information about possible evidence of George Zimmerman's racism. The DOJ held a conference with the Lawyers' Committee for Civil Rights Under Law asking for the group "to actively refer anyone who had information" on Zimmerman. "They said they would very aggressively investigate this case," said the group's president and executive director. Other groups included on the call: the ACLU and the NAACP Legal Defense and Educational Fund.[8]

And, of course, President Obama spoke out again. Originally, he'd ignored the facts and used his government to target Zimmerman. Now he ignored the facts again, and suggested—again, without any evidence—that Zimmerman was a vicious racist involved in racial profiling, and that racism plagued America at the deepest levels. After paying lip service to the system, he declared the verdict unfair: "You know, when Trayvon Martin was first shot I said that this could have been my son. Another way of saying that is Trayvon Martin could have been me 35 years ago. And when you think about why, in the African American community at least, there's a lot of pain around what happened here, I think it's important to recognize that the African American community is looking at this issue through a set of experiences and a history that doesn't go away. There are very few African American men in this country who haven't had the experience of being followed when they were shopping in a department store. That includes me. There are very few African American men who haven't had the experience of walking across the street and hearing the locks click on the doors of cars. That happens to me—at least before I was a senator. There are very few African Americans who haven't had the experience of getting on an elevator and a woman clutching her purse nervously and holding her breath until she had a chance to get off. That happens often."

This supposedly made the attempted railroading of Zimmerman just fine, according to Obama, since members of the black community had hurt feelings about phantom institutional racism. Instead of using his Justice Department to prosecute actual acts of racial profiling, Obama sent them on a goose chase to Sanford, Florida. And that, according to Obama, was justified: "And I don't want to exaggerate this, but those sets of experiences inform how the African American community interprets what happened one night in Florida. And it's inescapable for people to bring those experiences to bear. The African American community is also knowledgeable that there is a history of racial disparities in the application of our criminal laws—everything from the death penalty to enforcement of our drug laws. And that ends up having an impact in terms of how people interpret the case."

Obama sadly admitted that he had no more power to do anything about Zimmerman: "I know that Eric Holder is reviewing what happened down there, but I think it's important for people to have some clear expectations here. Traditionally, these are issues of state and local government, the criminal code. And law enforcement is traditionally done at the state and local levels, not at the federal level."

Obama concluded by once again justifying the racial pyre he had helped to prepare, and then lit via the power of his office: "if a white male teen was involved in the same kind of scenario . . . from top to bottom, both the outcome and the aftermath might have been different." Obama was right. So was Mark O'Mara. If a white male teen had been involved, Obama never would have been involved—and Zimmerman likely never would have been arrested or prosecuted. It took Obama's race-baiting, and the race-baiting of his official underlings, to put Zimmerman on trial before the world, without a shred of supporting evidence.[9]

THE CHARGES

The judiciary has defined federal criminal intimidation broadly. According to the Department of Justice, there is a debate among the courts about the scope of the relevant statute. Some courts have said that prosecution may be appropriate under 18 U.S. Code § 1503 anytime someone interferes "with the fair administration of justice if that conduct was undertaken with a corrupt motive." The Supreme Court seems to back this approach. The only true limitation under the clause is that all prohibited action must take place under the shadow of an upcoming judicial proceeding.

This clause is a catch-all, and includes crimes including suborning perjury, falsely testifying, attempting to influence a witness, altering documents, and the like.[10] The Obama administration, as we'll see, is far too fond of manipulating the justice system on behalf of its friends and against its enemies to avoid breaking the law.

THE RACIAL PROTECTION RACKET

The Zimmerman case wasn't the first time or the last time the Obama administration had perverted the justice system to target its enemies and help its friends, especially on issues of race. One particular group has received special treatment from the Obama administration: the New Black Panther Party. Obama's warm relationship with the NBP got started before his election, when two solid young members of law-abiding society stood outside a polling place in Philadelphia wearing military clothing and threateningly playing with their nightsticks. The Justice Department immediately leapt into action . . . to stop action. The whole thing was caught on tape. That merited no federal prosecution. But George Zimmerman—that white-Hispanic racist!—merited the department's full-scale attention.

J. Christian Adams, a Justice Department lawyer, later wrote, "The New Black Panther case was the simplest and most obvious violation of federal law of my Justice Department career." Nevertheless, he wrote, "Before a final judgment could be entered in May 2009, our superiors ordered us to dismiss the case. . . . Based on my firsthand experiences, I believe the dismissal of the Black Panther case was motivated by a lawless hostility toward equal enforcement of the law. Others still within the department share my assessment. The department abetted wrongdoers and abandoned law-abiding citizens victimized by the New Black Panthers." Thomas Perez, the assistant attorney general for civil rights, somehow came to the odd conclusion that the "facts and law" didn't support prosecution. Loretta King, Obama's head of the Civil Rights Division, "did not even read the internal Justice Department memorandums supporting the case and investigation," Adams reported. "Incredibly, after the case was dismissed, instructions were given that no more cases against racial minorities like the Black Panther case would be brought by the Voting Section."

New Black Panther Party activity wasn't restricted to Philadelphia. "We had indications that polling-place thugs were deployed elsewhere, not only in November 2008, but also during the Democratic primaries, where they targeted white Hillary Rodham Clinton supporters," Adams said. "Citizens would be shocked to learn about the open and pervasive hostility within the Justice Department to bringing civil rights cases against nonwhite defendants on behalf of white victims. Equal enforcement of justice is not a priority of this administration. Open contempt is voiced for these types of cases. Some of my co-workers argued that the law should not be used against black wrongdoers because of the long history of slavery and segregation. Less charitable individuals called it 'payback time.'" Adams ended up leaving the department in protest over its behavior.[11]

While leftists called Adams a liar, NBPP head Malik Shabazz freely admitted why the group hadn't been prosecuted: the Obama administration "owed us" some "favors" because they helped "deliver" Obama the presidency.[12] Shabazz also pointed out, "Justice Department leadership changed into the hands of a black man by the name of Eric Holder." That's no surprise. Holder reportedly carries a quote in his wallet: "Blackness is another issue entirely apart from class in America. No matter how affluent, educated and mobile [a black person] becomes, his race defines him more particularly than anything else. Black people have a common cause that requires attending to, and this cause does not allow for the rigid class separation that is the luxury of American whites." Holder once explained that quote thusly: "It really says that . . . I am not the tall U.S. attorney, I am not the thin United States attorney. I am the black United States attorney. And he was saying that no matter how successful you are, there's a common cause that bonds the black United States attorney with the black criminal or the black doctor with the black homeless person."[13]

The NBP didn't stop its lawbreaking. On March 24, before George Zimmerman's arrest, the New Black Panthers led a protest in Sanford, where member Mikhail Muhammad placed a ten-thousand-dollar bounty on Zimmerman. "An eye for an eye, a tooth for a tooth," Muhammad stated. He added, "Goddamnit, he should be fearful for his life. You can't keep killing black children, killing our children all over America. And we're supposed to take it easy? Supposed to play nice about it?" What happened? Nothing. Brother James J. Muhammad, national director of education for the Ordinary People Society New Black Panther Party, said, "We were never contacted by the Justice Department. We were never contacted to calm down."[14]

It wasn't enough for the Obama DOJ to drop all action against the New Black Panthers. President Obama got personally involved in one case in order to put pressure on a police department that had the temerity to arrest one of his friends. On June 16, 2009, Professor Henry Louis Gates Jr. of Harvard University arrived home in Cambridge, Massachusetts, and began to break into his home after his lock jammed. A neighbor called the police. She, of course, was later labeled a racist despite describing Gates and a companion this way: "One looked kind of Hispanic, but I'm not really sure. And the other one entered and I didn't see what he looked like at all."

When the police arrived, Gates was in his home; they asked for identification. He refused to provide it, and was booked for disorderly conduct by Sergeant Joseph Crowley for "exhibiting loud and tumultuous behavior." A black officer was present at the arrest, and later said he agreed with Crowley's actions. Gates then threatened the officer, and told him he had "no idea who he was messing with."[15]

That much, at least, was true.

Four days later, after the police dropped the charges, one of Gates's high-placed friends, President Obama, was asked about the incident. "I might be a little biased here," he said, because he was friends with "Skip Gates." He then admitted, "I don't know all the facts." But that didn't stop him from trying to push the notion that the Cambridge Police Department was racist: "Now, I don't know, not having been there and not seeing all the facts, what role race played in that. But I think it's fair to say, number one, any of us would be pretty angry; number two, that the Cambridge police acted stupidly in arresting somebody when there was already proof that they were in their own home; and, number three, what I think we know separate and apart from this incident is that there's a long history in this country of African-Americans and Latinos being stopped by law enforcement disproportionately. That's just a fact." He then said that the feds would work with police departments to target racism.[16] Later, Obama would call for a "beer summit" between Crowley and Gates. Gates would hand the officer a copy of his memoir, *Colored People*, then praise Obama as "very wise, very sage, very Solomonic."[17] How nice. President Obama has never injected himself without significant public pressure into a local criminal justice matter involving either a black perpetrator or a white victim (see Oklahoma murder victim Christopher Lane of Australia, for example).

"THE PRESIDENT WANTS ME TO TELL YOU IT'S TIME TO MOVE ON"

On June 12, 2009, President Barack Obama fired AmeriCorps inspector general Gerald Walpin. Walpin, who had been appointed by the Bush administration in 2007, had the temerity to step on the toes of one of Obama's close friends and political allies, former Phoenix Suns basketball star Kevin Johnson. But according to Obama, Walpin was fired for his incompetence. "[I]t is vital," Obama wrote, "that I have the fullest confidence in the appointees serving as Inspectors General. That is no longer the case with regard to this inspector general."

There was a reason Walpin lost Obama's confidence. And it had nothing to do with some supposed inability to write a brief.

AmeriCorps is a federally subsidized volunteer program. In April 2008, Walpin took charge of an investigation into allegations that St. HOPE, a California nonprofit headed by Johnson, had received a grant of $850,000. That grant was slotted for tutoring students, gutting and fixing buildings, and theater and art. Instead, according to Walpin's report, St. HOPE participated in "numerous potential criminal and grant violations, including diversion of federal grant funds, misuse of AmeriCorps members and false claims made against a taxpayer-supported Federal agency. The report found that AmeriCorps staff had been used to recruit for St. HOPE, for political activities connected to the Sacramento Board of Education election, and that AmeriCorps members even drove Johnson to personal appointments, washed his car, and did errands on his behalf." Johnson said Walpin was politically motivated, and suggested that St. HOPE had engaged in a few "administrative errors."[18]

Nonetheless, based on his findings, Walpin insisted that Johnson be suspended from involvement with AmeriCorps; his recommendation was accepted. He also sent a referral to the U.S. attorney of the Eastern District of California for possible prosecution. The U.S. attorney's office, led by Lawrence Brown, decided not to prosecute.

Then Johnson was elected mayor of Sacramento. And Obama was elected president.

The game began. Thanks to Johnson's suspension from AmeriCorps, a city attorney said that Sacramento could be cut off from federal stimulus funds. So Johnson and others pressured the inspector general's office to put the issue to bed and lift the suspension. Walpin refused, saying that Johnson hadn't even bothered to explain the AmeriCorps activities. Brown then stopped working with Walpin altogether, and instead decided to go around Walpin to talk with AmeriCorps board chair Alan Solomont, a major Obama donor. By this point, Michelle Obama's former chief of staff had joined AmeriCorps, too. Brown actually forced Johnson to hand over $72,836.50 in redress, and forced St. HOPE to pay back nearly $424,000. Then he handed Johnson a clean bill of health, prompting Walpin to complain that Brown had helped Johnson for political gain: "The suspension was lifted because, as one Corporation official put it, the Corporation could not 'stand in the way of Sacramento'—thereby effectively stating that, while Respondent Johnson was not sufficiently responsible to receive further Federal funds in his management position as a grantee, he suddenly became sufficiently responsible when elected Mayor of a city receiving substantially more federal funds." Walpin said the settlement sent the signal that acceptance of a grantee or its principal as 'responsible' can be purchased in a monetary settlement, overriding all evidence of wrongdoing previously found to warrant a suspension, without the presentation of any contradicting evidence."[19]

Walpin, upset, wrote a report for Congress and handed it over in April 2009. Less than two months later, Norman Eisen, special counsel to the president for ethics and government reform, called up Walpin, Walpin later explained. "Mr. Walpin," Eisen reportedly said, "the president wants me to tell you that he really appreciates your service, but it's time to move on. You can either resign, or I'll tell you that we'll have to terminate you." Eisen gave him one hour to consider, then called back forty-five minutes later demanding a response.[20]

Eisen said that it was "pure coincidence" that the resignation request came during the St. HOPE uproar. But that wasn't true. Thanks to a bill co-sponsored by Senator Barack Obama, President Obama had to explain his rationale for dumping Walpin. White House counsel Gregory Craig tried to use a complaint by Brown about Walpin as an excuse, but that excuse didn't hold water. As the *Wall Street Journal* pointed out, "the evidence suggests that [Obama's] White House fired a public official who refused to roll over to protect a Presidential crony."[21]

Later, an investigation by Senator Charles Grassley (R-IA) and Representative Darrell Issa (R-CA) would find that Walpin had actually uncovered allegations of more than financial impropriety. According to their report, Johnson had allegedly engaged in sexual misconduct toward St. HOPE students. "Mr. Johnson's attorney, Kevin Kiestand, approached at least one of the students describing himself only as 'a friend of Johnson's,' and 'basically asked me to keep quiet,'" the report stated. "[A]bout one week later, Kevin Johnson offered her $1,000 a month until the end of the program, which she refused to accept. Moreover, the OIG uncovered evidence of two other female St. HOPE students reporting Johnson for inappropriate sexual conduct towards them. These are not the first such allegations. Johnson was also accused of fondling a young woman in the mid 1990's, but no charges were ever filed." Grassley and Issa pointed out that the Justice Department did little or nothing to investigate the allegations, and that there was no evidence that the White House had, either. One of the St. HOPE teachers, who quit the school in anger over the cover-up of Johnson's activities, reported that a student had said Johnson "started massaging her shoulders and then reached over and touched her breasts." The teacher said that "St. HOPE sought to intimidate the student through an illegal interrogation and even had the audacity to ask me to change my story."[22]

"PROSECUTED, STRIPPED OF THEIR POSITIONS, COURT-MARTIALED, FIRED, DISHONORABLY DISCHARGED"

The Obama administration had no comment about the allegations of sexual impropriety from their favorite Sacramento mayor. The same held true for their ally in San Diego: when longtime Democratic congressman and San Diego mayor Bob Filner came under fire for allegedly sexually harassing dozens of women during his time in the mayoral office, Obama remained silent.

But when a report broke in May 2013 suggesting that sexual assaults in the military had skyrocketed by more than one-third since 2010, Obama just had to sound off. "When you engage in this kind of behavior that's not patriotic—it's a crime. And we have to do everything we can to root this out," Obama said in South Korea. He said he wanted alleged victims to "hear directly from their commander in chief that I've got their backs. I will support them. And we're not going to tolerate this stuff and there will be accountability. If people have engaged in this behavior, they should be prosecuted." He concluded, "I don't want just more speeches or awareness programs or training but, ultimately, folks look the other way. If we find out somebody is engaging in this stuff, they've got to be held accountable—prosecuted, stripped of their positions, court-martialed, fired, dishonorably discharged. Period. It's not acceptable."[23]

This was an eminently reasonable position for a layperson. It was also illegal for the president of the United States to say it.

In June 2013, Navy judge Commander Marcus Fulton issued a ruling stating that Obama's comments could let two alleged sexual assault defendants off the hook thanks to Obama exerting unlawful command influence. The judge wrote, "A member of the public would not hear the President's statement to be a simple admonition to hold members accountable. A member of the public would draw the connection between the 'dishonorable discharge' required by the President and a punitive discharge approved by the convening authority. The strain on the system created by asking a convening authority to disregard [Obama's] statement in this environment would be too much to sustain public confidence." In short, Obama's words brought into doubt the objectivity of the military courts, which fall directly under Obama's jurisdiction. His words could be taken as an order rather than a commentary.[24] Defense attorneys for those accused of sexual assault in the military immediately announced they would cite Obama's words in defense of their clients.[25]

That same week, Secretary of Defense Chuck Hagel quietly sent out a one-page memo attempting to mitigate the damage Obama had done. The memo stated, "There are no expected or required dispositions, outcomes or sentences in any military justice case, other than what result from the individual facts and merits of a case and the application to the case of the fundamentals of due process of law." Lieutenant General Curtis Scaparrotti, director of the Joint Staff, explained that as a result of Obama's comments, "we believed it was necessary . . . to make a statement, simply to ensure that commanders understood that they act independently, based on the merits of a case, and to ensure that there's no taint in any of the jurisdiction that takes place or any of the cases that are ongoing now." The memo, lawyers said, likely wouldn't accomplish its goal, leaving sexual assault perpetrators the Obama Defense.[26]

"THE ONLY THING BETWEEN YOU AND THE PITCHFORKS"

President Obama's threats aren't relegated to members of the military, inspectors general, or Cambridge police officers. President Obama is all too happy to use the power of his office to leverage concessions from the business community. With the economy in shambles thanks to the economic collapse of 2008, President Obama decided to target businesses. On April 3, 2009, Obama met with thirteen bank CEOs. There was no food, one glass of water per person, and no refills. He casually informed the bank CEOs that they would have to slash salaries. "My administration," Obama sneered, "is the only thing between you and the pitchforks."[27]

And the administration wasn't shy about ginning up the pitchforks.

To that end, Obama's government did nothing to investigate seven hundred Service Employees International Union members invading the front yard of bank executive Greg Baer, deputy general counsel of Bank of America, whose son, *Forbes*' Nina Easton reported, "locked himself in the bathroom." When Baer's son called the police, they didn't even respond. "Intimidation was the whole point of this exercise, and it worked—even on the police," Easton later wrote. "A trio of officers who belatedly answered our calls confessed a fear that arrests might 'incite' these trespassers."[28] Union violence has become disturbingly common under President Obama, and has gone largely unprosecuted.

President Obama also praised the Occupy Wall Street movement. Even as they illegally occupied public areas, destroyed private property, and engaged in crimes ranging from rape to attempted terrorism, Obama said that he was "on their side." He contrasted those selfless Occupiers with "people who are irresponsible, who are reckless, who don't feel a sense of obligation to their communities and their companies and their workers. . . ." Those Wall Street folks, he added, could not be "rewarded."[29]

But while Obama encouraged animus toward the 1 percent, he used the power of the government to protect his rich Wall Street friends. Despite the fact that some of the worst offenders in terms of taking unsustainable risks were located at major Wall Street firms like Goldman Sachs, the Obama administration shied away from prosecuting any of those firms. That's because those same firms were some of Obama's biggest campaign donors: in 2008, Goldman's political action committee and individual contributors gave nearly $1 million to Obama.[30] Overall, the Obama campaign raised $16 million from Wall Street, compared to $9 million for that evil Republican corporate fat cat John McCain.[31]

During the recession, Goldman Sachs cleaned up thanks to its short-selling, even as it took $12.9 billion in a bailout of American International Group in 2008. If AIG had been allowed to go bankrupt, Goldman would have made just $2.3 billion.[32] In 2009, Goldman had one of the most profitable years in its history, and forwent billions in cash bonuses only thanks to public outrage.[33] How did Goldman clean up during one of the worst economic crises in American history? A congressional report found that the company "used net short positions to benefit from the downturn in the mortgage market, and designed, marketed, and sold CDOs [collateralized debt obligations] in ways that created conflicts of interest with the firm's clients and at times led to the bank's profiting from the same products that caused substantial losses for its clients." Goldman had to pay a $550 million fine to the Securities and Exchange Commission for misconduct.

But that didn't mean that the Justice Department would prosecute. Instead, they released a statement: "Based on the law and evidence as they exist at this time, there is not a viable basis to bring a criminal prosecution with respect to Goldman Sachs or its employees in regard to the allegations set forth in the report." David Wells, spokesman for Goldman Sachs, smiled and said, "We are pleased that this matter is behind us."[34]

What happened to the prosecution? Peter Boyer and Peter Schweizer reported for *Newsweek* that just as the congressional report was released, suspiciously, "several Goldman executives and their families made large donations to Obama's Victory Fund and related entities, some of them maxing out at the highest individual donation allowed, $35,800, even though 2011 was an electoral off-year. Some of these executives were giving to Obama for the first time."[35]

It wasn't just Goldman getting off the hook. Virtually no Wall Street executives were prosecuted, despite routinely lying to clients about the risk inherent in their investment recommendations. Overall, financial fraud prosecutions dropped dramatically, a full 39 percent since 2003. Eric Holder's job prior to joining the Obama Justice Department as attorney general had him working at white-shoe law firm Covington & Burling, which just happened to represent Goldman Sachs, JPMorgan Chase, Citigroup, Bank of America, Wells Fargo, and Deutsche Bank. Lanny Breuer, who ran the Criminal Division at Justice, came from Covington, too.[36]

As Glenn Greenwald of the *Guardian* wrote, "the Obama justice department, in particular the Chief of its Criminal Division, Lanny Breuer, never even tried to hold the high-level criminals accountable. . . . Obama justice officials both shielded and feted these Wall Street oligarchs." This despite the fact that even Alan Greenspan, a libertarian-leaning, easy-money former chair of the Federal Reserve Board, said that a lot of Wall Street financial activity in the lead-up to the recession "was just plain fraud." Even the *New York Times* complained that the Justice Department's decision not to prosecute "defied common sense."[37]

It's good to be a Friend of Obama. But getting on Obama's wrong side means facing the wrong side of the law for business.

The Obama administration has used its regulatory power to blackmail businesses into handing over cash for Obamacare. In May 2013, after Congress refused to appropriate funds to help implement the gargantuan tar pit that is Obamacare, Secretary of Health and Human Services Kathleen Sebelius went to officials in the health industry to "request" donations for publicizing Obamacare. The *Washington Post* reported, "Over the past three months, Sebelius has made multiple phone calls to health industry executives, community organizations and church groups and asked that they contribute whatever they can to nonprofit groups that are working to enroll uninsured Americans and increase awareness of the law, according to an HHS official and an industry person familiar with the secretary's activities."

The department claimed it did nothing wrong. But under the law, requesting donations from companies under your jurisdiction is problematic. "To solicit funds from health-care executives to help pay for the implementation of the President's $2.6 trillion health spending law is absurd," Senator Orrin Hatch (R–UT) complained. Justice Department regulations prohibit fund-raising from "a subordinate or from someone who has or seeks business with the Department." One of the *Post*'s sources stated that "there was a clear insinuation by the administration that the insurers should give financially to the nonprofits."[38]

Then there was the infamous British Petroleum oil spill in the Gulf of Mexico in April 2010. Secretary of the Interior Ken Salazar immediately stated, "our job basically is to keep the boot on the neck of British Petroleum." White House press secretary Robert Gibbs agreed: "We will keep our, as Secretary Salazar said, our boot on the throat of BP to ensure that they're doing all that they—all that is necessary, while we do all that is humanly possible to deal with this incident." British prime minister David Cameron complained that Obama's thuggish behavior over BP would shortchange British pensioners.[39] Finally, Obama called BP executives to the White House, where he blithely informed them they would pony up $20 billion to pay damages. No trial, no due process. Just cash up front. "The president said he's concerned about those workers. He asked if there was something we could do as a voluntary gesture," said BP lawyer Jamie Gorelick. In return, Obama gave a brief statement talking about the financial health of BP, which had been in a stock nosedive.[40]

EXECUTIVE TYRANNY

The Obama administration's obstruction of justice has been most egregious with regard to enforcement of federal and state immigration law. Early on in his presidency, President Obama decided that he would fight against federal immigration law as hard as possible. When Arizona passed a series of state laws attempting to help the federal government *enforce* state law, Obama's Justice Department promptly sued the state. Obama accused Arizona of making it "really tough on people who look like they, quote, unquote look like illegal immigrants. . . . Now suddenly if you don't have your papers and you took your kid out to get ice cream, you're going to be harassed, that's something that could potentially happen."[41] Obama said that Arizona law designed to help the feds would actually "undermine basic notions of fairness that we cherish as Americans."[42] Attorney General Holder then admitted he hadn't read the Arizona law, but would sue anyway; homeland security secretary and former Arizona governor Janet Napolitano said she hadn't read it, either, but called it "bad law enforcement law."[43]

The Obama administration's decision to fight state law cracking down on illegal immigration contrasted sharply with Obama's illegal decision to stop the federal government from prosecuting so-called DREAMers, young illegal immigrants who had come to the country as children. In June 2012, with no authorization from Congress to do so, Obama simply declared that the executive branch would cease deporting anyone who had come to the country under age sixteen, had been in the country for over five years, and was under age thirty. Those convicted of small misdemeanors would not be deported. "They pledge allegiance to our flag," Obama said. "They are Americans in their hearts, in their minds, in every single way but one: on paper." Incredibly, Napolitano simultaneously claimed that this did not constitute "amnesty." Instead, she said, "It is an exercise of discretion so that these young people are not in the removal system. It will help us continue to streamline immigration enforcement and ensure that resources are not spent pursuing the removal of low-priority cases involving productive young people." Obama then blamed Congress for his own executive tyranny: "I've said time and time again to Congress, send me the Dream Act, put it on my desk, and I will sign it right away."

Nothing in the Constitution gave Obama the authority to allow selective prosecution of different types of illegal immigrants. If he wanted to push immigration reform, he could have done it throughout his presidency. Instead, he acted unilaterally in order to boost his reelection effort, in the process cutting the ground out from under law enforcement. Representative Peter King (R-NY) said that he would seek "an immediate review into the possibility that DHS will direct Border Patrol agents to conduct selective enforcement." And Representative Lamar Smith (R-TX) said that the decision "blatantly ignores the rule of law that is the foundation of our democracy."[44] According to Chris Crane, president of the National Immigration and Customs Enforcement Council, the union for border agents, "There is no burden for the alien to prove anything." Crane said that prosecutors were treating DREAMers as immune to virtually all prosecution. One illegal immigrant, Crane recalled, had been arrested on four charges, including felonies. Prosecutors said, "He's a DREAMer. Release him."[45]

President Obama's view that he could unilaterally decide which criminal laws to enforce extended to marijuana, as well. Despite blatant conflict between federal marijuana laws (idiotically declared constitutional by the Supreme Court in 2005's *Gonzales v. Raich*)[46] and state laws allowing marijuana, the Department of Justice declared that it would not challenge state laws allowing pot use and distribution. Federal prosecutors were told to let certain crimes go based on the Obama administration's sole determination that duly-enacted law simply wasn't important. "While the prosecution of drug traffickers remains an important priority, the president and the administration believe that targeting individual marijuana users, especially those with serious illnesses and their caregivers, is not the best allocation of federal government resources," said White House deputy press secretary Josh Earnest. Peter Bensinger, former head of the Drug Enforcement Administration, rightly said, "He's not just abandoning the law, he's breaking the law. . . . He's telling the world we don't really follow the law here."[47]

For good measure, Obama also unilaterally delayed the implementation of the most important part of Obamacare—the employer mandate, the section of Obamacare requiring employers to cover their employees' health care—until beyond the 2014 election cycle. Obama's national waiver violated every element of the law. Congress did not give the Obama administration the ability to waive enforcement of Obamacare by the Treasury Department; in fact, the statute contained specific penalties designed for 2014. That didn't stop Obama's Treasury Department from declaring that "the employer shared responsibility payments . . . will not apply for 2014. Any employer shared responsibility payments will not apply until 2015." Congress also didn't give Treasury the ability to waive reporting requirements by business. But that didn't matter to the Obama administration. Treasury stated, "The Administration . . . will provide an additional year before the [Affordable Care Act] mandatory employer and insurer reporting requirements begin."[48]

PROTECTING THE PIMPS

Barack Obama got to know the Association of Community Organizations for Reform Now early in his career in Chicago. He represented them in cases as a lawyer. He worked at the ACORN offshoot "Project Vote," training workers. He served on the board of the Woods Fund when that group gave ACORN grants. In 2007, Obama spoke to ACORN directly. "I've been fighting alongside ACORN on issues you care about my entire career," he said. "Even before I was an elected official, when I ran Project Vote voter registration drive in Illinois, ACORN was smack dab in the middle of it, and we appreciate your work."[49] Andy Stern, head of the SEIU and board member at ACORN,[50] was the single most common visitor to the White House early in Obama's presidency.

ACORN was publicly funded. But its political wing endorsed Obama in February 2008 for the presidency. And it had a long history of association with voter fraud.[51] In July 2007, ACORN was forced to settle Washington's case against it for voter fraud after seven workers submitted thousands of false registrations. The names included "Frekkie Magoal" and "Fruto Boy Crispila." As Michelle Malkin points out, "The group's vandalism on electoral integrity is systemic. ACORN has been implicated in similar voter fraud schemes in Missouri, Ohio, and at least 12 other states." The group was also involved in mortgages using cash not reported to the IRS.[52] In brief, ACORN was one of the worst political groups in the country.

It took two citizen journalists to take them down. When Andrew Breitbart distributed a series of video exposés on ACORN's activities produced by activists James O'Keefe and Hannah Giles—videos depicting O'Keefe and Giles portraying themselves as a pimp and prostitute, and receiving tax advice from ACORN employees on setting up a brothel for underage girls—Congress quickly withdrew funding. The feds quickly absolved ACORN of criminal wrongdoing with federal funds.[53]

But that wasn't the end of the story. Not only did the Obama administration not investigate ACORN's activities in any serious way for violations of federal law, but the Obama administration attempted to resurrect ACORN through its various fragmented offshoots. In March 2011, the U.S. Department of Housing and Urban Development gave $80,000 to the Affordable Housing Centers of America, a onetime ACORN affiliate. Naturally, the Government Accountability Office said that AHCOA wasn't "directly or indirectly under the control of ACORN." The government website, however, said differently, listing the organization as "ACORN Housing Corporation Inc.," and giving the same address as ACORN's old New Orleans office. An internal HUD report from September 2010 said ACORN Housing was "now operating as Affordable Housing Centers of America."[54]

That same year, the Obama administration created a foreclosure relief program funded to the tune of $7.6 billion. A full $445.6 million went to the Illinois Housing Development Authority, run by former ACORN Housing Chicago operations manager Joe McGavin.[55]

In 2013, the White House hired a nonprofit group called the Center for Community Change to run its Obamacare youth video contest, created to promote outreach on the Affordable Care Act. The Center for Community Change is run by Deepak Bhargava, the top governmental affairs official for ACORN from 1992 to 2002. "The fact that the Obama administration is putting a senior staffer of the now defunct and notoriously corrupt ACORN in charge of giving away cash to bribe young Americans into accepting Obamacare is cause for grave concern," Representative Paul Gosar (R-AZ) observed.[56]

Far from being dead, ACORN has merely morphed. As former ACORN CEO Bertha Lewis said, "these entities are carrying on ACORN's work of organizing low- and moderate-income folks. . . . [We have created] bullet-proof community-organizing Frankensteins that they're going to have a very hard time attacking." That's particularly true with an administration fully committed to overlooking the corruption and criminality of its allies. "Barack Obama is truly 'the president from ACORN,'" Judicial Watch's Tom Fitton said.[57]

CLOSING ARGUMENT

The charge of governmental corruption is about the worst charge that an administration can face. Such corruption fundamentally undermines the entire purpose of government, transforming it into a mafia-like organization with the power of force behind it. The only thing separating American government from thugocracies like Russia is our willingness to hold our politicians accountable.

And that distinction is disappearing.

In 2000, a young Russian politician named Vladimir Putin was running for president to replace the ailing Boris Yeltsin. His chief opposition in the media came from NTV, a network owned by one Vladimir Gusinsky. Just before the crucial election that would put the former KGB strongman Putin in power, Gusinsky's NTV ran an exposé on the thwarted bombing of an apartment building in Ryazan the year before. The special alleged that the Russian security service, FSB—a service run largely by Putin—had set up the bombing as a way to push Putin's political ambitions and cast aspersion on Islamist terrorists in Chechnya.

Putin struck back. Hard. The Russian information minister, Mikhail Lesin, said that NTV had "crossed the line" and become "outlaws." Four days after Putin gained office, FSB troops invaded NTV headquarters heavily armed. Putin then leveraged NTV's biggest creditor, the state-owned energy giant Gazprom, to call in NTV's loans. Finally, Putin told Gusinsky that he could either hand over NTV to the state directly, or end up in court for fraud. As Putin biographer Angus Roxburgh of BBC News reported, "It was blackmail." Gusinsky handed over the company. The largest independent television channel in Russia became a government-owned subsidiary.

Using the power of law to leverage against allies and to protect friends is the essence of tyranny. The Obama administration has practiced and perfected such tyranny. Whether hunting down George Zimmerman or protecting the New Black Panthers to boost racial animus, protecting Kevin Johnson or firing Gerald Walpin to save friends' political hides, or unilaterally declaring the power to make and break duly enacted law at will, the Obama administration has destroyed the concept of fair and objective justice at the federal level. It is no wonder that Americans' trust in government continues to decline further and further each year. Who would trust a thug government that could destroy due process for political purposes?

No such government deserves the trust of its people. That is why the RICO Act explicitly contains obstruction of justice as a predicate offense: if the justice system is perverted by a criminal enterprise, all faith in our democracy is lost. Unfortunately, that is exactly what is happening.

In September 2012, President Obama declared the ability of the executive branch to target American citizens who became anti-American terrorists with drone strikes. Attorney General Eric Holder said that no judicial intervention was necessary for such strikes to occur. "Due process and judicial process are not one and the same, particularly when it comes to national security," Holder stated. "The Constitution guarantees due process, it does not guarantee judicial process." President Obama added, "It's very important for the president and the entire culture of our national security team to continually ask tough questions about, are we doing the right thing, are we abiding by rule of law, are we abiding by due process." He went on to suggest that the government should "set up structures and institutional checks, so that, you know, you avoid any kind of slippery slope into a place where we're not being true to who we are."[58]

What did that due process look like?

Nobody really knew. The best description of the process came from a leaked report in the *New York Times*: "Mr. Obama is the liberal law professor who campaigned against the Iraq war and torture, and then insisted on approving every new name on an expanding 'kill list,' poring over terrorist suspects' biographies on what one official calls the macabre 'baseball cards' of an unconventional war. When a rare opportunity for a drone strike at a top terrorist arises—but his family is with him—it is the president who has reserved to himself the final moral calculation."[59]

President Obama may target the right people. He may do the right thing. But his willingness to pervert the judicial process speaks to a man hungry for power—and a man willing to do anything to achieve his desired political ends.

CONCLUSION

★

merica has seen criminal administrations before. Over the course of American history, dozens of federal officials have been convicted of offenses based on corruption, including one cabinet secretary (Albert B. Fall, secretary of the interior under Warren G. Harding), four senators (two Democrats and two Republicans), and thirty-one members of Congress (twenty-five of them Democrats). Far more have deserved jail time. Presidents, too, have deserved jail time. In fact, it is difficult to name a president over the last several decades who has *not* risked prosecution, from Nixon to Clinton and from JFK to George W. Bush.

But there is one president who has topped them all. He has turned his administration into a hotbed of corruption, all the while claiming ignorance. His administration has been responsible for deaths, constitutional violations, and the dissolution of American power on the world stage. It is no wonder that trust in American government has hit all-time lows under President Obama.

President Obama has not hesitated to turn his administration into the most corrupt and criminal of all time. Stacking his administration with cronies and hungry bureaucrats in his legalized criminal syndicate, Obama merely sets out the end goals and lets his goons take care of the rest. He offers them protection, advancement, and the chance to change the lives of millions. He offers them both personal and collective salvation. All it will cost is a few souls who oppose his agenda, or who inconveniently find themselves in the way.

The White House's gun smuggling throughout the Middle East,

and its predictably murderous results in Benghazi, Libya, are unsurpassed in the annals of Oval Office treachery—the active cover-up of events, the attempt to quash the truth from coming out, the retaliation against would-be whistle-blowers, and the continuance of a policy of appeasement finds no parallel in American history. Jimmy Carter and his administration were incompetent; Barack Obama's administration is malevolent. George W. Bush's administration relied on bad intelligence and worse postwar planning, but at least he chose the correct side in the war on terror. President Obama's quest to weaken America on the international stage found its apex in the death of four Americans, including an American ambassador, followed by an attempt to cast American free speech as the culprit for such evil. Benghazi represented the flash point for Obama's vaunted Arab Spring: the rise of Islamism, the decline of American power, and the "blame America first" mentality of a cowardly internationalist with delusions of grandeur.

The Fast and Furious scandal sprang from the bowels of the antigun hysteria of the administration. Willingness to overlook the obvious risks of handing heavy weaponry to Mexican drug cartels—or purposeful decisions to ramp up that risk—ended in the realization of many Americans' worst nightmare: an even more out-of-control Mexican murder business unhesitating in its desire to kill and maim everyone in its path, including American border agents like Brian Terry. The administration has tried to cast Second Amendment advocates as the villains of a story the administration itself created, meanwhile letting the real culprits keep their jobs or their pensions. The Reagan administration smuggled guns. But those guns never ended up killing Americans.

The Obama administration's use of the IRS is hardly unprecedented (see FDR, JFK, Nixon, and Clinton), but its very obviousness demonstrates the unconcern with which the administration violates the law. The Obama team has derided the IRS's targeting of conservatives as a "phony scandal," and has attempted to grow the IRS to unrivaled proportions. Tax law became a vehicle for leftist social engineering back during the Wilson administration. Nothing has changed. It's just gotten more obvious, and more dangerous. The hallmarks of tin-pot dictatorship are stamped all over the president's desk.

No administration has been more tenacious in pursuing leakers than the Obama administration—but only when those leaks harm the administration itself. When leaks *help* the administration, however, no administration has been more willing to destroy the national security of America and its allies for political gain than the Obama White House. Whether it is leaking Israeli national security information in order to stymie an attack on Iran's nuclear facilities, or leaking information about the Osama bin Laden raid and endangering Navy SEALs in order to prop up the president's flagging reelection efforts, the Obama administration has made a game of revealing self-serving classified information while targeting even *journalists* who inform the public of classified information harmful to the Obama image. Many Americans reacted in anger when Richard Armitage revealed the identity of CIA analyst Valerie Plame during the debate over the war in Iraq. Former vice presidential adviser Scooter Libby wrongly ended up in prison over that case; Valerie Plame and her husband, Joe Wilson, ended up with a terrible Hollywood movie about them starring Naomi Watts and Sean Penn. Nobody has gone to prison over the Obama administration's leaks. But men and women are already dead because of those leaks—and more men and women will die because of the Obama administration's leaks.

While the Obama administration is profligate with classified information, they are happy to seize our personal information. When Edward Snowden revealed to the American public the extent of the government's surveillance of the American people, we reacted with shock and horror. Perhaps we shouldn't have. Perhaps we should have recognized that the Patriot Act would be perverted to allow government almost unlimited power; perhaps we should have considered the possibility that a government powerful enough to gather all our information for our protection could also be large enough to use that information to our detriment. But Americans could not have foreseen an administration switching sides in the war on terror, ignoring obvious markers of terrorism like association with known terrorists overseas (Nidal Hassan, the Fort Hood shooter, communicated with terrorist cleric Anwar al-Awlaki, and the government knew about it), and yet simultaneously insisting that it needed all our Gchats in order to keep us safe. Thanks to the Obama administration's terrible record of targeting its opposition, Americans do not feel safe in its hands. They feel even less safe knowing that the government has the power to monitor us, keystroke by keystroke.

Bribery is the key to the Obama administration's success. While Obama's 2012 Republican opponent, Mitt Romney, complained that 47 percent of Americans were dependent on the government and therefore likely to back Obama, that was a sin against the American people. The truth is that a vast swath of Americans take government benefits not because they want to, but because they have to. And they are not the Americans who control the direction of American politics. Those who do are our political elites, who have been bribed in ways heretofore unseen in American politics. The Obama administration bribes the unions, who will see millions of new government union members thanks to the bureaucratic class created by Obamacare—and who receive waivers from that same godawful program. And those unions pay him back in votes. The Obama administration cows businesses into doing its bidding via the power of threats and regulation. And those businesses pay up their lunch money. The Obama administration pays off the environmental lobby while putting its boot on the throat of the energy industry, and pays off Hollywood while seeking to leech the lifeblood of major industry. The outright bribery of the Obama administration has turned America from a republic to a massive kleptocracy.

The ultimate mark of corruption lies in the use of government power to target political opposition. The Obama administration hasn't just done that through the IRS. It has done so through the Department of Justice—the single most corrupt branch of the single most corrupt White House. Whether urging the public to string up George Zimmerman while leveraging federal resources to push local prosecution, or clearing the field for criminal FOO—Friends of Obama—the department has become the perverse instrument of tyranny.

For all of these crimes and many more, there have been no consequences whatsoever for the Obama administration, despite Obama's repeated avowals that such corruption and abuse of power would be punished.

Here's White House press secretary Jay Carney on Obama's response to Benghazi: "He is very interested in bringing the perpetrators to justice and ensuring that we find out what happened, why it happened and taking steps to ensure that it never happens again."[1] Promise unfulfilled.

Obama on Fast and Furious: "People who have screwed up will be held accountable."[2] Promise unfulfilled.

Obama on the IRS scandal: "[P]eople have to be accountable and it's got to be fixed."[3] Promise unfulfilled.

Obama on leaks: "I am troubled by the possibility that leak investigations could chill the investigative journalism that holds government accountable. Journalists should not be at legal risk for doing their jobs."[4] Promise unfulfilled.

Obama on the NSA scandal: "I am tasking this independent group to step back and review our capabilities—particularly our surveillance technologies. And they'll consider how we can maintain the trust of the people, how we can make sure that there absolutely is no abuse in terms of how these surveillance technologies are used." The group starred perjurer director of national intelligence James Clapper.[5] Promise unfulfilled.

Obama on corruption in government: "My Administration is committed to creating an unprecedented level of openness in Government. We will work together to ensure the public trust and establish a system of transparency, public participation, and collaboration."[6] Promise unfulfilled.

Obama to Americans on perversion of justice: "Ask yourself your own questions about, am I wringing as much bias out of myself as I can?"[7] Obama certainly isn't.

OBAMA'S PLAUSIBLE DENIABILITY

So how is Obama able to get away with this vast bevy of untruths about his own administration? Plausible deniability—the ability to claim ignorance on subjects on which Obama is intimately involved, and with regard to which his interests have been undeniably forwarded. It's the name of the game in Chicago politics. It's how some members of the Daley family have been able to avoid prison for decades, despite widespread suspicion of corruption. It's why those who breach that rule *do* wind up in prison, from Representative Jesse Jackson Jr. to Governor

Rod Blagojevich. And it's why President Obama claims ignorance on every major scandal to hit his administration.

Here's Obama on Benghazi, after being asked if it had changed his mind at all about his faux Arab Spring: "This is going to be a rocky path. The question presumes that somehow we could have stopped this wave of change."[8] It was unforeseeable.

Obama on Fast and Furious: "This is a pretty big government, the United States government. I've got a lot of moving parts." Obama also said that he first heard about Fast and Furious "on the news."[9] He had no knowledge.

Obama on the IRS scandal: "I first learned about it through the same news reports other people learned from."[10] Once again, no knowledge.

Obama press secretary Carney on the Justice Department targeting journalists who worked with leakers: "Other than press reports, we have no knowledge of any attempt by the Justice Department to seek phone records of the Associated Press. . . . [Obama] found out about the news reports yesterday on the road."[11] Good thing Obama watches the news, or he'd never know about anything.

Obama on the NSA scandal: "We don't have domestic spying."[12] Oops.

Obama top adviser David Axelrod on Solyndra: "I don't know anybody associated with Solyndra and I know nothing about the project." Former White House chief of staff Rahm Emanuel also claimed ignorance.[13]

Obama press secretary Carney on the trial of Kermit Gosnell, black abortionist and murderer in Philadelphia: "The president does not and cannot take a position on an ongoing trial, so I won't, as well." Except, of course, for George Zimmerman, Henry Louis Gates Jr., and any other trial that tickles his fancy.[14]

Yet somehow Obama was intimately involved with the circumstances surrounding the killing of Osama bin Laden, the bailout of General Motors, and the circumstances surrounding the Arizona immigration law. Obama is surprisingly well informed, but only when he wants to be. Otherwise, he's about as knowledgeable as Al Capone was about his finances. Which is to say, perfectly well informed, but able to deny he'd ever heard of whiskey.

THE WILLING ACCOMPLICES

And yet the media seem not to care. That's because we are watching the death of the modern media, slain by their own hand; as they watch their Juliet, President Obama, slay America's democratic process on the altar of liberalism, they prepare their own suicide Romeo-esque capsule. At all costs, they have decided, they must defend the Obama administration, which pledges to dismantle inequality, "level the playing field," and make the world an all-around fairer place. President Obama has the support of the media in ways his predecessors would have found astonishing. If President Reagan was the Teflon president, Obama is the BAM president—aluminum magnesium boride, one of the most slippery substances on the planet. How else could Obama maintain such high personal approval ratings at the same time he holds such low policy ratings?

In 2011, political science professor Tim Groseclose of the University of California, Los Angeles concluded that if the rest of the media was as biased as the *New York Times* in 2008, they were worth 8 percent to Obama.[15] That's an understatement. Not a single major scandal of the Obama administration has been broken by the mainstream media. Benghazi has been actively buried by virtually everyone but Jake Tapper of CNN and Sharyl Attkisson of CBS News—and Attkisson came under attack from her own network. The media was far more concerned with Mitt Romney's comments about Benghazi than the Obama administration's conduct before or after the September 11, 2012, attacks. That's because the media believes in Obama's vision of foreign policy, involving a diminished America on the world stage.

The Fast and Furious scandal only found the light of day thanks to the conservative blogosphere, including Katie Pavlich of Townhall and Matthew Boyle of Breitbart, and the tenacity of Senator Charles Grassley (R-IA) and Representative Darrell Issa (R-CA). Members of the media were unwilling to undercut Obama's credibility on two of his key political issues: open borders and gun control.

The media downplayed all questions about IRS behavior under Obama for years, instead declaring over and over that conservative nonprofits were gaming the system. Only when the IRS itself admitted discrimination did coverage come—and even then, the media attempted to downplay the revelations.

The NSA scandal broke only after American media rejected the stories—Edward Snowden went to the *Washington Post* first with slides about the PRISM program, and only after the *Post* rejected him did he give all his material to Glenn Greenwald of the *Guardian*.

Justice Department targeting of journalists, including members of the Associated Press, wasn't broken by the Associated Press—the department broke that scandal itself in a letter to the AP. As to the Obama administration's regular pattern of pro-administration leaks, the media largely grinned and took the scoops without questioning the inconsistency of an administration targeting some journalists but rewarding others.

Coverage of Obama administration bribery and corruption has been notoriously absent from mainstream media reports, at least until prompted by conservatives monitoring that corruption.

And as for Obama's manipulation of the justice system, the media have been particularly eager to jump on Obama's bandwagon—it was members of the media who pushed forward the Zimmerman trial, ignored the New Black Panthers, and treated Gerald Walpin as an old nut rather than as an effective inspector general. The media also allowed Obama to pass himself off as an Occupy Wall Street man of the people all the while paying off his Wall Street buddies.

Media malfeasance has reached new heights under this administration. No wonder the Obama syndicate has gotten away with its crimes.

CLOSING ARGUMENT

If we had an honest attorney general, President Obama and many of his subordinates would find themselves at the defendants' table. Senator John McClellan (D-AR), the moving force behind the RICO bill, said while introducing it, "The problem, simply stated, is that organized crime is increasingly taking over organizations in our country, presenting an intolerable increase in deterioration of our Nation's standards. Efforts to dislodge them so far have been of little avail. To aid in the pressing need to remove organized crime from legitimate organizations in our country, I have thus formulated this bill." The goal was to blot out the "cancer" of organized crime "by direct attack, by forcible removal and prevention of return." That is the case against the Obama administration in a nutshell: an administration that has put itself above and beyond the law, that has perverted the mechanisms of government to enrich itself and the mechanisms of justice to protect itself.

The Obama administration has motive: transformation of the American ideal.

It has means: the government.

And it has the opportunity, provided to it by an American people kept ignorant by media lapdogs about the nature of its lawless overlords.

We can continue to deny that any of this criminality exists. We can channel J. Edgar Hoover, telling ourselves that there is no mafia. We can blind ourselves to the loss of our government, to the destruction of our constitutional system. We can tell ourselves it's all a myth, a dream, a nasty attempt to take down the nation's first black president.

Or we can tell ourselves the truth. Consolidated government means consolidated power; consolidated power means consolidated corruption. As Thomas Jefferson wrote in his *Notes on the State of Virginia*, "Mankind soon learns to make interested uses of every right and power which they possess, or may assume . . . our assembly [should not] be deluded by the integrity of their own purposes, and conclude that these unlimited powers will never be abused, because themselves are not disposed to abuse them. They should look forward to a time, and that not a distant one, when a corruption in this, as in the country from which we derive our origin, will have seized the head of government, and be spread by them through the body of the people; when they will purchase the voices of the people, and make them pay the price."

Jefferson concluded, "The time to guard against corruption and tyranny, is before they shall have gotten hold of us. It is better to keep the wolf out of the fold, than to trust to drawing his teeth and claws after he shall have entered."[16]

We didn't stop the wolf. It runs our government.

So what do we do about it?

First, Americans should, if they can find enough evidence, pursue litigation against the federal government. Holder's Justice Department will never sign off on a RICO prosecution of the Obama administration under any conceivable scenario, but that does not mean that the administration must go without repercussion. RICO provides for civil lawsuits, designed to turn American citizens into "private attorneys general," according to the Supreme Court, "undertaking litigation in the public good." Successful RICO plaintiffs win triple damages.[17] Historically, the courts have found that RICO actions against the government should not be allowed for a wide variety of reasons—but action against specific government agents has been allowed. Charges of bribery have been particularly successfully against particular government officials. It has been successfully argued before that specific branches of government also constitute "enterprises" for purposes of RICO.[18]

Second, we must elect enough congresspeople who are willing to hold the Obama administration accountable for its sins. Impeachment of the president is not on the table. But forcing him to fire and prosecute the lower-level officials on whom the president shifts blame would be a good start. The first to go should be Attorney General Eric Holder, whose Justice Department has been a fetid swamp of graft, fraud, and venality.

Congress must also pursue legislation to fills the massive gap that exists in the law to combat public corruption. A criminal administration can do virtually anything, without any sort of real consequences. Impeachment is rarely used—in the entire history of the United States, there have been just nineteen House impeachments, and just eight of those ended with full removal after a Senate trial. No doubt the founders intended impeachment to be utilized far more often than it has been—as Hamilton wrote in *Federalist No. 65*, "The subjects of its jurisdiction are those offenses which proceed from the misconduct of public men, or, in other words, from the abuse or violation of some public trust." But in practice, impeachment has been a failure. And we have seen that the executive branch cannot police itself. Every lame-duck president therefore has the ability to be as corrupt as he or she wants to be, given that he or she is not subject to reelection.

Congress should therefore expand the jurisdiction of RICO lawsuits to allow legal remedies against the executive branch. This would be hotly debated, and no doubt would be seen as compromising the power of the commander in chief. But the balance of power between the people and the executive branch has grown so skewed that there is little choice but to make the executive branch far more subject to direct action by the people. Why shouldn't the family of Brian Terry be able to lodge a RICO suit against the Obama administration? Why shouldn't the families of the slain from Benghazi, or the Americans spied on by the Bush and Obama administrations, or the organizations targeted by the IRS be given leeway to use the power of discovery—within rational national security limits, naturally—to bring public officials to some form of justice?

The alternative is an unanswerable government in which corrupt bargains between corrupt officials predominate, protected by the barrier of plausible deniability. The American people are left out in the cold.

Finally, Americans should recognize that much of the corruption of the Obama administration is endemic to the business of unchecked government. A government this large cannot be controlled. It is bound to run roughshod over the ordinary citizen. The Founders knew that; that's why they counted on checks and balances to stop the growth of government. But over the centuries, our form of government changed; those checks and balances fell away. Now we face the specter of naked power, and we should not be surprised to find that it is arbitrary and cruel.

The current state of the country is the most damning indictment of the Obama administration. And that administration will be repeated ad infinitum unless the American people stand up and seize their liberty. The Founders put their belief in representative government in the notion that men were neither good nor evil; as Hamilton wrote, "This supposition of universal venality in human nature is little less an error in political reasoning, than the supposition of universal rectitude. . . . [T]here is a portion of virtue and honor among mankind, which may be a reasonable foundation of confidence; and experience justifies the theory." But in a representative democracy, that portion of virtue and honor must begin with us. If we wish our representatives to be honest, we must be honest enough to dispense with the notion of a government that gives us everything without costing us our souls.

For at root, it is the soul of the nation that is at stake. "The government is us," President Obama is fond of saying. He's wrong. But if we allow our government to become ever bigger and ever more corrupt because we *want* it to be bigger and demand that it be more corrupt, Obama becomes right. And the victory of Obama's ideal of government—unaccountable, unscrupulous, and unending—would mean that we all stand guilty for the destruction of the country itself.

ACKNOWLEDGMENTS

★

I am blessed in my life to be surrounded by wonderful people who provide me the strength, aid, and inspiration to fight every day.

On a professional level, my agent, Frank Breeden, is a calming voice and a professional bulldog; my editor, Mitchell Ivers, is a grinding stone who constantly sharpens and perfects. David Limbaugh has been a lifelong friend and an incredible source of advice.

David Horowitz and all the folks at the David Horowitz Freedom Center, especially Mike Finch and the members of the board, are not only wellsprings of information and support, they are life guides whose fighting spirit infuses the center with purpose and cause. Thanks also to the staff of troopers at TruthRevolt, who engage in the war for American ideals around the clock. Winning is all that matters, and they are dedicated to victory.

If David was one of my intellectual godfathers, Andrew Breitbart was the other. Larry Solov, Steve Bannon, and Alex Marlow of Breitbart News have gallantly carried on the task of pushing forward Andrew's legacy.

I am blessed to work with Phil Boyce, Terry Fahy, Chuck Tyler, and all the executives at Salem Communications, as well as my extraordinarily talented cohosts, Brian Whitman and Elisha Krauss, every morning on KRLA 870 AM in Los Angeles.

Thanks to Jason Antebi for believing in me enough to put me on in a terrific market like Seattle. It's a pleasure and a privilege to fight for conservatism 3–6 p.m. every day on KTTH 770 AM.

On a personal level, I could not be luckier than to have a best friend like Jeremy Boreing, who is not only a dramatically underappreciated asset to the conservative movement, but a brilliant thinker and film-maker who, with any justice, won't be underappreciated for long.

My in-laws, Shmuel and Sima Toledano, are pillars of strength for me and my wife and child. Their enthusiasm gives us an example to follow in celebrating God with joy.

My sisters are all stars in their respective fields, and I couldn't be prouder to be their brother. More than that, their constant good humor and warrior spirit is a tribute to my parents and to the American and Jewish people.

My parents are, simply put, the greatest parents on the planet. Whether they're cooking Shabbat meals for us when we're too tired to move or babysitting so that Mor and I can go to a movie, whether they're giving us advice or listening to us complain, I couldn't be more blessed by God than to have them in my life each day.

Finally, my wife is a true *aishet chayil*, a woman of valor. She somehow achieves the impossible, balancing not only her own ambitions as a future doctor with being the best mother in the entire world, but somehow balancing both of those with being my partner in this exciting, irritating, and ultimately deeply rewarding battle. Without her, I could not push forward. With her, I cannot fail to do so.

And as for my baby, Leeya Eliana—God has blessed me and my wife more than we ever thought possible. She was born during President Obama's State of the Union address, ignoring his prevarications and instead bringing light to the world—and getting me out of covering that monstrosity in the process. If her birth is any indicator, she'll keep standing up for truth.

Thanks to God for my life, my wife, my child, and my mission.

NOTES

★

Introduction

1 "Well, Time to Go Out in Front of a Bunch of People and Lie to Them," TheOnion.com, June 25, 2013.

2 "Press Briefing by Press Secretary Jay Carney, 7/23/2013," WhiteHouse. gov, July 23, 2013, http://www.whitehouse.gov/the-press-office/2013/07/23 /press-briefing-press-secretary-jay-carney-7232013.

3 *In re Yamashita*, 327 U.S. 1 (1946).

4 Nathan Koppel, "They Call It RICO, and It Is Sweeping," WSJ.com, January 20, 2011, http://online.wsj.com/article/SB1000142405274870488130457609411 0829882704.html.

5 Ibid.

6 Donald J. Rebovich, Kenneth R. Coyle, and John C. Schaaf, "Local Prosecution of Organized Crime: The Use of State RICO Statutes," U.S. Department of Justice National Institute of Justice, October 1993.

7 U.S. Department of Justice, "Organized Crime and Racketeering," U.S. Attorneys Manual, http://www.justice.gov/usao/eousa/foia_reading_room /usam/title9/110mcrm.htm.

8 *Annulli v. Pannikkar*, 200 F.3d 189, at 200 (3d Cir. 1999).

9 "Kwame Kilpatrick Ran Racket as Detroit Mayor with Extortion, Bribery, Kickbacks, Jury Decides," *Detroit Free Press*, March 11, 2013, http:// www.freep.com/article/20130311/NEWS0102/303110133/Ex-mayor -Kilpatrick-Ferguson-guilty-racketeering-conspiracy-extortion-?odyssey= mod%3C/p%3E%3Cp%3Edefcon%3C/p%3E%3Cp%3Etext%3C /p%3E%3Cp%3EFRONTPAGE.

10 *Agency Holding Corp. v. Malley-Duff & Associates*, 483 U.S. 143, 151 (1987).

11 Gregory P. Joseph, "RICO Enterprise after *Boyle*," JosephNYC.com, 2009, http://www.josephnyc.com/articles/viewarticle.php?64.

12 "Policy Statement of the Department of Justice on Its Relationship and Coordination with the Statutory Inspectors General of the Various Departments and Agencies of the United States," Department of Justice Criminal Resource Manual Section 934, www.justice.gov/usao/eousa/foia_reading _room/usam/title9/crm00934.htm.

13 Alexander Hamilton, *The Federalist No. 70, Independent Journal*, March 15, 1788.

14 Woodrow Wilson, "The Study of Administration," *Political Science Quarterly*, July 1887, http://www.heritage.org/initiatives/first-principles/primary -sources/woodrow-wilson-on-administration.

15 Woodrow Wilson, "What Is Progress?," 1912 campaign speech.

16 "Historical Federal Workforce Tables: Total Government Employment Since 1962," Office of Personnel Management, http://www.opm.gov/policy-data -oversight/data-analysis-documentation/federal-employment-reports/historical -tables/total-government-employment-since-1962/.

17 William English Walling, *State Socialism, Pro and Con* (New York: Henry Holt, 1917), xiv.

18 "Poll Chart: Obama Job Approval," HuffingtonPost.com, January 5, 2013, http://elections.huffingtonpost.com/pollster/obama-job-approval.

19 "Poll Chart: Obama Job Approval—Economy," HuffingtonPost.com, August 2, 2013, http://elections.huffingtonpost.com/pollster/obama-job -approval-economy.

20 "Poll Chart: Obama Job Approval—Health," HuffingtonPost.com, August 2, 2013, http://elections.huffingtonpost.com/pollster/obama-job -approval-health.

21 "Poll Chart: Obama Job Approval—Foreign Policy," HuffingtonPost.com, August 2, 2013, http://elections.huffingtonpost.com/pollster/obama-job -approval-foreign-policy.

22 Nate Silver, "Is Democratic Criticism on NSA Hurting Obama's Approval Rating?," NYTimes.com, June 17, 2013, http://fivethirtyeight.blogs.nytimes.com/2013 /06/17/is-democratic-criticism-on-n-s-a-hurting-obamas-approval-rating/.

23 Lyneka Little, "Jay-Z Declares 'My Presence is Charity,'" WSJ.com, July 29, 2013, http://blogs.wsj.com/speakeasy/2013/07/29/jay-z-declares-my -presence-is-charity/.

24 Kyle Becker, "Obama: 'I Am Constrained by a System That Our Founders Put in Place,'" IJReview.com, April 4, 2013, http://www.ijreview.com/2013/04 /45095-obama-i-am-constrained-by-a-system-that-our-founders-put-in-place/.

25 "Obama Taking Executive Action on Guns After Senate Vote," FoxNews .com, April 20, 2013, http://nation.foxnews.com/gun-control/2013/04/20 /obama-taking-executive-action-guns-after-senate-vote.

26 Julie Mason, "Obama Tells Hispanic Roundtable He Can't Fix Immigration Alone," Politico.com, September 28, 2011, http://www.politico.com/news /stories/0911/64635.html. (The DREAM Act is a federal bill intended to provide benefits to the non-citizen children of illegal immigrants that are normally reserved for American citizens.)

27 Peter Grier, "Obama on Immigration Reform: I'll Act if Congress Doesn't," CSMonitor.com, January 29, 2013, http://www.csmonitor.com/USA/Politics /2013/0129/Obama-on-immigration-reform-I-ll-act-if-Congress-doesn-t.

28 Daniel Henninger, "Obama's Creeping Authoritarianism," WSJ.com, July 31, 2013, http://online.wsj.com/article/SB10001424127887324136204578 639953580480838.html.?mod=WSJ_Opinion_LEADTop.

29 Nicholas Ballasy, "Obama: As president, 'You Can't Do Things by Yourself,'" DailyCaller.com, February 26, 2013, http://dailycaller.com/2013/02/26 /obama-as-president-you-cant-do-things-by-yourself-video/.

30 Associated Press, "Obama Learned of IRS Targeting from News Reports: Aide," HuffingtonPost.com, May 19, 2013, http://www.huffingtonpost.com /2013/05/19/obama-irs-targeting_n_3302449.html.

31 Jay Carney, White House Press Briefing, October 23, 2013.

32 Jay Carney, White House Press Briefing, May 14, 2013.

33 Jay Carney, White House Press Briefing, July 15, 2011.

34 "Obama Unaware as U.S. Spied on World Leaders: Officials," WSJ.com, October 27, 2013, http://online.wsj.com/news/articles/SB1000142405270 2304470504579162110180138036?mod=djemalertNEWS.

35 "President Obama Says Romney Should Answer Bain Capital Questions," WJLA.com, July 13, 2012, www.wjla.com/articles/2012/07/president -obama-says-romney-should-answer-bain-capital-questions-77842.html.

36 Tim Arango, "Ex-Prosecutor's Book Accuses Bush of Murder," NYTimes .com, July 7, 2008, http://www.nytimes.com/2008/07/07/business/media /07bugliosi.html.

37 Noel Sheppard, "Chris Matthews: 'Obama Is the Perfect Father, the Perfect Husband, the Perfect American,'" Newsbusters.org, July 17, 2012, http://newsbusters.org/blogs/noel-shepard/2012/07/17/chris-matthews-obama -perfect-father-perfect-husband-perfect-american.

38 Amie Parnes and Ian Swanson, "Obama Adviser Didn't Threaten Woodward, Says White House," TheHill.com, February 28, 2013,http://thehill.com/homenews /administration/285549-sperling-didnt-threaten-woodward-says-white-house.

39 David Jackson, "New Sequester Battle: Woodward vs. White House," *USA Today*, February 28, 2013, http://www.usatoday.com/story/theoval/2013/02 /28/obama-woodward-white-house/1953105/, and Ron Fournier, "Why Bob Woodward's Fight with the White House Matters to You," National -Journal.com, May 30, 2013, http://www.nationaljournal.com/politics/why -bob-woodward-s-fight-with-the-white-house-matters-to-you-20130228.

40 John Nolte, "Mainstream Media Did Not Break Even One of Four Obama Scandals," Breitbart.com, June 6, 2013, http://www.breitbart.com /Big-Journalism/2013/06/06/.Mainstream-Media-Did-Not-break-Even-One-of -Four-Obama-Scandals.

41 Frank J. Marine et al., *Criminal RICO: 18 USC §§ 1961–1968* (5th rev. ed., October 2009), 3–5.

Count 1: Espionage

1 James Nye and Beth Stebner, "'Their Sacrifice Will Never Be Forgotten,'" *Daily Mail* (U.K.), September 14, 2012, http://www.dailymail.co.uk/news /article-2203298/Victims-Benghazi-massacre-return-home-Obama-Clinton -pay-tribute.html.

2 "President's Schedule—September 14, 2012," WhiteHouse.gov, http://www .whitehouse.gov/schedule/president/2012-09-14.

3 Nicholas D. Kristof, "Obama: Man of the World," *New York Times*, March 6, 2007, http://www.nytimes.com/2007/03/06/opinion/06kristof.html.

4 President Barack Obama, "Text: Obama's Speech in Cairo," *New York Times*, June 4, 2009, http://www.nytimes.com/2009/06/04/us/politics/04obama .text.html.?pagewanted=all&_r=0.

5 "Muslim Brotherhood Members to Attend Obama's Cairo Speech," FoxNews.com, June 3, 2009, http://www.foxnews.com/politics/2009/06/03 /muslim-brotherhood-members-attend-obamas-cairo-speech/.

6 Marc Ambinder, "'Brotherhood' Invited to Obama Speech by U.S.," The-Atlantic.com, June 3, 2009, http://www.theatlantic.com/politics/archive /2009/06/-brotherhood-invited-to-obama-speech-by-us/18693/.

7 "Is Talking to the Taliban the Right Approach?," CNN.com, March 9, 2009, http://edition.cnn.com/2009/POLITICS/03/09/obama.taliban/.

8 Josh Lev, "Fact Check: Was Obama 'Silent' on Iran 2009 Protests?," CNN.com, October 9, 2012, http://edition.cnn.com/2012/10/08/politics /fact-check-romney-iran.

9 Spencer Ackerman, "U.S. Had Helo Deal with Ousted Tunisian Dictator," Wired.com, January 14, 2011, http://www.wired.com/dangerroom/2011/01 /u-s-copter-sales-cant-save-wiki-ousted-tunisian-dictator/.

10 Patrick Goodenough, "Obama Says He 'Stood with' Tunisians and Egyptians, but He Was Wary at the Time," CNSNews.com, October 23, 2012, http://cnsnews.com/news/article/obama says-he-stood-tunisians-and-egyptians-he-was-wary-time.

11 Christopher Alexander, "Tunisia's Protest Wave: Where It Comes from and What It Means," ForeignPolicy.com, January 3, 2011, http://mideast.foreignpolicy.com/posts/2011/01/02/tunisia_s_protest_wave_where_it_comes_from_and_what_it_means_for_ben_ali.

12 Goodenough, "Obama Says He 'Stood with' Tunisians and Egyptians, but He Was Wary at the Time."

13 Tarek Amara, "Tunisian Islamists, Secularists Gird for Rival Shows of Strength," Reuters, August 13, 2013, http://www.reuters.com/article/2013/08/13/us-tunisia-crisis-idUSBRE97C0D220130813.

14 Goodenough, "Obama Says He 'Stood with' Tunisians and Egyptians, but He Was Wary at the Time."

15 Matthew Shaffer, "Obama's Speech After Mubarak's Resignation," NationalReview.com, February 11, 2011, http://www.nationalreview.com/egypt-watch/259611/obamas-speech-after-mubaraks-resignation-matthew-shaffer.

16 Raymond Ibrahim, "Behind Benghazi: Muslim Brotherhood and Obama Administration," HumanEvents.com, August 16, 2013, http://www.humanevents.com/2013/08/16/behind-benghazi-muslim-brotherhood-and-obama-administration/.

17 Glenn Kessler, "Hillary Clinton's Uncredible Statement on Syria," *Washington Post*, April 4, 2011, http://www.washingtonpost.com/blogs/fact-checker/post/hillary-clintons-uncredible-statement-on-syria/2011/04/01/AFWPEYaC_blog.html.

18 Joby Warrick, "Some Now Question U.S. Deal That Brought Gaddafi Back into Diplomatic Fold," *Washington Post*, February 25, 2011, http://www.washingtonpost.com/wp-dyn/content/article/2011/02/24/AR2011022407829.html.

19 "Libyan Uprising One-Year Anniversary: Timeline," *Telegraph* (U.K.), February 17, 2012, http://www.telegraph.co.uk/news/worldnews/africaandindianocean/libya/9087969/Libyan-uprising-one-year-anniversary-timeline.html.

20 "We Came, We Saw, He Died," *Daily Mail Online*, October 21, 2011, http://www.dailymail.co.uk/news/article-2051826/We-came-saw-died-What-Hillary-Clinton-told-news-reporter-moments-hearing-Gaddafis-death.html.

21 Eli Lake, "Al Qaeda Offers Aid to Rebels in Libya," *Washington Times*, February 24, 2011, http://www.washingtontimes.com/news/2011/feb/24/al-qaeda-offers-aid-to-rebels-in-libya/?page=all.

22 Praveen Swami, Nick Squires, and Duncan Gardham, "Libyan Rebel Commander Admits His Fighters Have al-Qaeda Links," *Telegraph* (U.K.), March 25, 2011, http://www.telegraph.co.uk/news/worldnews/africaandindianocean/libya/8407047/Libyan-rebel-commander-admits-his-fighters-have-al-Qaeda-links.html.

23 "Al Qaeda May Already Be Among Libya's Rebels," CBSNews.com, March 30, 2011, http://www.cbsnews.com/8301-503543_162-20048982-503543/al-qaeda-may-already-be-among-libyas-rebels/.

24 Christopher Ayad, "'We Are Simply Muslim': Libyan Rebel Chief Denies Al-Qaeda Ties," Time.com, September 4, 2011, http://www.time.com/time/world/article/0,8599,2091744,00.html.

25 Jean-Pierre Perrin, "Top Libyan Rebel Leader Has Deep Al Qaeda Ties," WorldCrunch.com, August 29, 2011, http://www.worldcrunch.com/top-libyan-rebel-leader-has-deep-al-qaeda-ties/world-affairs/top-libyan-rebel-leader-has-deep-al-qaeda-ties/c1s3661/.

26 "Congress Members Grill Administration Officials on Libya Mission," CNN.com, March 31, 2011, http://edition.cnn.com/2011/POLITICS/03/30/congress.libya.briefing/index.html.

27 Tom Curry, "Obama, Libya, and the Authorization Conflict," NBCNews.com, March 22, 2011, http://www.nbcnews.com/id/42201792/ns/politics/t/obama-libya-authorization-conflict/#.UgqTx2DrOR8.

28 "Bipartisan Congress Rebuffs Obama on Libya Mission," *Washington Times*, June 3, 2011, http://www.washingtontimes.com/news/2011/jun/3/bipartisan-congress-rebuffs-obama-libya-mission/.

29 Jeffrey M. Jones, "Americans Shift to More Negative View of Libya Military Action," Gallup.com, June 24, 2011, http://www.gallup.com/poll/148196/americans-shift-negative-view-libya-military-action.aspx.

30 Elisabeth Bumiller and Thom Shanker, "U.S. Is Unlikely to Arm Libyan Rebels, Obama Aides Say," *New York Times*, March 31, 2011, http://www.nytimes.com/2011/04/01/world/africa/01military.html.?pagewanted=all.

31 "Yes, We Can: Obama Waives Anti-Terrorism Provisions to Arm Syrian Rebels," RT.com, September 17, 2013, http://rt.com/usa/obama-terrorist-arms-supply-966/.

32 Karen DeYoung and Greg Miller, "In Libya, CIA Is Gathering Intelligence on Rebels," *Washington Post*, March 30, 2011, http://www.washingtonpost.com/world/in-libya-cia-is-gathering-intelligence-on-rebels/2011/03/30/AFLyb25B_story.html.

33 Jake Tapper, Jon Karl, and Russell Goldman, "President Obama Authorizes Covert Help for Libyan Rebels," ABCNews.com, March 30, 2011, http://abcnews

.go.com/International/president-obama-authorizes-covert-libyan-rebels/storyNew
?id=13259028&singlePage=true.

34 James Risen, Mark Mazzetti, and Michael S. Schmidt, "U.S.-Approved Weapons Transfer Ended Up with Libyan Jihadis," NYTimes.com, December 5, 2012, http://www.nytimes.com/2012/12/06/world/africa/weapons-sent-to-libyan -rebels-with-us-approval-fell-into-islamist-hands.html.?pagewanted=all.

35 Rod Nordland and Scott Shane, "Libyan, Once a Detainee, Is Now a U.S. Ally of Sorts," NYTimes.com, April 24, 2011, http://www.nytimes.com/2011/04 /25/world/guantanamo-files-libyan-detainee-now-us-ally-of-sorts.html.?hp=& adxnnl=1&adxnnlx=1347728400-2My68hL/Qqy52SG0reimIg&_r=1.

36 Ibid.

37 Senator Rand Paul, "Hold Obama Accountable for Benghazi Cover-up," NewsMax.com, August 7, 2013, http://www.newsmax.com/Newsfront/rand -paul-hillary-benghazi/2013/08/07/id/519270.

38 AWR Hawkins, "Attorney for Whistleblower: 400 U.S. Missiles Stolen in Benghazi," Breitbart.com, August 12, 2013, http://www.breitbart.com/Big -Peace/2013/08/12/Attorney-For-Benghazi-Whistleblower-400-U-S-Missiles -Stolen-In-Benghazi-Annex-Involved.

39 Sheera Frenkel Antakya, "Syrian Rebels Squabble over Weapons as Biggest Shipload Arrives from Libya," Times of London, September 14, 2012, http:// www.thetimes.co.uk/tto/news/world/middleeast/article3537770.ece.

40 Paul, "Hold Obama Accountable for Benghazi Cover-up."

41 Eric Schmitt, "CIA Said to Aid in Steering Arms to Syrian Opposition," New York Times, June 21, 2012, http://www.nytimes.com/2012/06/21/world /middleeast/cia-said-to-aid-in-steering-arms-to-syrian-rebels.html.?pagewanted =all.

42 Ben Swann, "One-on-One with President Obama: Why Is the U.S. Supporting Al Qaeda in Syria," September 11, 2012, http://www.youtube.com /watch?feature=player_detailpage&v=_h_D_oAtnLI#t=122s.

43 Perry Chairamonte, "Egypt Claims Jihadists Fired U.S. Hellfire Missile at Government Office,"FoxNews.com, August 5, 2013, http://www.foxnews .com/world/2013/08/05/us-made-hellfire-missile-believed-to-have-been-used -in-insurgent-attack-on/.

44 Risen, Mazzetti, and Schmidt, "U.S.-Approved Weapons Transfer Ended Up with Libyan Jihadis."

45 Praveen Swami, Nick Squires, and Duncan Gardham, "Libyan rebel commander admits his fighters have al-Qaeda links," Telegraph (U.K.), March 25, 2011, http:// www.telegraph.co.uk/news/worldnews/africaandindian ocean/libya/8407047/ Libyan-rebel-commander-admits-his-fighters-have-al-Qaeda-links.html.

46 Terence P. Jeffrey, "Hillary Clinton: Al-Qaida Got Arms out of Post-Revo-
    lutionary Libya," CNSNews.com, April 17, 2013,http://cnsnews.com/blog
    /terence-p-jeffrey/hillary-clinton-al-qaida-got-arms-out-post-revolutionary-libya.

47 Aaron Klein, "This Is What Benghazi 'Consulate' *Really* Was," WND.com, Octo-
    ber 16, 2012, http://www.wnd.com/2012/10/this-is-what-benghazi-consulate
    -really-was/.

48 Aaron Klein, "Sources: Slain U.S. Ambassador Recruited Jihadists,"
    WND.com, September 24, 2012, http://www.wnd.com/2012/09
    /sources-slain-u-s-ambassador-recruited-jihadists/.

49 Ben Shapiro, "BenghaziGate: Obama Admin Knew Libyan Terrorists Had
    U.S.-Provided Weapons," Breitbart.com, December 5, 2012, http://www
    .breitbart.com/Big-Peace/2012/12/05/NYT-Benghazi-weapons-funneled.

50 Adrian Blomfield, Damien McElroy, and Ruth Sherlock, "Islamists Blamed for
    Killing General Abdel Fattah Younes as Libya's Rebels Face Up to Enemy Within,"
    Telegraph (U.K.), July 30, 2011, http://www.telegraph.co.uk/news/worldnews
    /africaandindianocean/libya/8673021/Islamists-blamed-for-killing-General
    -Abdel-Fattah-Younes-as-Liyas-rebels-face-up-to-enemy-within.html.

51 John Rosenthal, "Newsmax Exclusive: U.S. Hired al-Qaeda-Linked Group
    to Defend Benghazi Mission," Newsmax.com, May 3, 2013, http://www
    .newsmax.com/Newsfront/benghazi-consulate-protected-alqaida/2013/05
    /02/id/502565.

52 Jeryl Bier, "State Dept. Report Lists 6 Terror Attacks Last Year in Benghazi
    Before 9/11 Attack," WeeklyStandard.com, May 31, 2013, http://www
    .weeklystandard.com/blogs/state-dept-report-lists-6-terror-attacks-last-year
    -benghazi-911-attack_732051.html.

53 Mel Frykberg, "British Say Weapons They Left at U.S. Consulate in
    Benghazi Are Missing," McClatchyDC.com, October 12, 2012, http://
    www.mcclatchydc.com/2012/10/12/171421/british-say-weapons-they-left
    .html.#.UgrnYWDrOR8.

54 Jeryl Bier, "State Dept. Report Lists 6 Terror Attacks Last Year in Benghazi
    Before 9/11 Attack," WeeklyStandard.com, May 31, 2013, http://www
    .weeklystandard.com/blogs/state-dept-report-lists-6-terror-attacks-last-year
    -benghazi-911-attack_732051.html.

55 "Interim Progress Report for the Members of the House Republican Confer-
    ence on the Events Surrounding the September 11, 2012, Terrorist Attacks
    in Benghazi, Libya," April 23, 2013, http://oversight.house.gov/wp-content
    /uploads/2013/04/Libya-Progress-Report-Final-1.pdf. Subsequently referred
    to as "Interim Progress Report."

56 Rosenthal, "Newsmax Exclusive: U.S. Hired al-Qaeda-Linked Group to De-
    fend Benghazi Mission."

57   Eric Allan Nordstrom, "Prepared Statement at the Request of Chairman Issa and the Committee on Oversight & Government Reform," Hearing on Security Failures in Benghazi, Tripoli on September 11, 2012, October 10, 2012, http://oversight.house.gov/wp-content/uploads/2012/10/2012-10-09-NORDSTROM-Written-Statement-Final1.pdf.

58   Jake Tapper, "U.S. Security Official in Libya Tells Congressional Investigators About 'Inappropriately Low' Security at Benghazi Post," ABCNews.com, October 10, 2012, http://abcnews.go.com/blogs/politics/2012/10/u-s-security-official-in-libya-tells-congressional-investigators-about-inappropriately-low-security-at-benghazi-post/.

59   "Interim Progress Report."

60   "CNN Finds, Returns Journal Belonging to Late U.S. Ambassador," CNN.com, September 23, 2012, http://www.cnn.com/2012/09/22/world/africa/libya-ambassador-journal/index.html.

61   "Interim Progress Report."

62   Pat Buchanan, "The Smoking Gun of the Benghazi Cover-up," WND.com, November 1, 2012, http://www.wnd.com/2012/11/the-smoking-gun-of-the-benghazi-cover-up/.

63   Documents released by House Committee on Oversight and Government Reform, October 19, 2012, http://oversight.house.gov/wp-content/uploads/2012/10/DEI-to-BHO-10-19-2012-attachments.pdf.

64   Jonathan Easley, "Report: Officials Say Stevens Turned down Extra Benghazi Security," TheHill.com, May 15, 2013, http://thehill.com/blogs/blog-briefing-room/news/299807-report-officials-say-stevens-turned-down-extra-benghazi-security.

65   Harald Doornbos and Jenan Moussa, "'Troubling' Surveillance Before Benghazi Attack," ForeignPolicy.com, November 1, 2012, http://www.foreignpolicy.com/articles/2012/11/01/troubling_surveillance_before_benghazi_attack.

66   "CNN Finds, Returns Journal Belonging to Late U.S. Ambassador," CNN.com, September 23, 2012, http://www.cnn.com/2012/09/22/world/africa/libya-ambassador-journal/index.html.

67   Doornbos and Moussa, "'Troubling' Surveillance Before Benghazi Attack."

68   "Interim Progress Report."

69   Jake Tapper, "Documents Back Up Claims of Requests for Greater Security in Benghazi," ABCNews.com, October 19, 2012, http://abcnews.go.com/blogs/politics/2012/10/documents-back-up-claims-of-requests-for-greater-security-in-benghazi/.

70   Thomas Joscelyn, "Al Qaeda Responsible for 4 Attacks on U.S. Embassies in

September," *Weekly Standard,* October 3, 2012, http://www.weeklystandard
.com/print/blogs/al-qaeda-responsible-4-attacks-us-embassies-september
_653460.html.

71 Matt Bradley and Dion Nissenbaum, "U.S. Missions Stormed in Libya,
Egypt," *Wall Street Journal,* September 12, 2012, http://online.wsj.com
/article/SB10000872396390444017504577645681057498266.html.?mod=
WSJ_hpp_MIDDLENexttoWhatsNewsThird.

72 Byron Tau, "U.S. Embassy in Cairo Condemns Muhammed Video,"
Politico.com, September 11, 2012, http://www.politico.com/politico44/
2012/09/after-attack-us-embassy-in-cairo-apologizes-for-unspecified-135222
.html.

73 Sheera Frenkel Antakya, "Syrian Rebels Squabble Over Weapons as Biggest Shipload Arrives from Libya," *Times of London* (U.K.), September
14, 2012, http://www.thetimes.co.uk/tto/news/world/middleeast/article3537770
.ece.

74 Hayley Peterson and Jill Reilly, "Drones Were Circling Above U.S. Consulate
During Libya Attack but Officials Decided NOT to Mount a Rescue Mission,"
Daily Mail (U.K.), October 19, 2012, http://www.dailymail.co.uk/news
/article-2220153/Christopher-Stevens-Ambassador-pleaded-extra-security
-Libya-hours-killed.html.

75 Jennifer Griffin, "EXCLUSIVE: CIA Operators Were Denied Request for
Help During Benghazi Attack, Sources Say," FoxNews.com, October 26, 2012,
http://www.foxnews.com/politics/2012/10/26/cia-operators-were-denied-request
-for-help-during-benghazi-attack-sources-say/#ixzz2AQF4OlER.

76 "Interim Progress Report."

77 Ibid.

78 Peterson and Reilly, "Drones Were Circling Above U.S. Consulate During
Libya Attack."

79 Griffin, "EXCLUSIVE: CIA Operators Were Denied Request for Help."

80 Sharyl Attkisson, "Officials on Benghazi: 'We Made Mistakes, but Without
Malice,'" CBSNews.com, May 17, 2013,http://www.cbsnews.com/8301-250
_162-57584921/officials-on-benghazi-we-made-mistakes-but-without-malice/.

81 "Interim Progress Report."

82 Ashley Fantz, "Panetta, Dempsey Defend U.S. Response to Benghazi Attack," CNN.com, February 7, 2013, http://www.cnn.com/2013/02/07/us
/panetta-benghazi-hearing.

83 "Transcript: Whistle-blower's Account of Sept. 11 Libya Terror Attack,"
FoxNews.com, May 8, 2013, http://www.foxnews.com/politics/2013/05/08
/transcript-whistle-blower-account-sept-11-libya-terror-attack/.

84 Fantz, "Panetta, Dempsey Defend U.S. Response to Benghazi Attack."

85 "Transcript: Whistle-blower's Account of Sept. 11 Libya Terror Attack," FoxNews.com, May 8, 2013, http://www.foxnews.com/politics/2013/05/08 /transcript-whistle-blower-account-sept-11-libya-terror-attack/.

86 Dustin Walker, "Pentagon: Special Forces Would Not Have Saved Lives in Benghazi," RealClearDefense.com, May 8, 2013, http://www.realcleardefense .com/articles/2013/05/08/pentagon_special_forces_would_not_have_saved _lives_in_benghazi_106587.html.

87 Nordstrom, "Prepared Statement at the Request of Chairman Issa and the Committee on Oversight & Government Reform."

88 Kerry Picket, "Benghazi Attack Eyewitness: Help Was Available," Breitbart .com, April 29, 2013, http://www.breitbart.com/Big-Government/2013/04 /29/Benghazi-Attack-Eyewitness-Help-Was-Available.

89 Fred Lucas, "Obama Has Touted Al Qaeda's Demise 32 Times Since Benghazi Attack," CNSNews.com, November 1, 2012, http://cnsnews.com/ news/article/obama-touts-al-qaeda-s-demise-32-times-benghazi-attack-0.

90 "Remarks by the President on the Deaths of U.S. Embassy Staff in Libya," Office of the White House Press Secretary, September 12, 2012, http://www.whitehouse.gov/the-press-office/2012/09/12/remarks-president -deaths-us-embassy-staff-libya.

91 Joel B. Pollak, "Proof: Obama Refused to Call Benghazi 'Terror,' CBS Covered Up," Breitbart.com, November 5, 2012, http://www.breitbart .com/Big-Journalism/2012/11/05/Proof-Obama-Refused-to-Call-Benghazi -Terror-CBS-Covered-Up.

92 "Interim Progress Report."

93 "GOP Rep: Hillary Screamed at Congressman for Calling Benghazi Attack 'Terrorism,'" Breitbart.com, August 15, 2013, http://www.breitbart.com /Breitbart-TV?id=%7B426EEBE8-26A9-48BE-BCCB-CD6EB7EA3022%7D &title=GOP-Rep-Hillary-Clinton-Attacked-Congressman-Two-Days-After -Benghazi-For-Daring-to-Call-It-Terrorism.

94 Benjy Sarlin, "State Dept. Confirms Death in Libya; Romney Attacks 'Disgraceful' White House," TalkingPointsMemo.com, September 11, 2012, http://2012.talkingpointsmemo.com/2012/09/state-dept-confirms-death-in -libya-romney-attacks-disgraceful-white-house.php.

95 "Father of ex-SEAL: Those Who Denied Request for Help at Consulate 'Murderers of My Son,'" FoxNews.com, October 26, 2012, http:// www.foxnews.com/politics/2012/10/26/father-seal-killed-in-libya-says-clinton -vowed-to-arrest-and-prosecute/.

96 'Danger to the Community': Feds Arrest Obama's Scapegoated Filmmaker,"

September 27, 2012, http://www.breitbart.com/Big-Hollywood/2012/09/27 /anti-muslim-filmmaker-arrested.

97 Sharyl Attkisson, "Emails Detail Unfolding Benghazi Attack on Sept. 11," CBSNews.com, October 23, 2012, http://www.cbsnews.com/8301-18563 _162-57538689/emails-detail-unfolding-benghazi-attack-on-sept-11/?tag= AverageMixRelated.

98 "Flashback: What Susan Rice Said About Benghazi," WSJ.com, November 16, 2012, http://blogs.wsj.com/washwire/2012/11/16/flashback-what-susan-rice-said -about-benghazi/.

99 Jonathan Karl and Chris Good, "The Benghazi Emails: Talking Points Changed at State Dept.'s Request," ABCNews.com, May 15, 2013, http:// abcnews.go.com/Politics/benghazi-emails-talking-points-changed-state-depts -request/story?id=19187137&singlePage=true.

100 "Interim Progress Report."

101 Ben Shapiro, "White House: Benghazi Talking Points Edits Not Politically Motivated," Breitbart.com, May 10, 2013, http://www.breitbart.com/Big -Peace/2013/05/10/Carney-WH-Benghazi-political-talking-points.

102 "Interim Progress Report."

103 "Obama's Speech to the United Nations General Assembly—Text," New York Times, September 25, 2012, http://www.nytimes.com/2012 /09/26/world/obamas-speech-to-the-united-nations-general-assembly-text. html.?pagewanted=all&_moc.semityn.www.

104 Ben Shapiro, "Obama: Benghazi Murders 'Not Optimal,'" Breitbart.com, October 18, 2012, http://www.breitbart.com/Big-Government/2012/10/18 /Obama-Benghazi-murders-not-optimal.

105 "In Context: Hillary Clinton's 'What Difference Does It Make' Comment," Politifact.com, May 8, 2013, http://www.politifact.com/truth-o-meter /article/2013/may/08/context-hillary-clintons-what-difference-does-it-m/.

106 Noah Rothman, "Benghazi Whistleblower Reacts to Hillary Clinton Saying 'What Difference Does It Make?': A Lot," Mediaite.com, May 8, 2013, http:// www.mediaite.com/tv/benghazi-whistleblower-reacts-to-hillary-clinton-saying -what-difference-does-it-make-a-lot/.

107 Ben Shapiro, "WH: Obama 'Has Not Participated' in Benghazi Investigation," Breitbart.com, November 1, 2012, http://www.breitbart.com/Big -Peace/2012/11/01/Obama-not-interested-investigation-Benghazi.

108 "Accountability Review Board Report—U.S. Department of State," December 18, 2012, http://www.state.gov/documents/organization/202446.pdf.

109 Eliana Johnson, "Pickering Defends Decision Not to Interview Hillary for ARB Report," NationalReview.com, May 12, 2013, http://www.nationalreview

.com/corner/348058/picking-defends-decision-not-interview-hillary-arb-report.

110 Victoria Toensing, "Administration Relying on Shoddy Benghazi Report to Absolve Itself of Blame," WeeklyStandard.com, May 12, 2013, http://www .weeklystandard.com/print/blogs/administration-relying-shoddy-benghazi-report-absolve-itself-blame_722379.html.

111 "Accountability Review Board Report—U.S. Department of State," December 18, 2012, http://www.state.gov/documents/organization/202446.pdf.

112 Josh Rogin, "Congress: Hillary's Benghazi Investigation Let Top Officials Escape Blame," TheDailyBeast.com, September 15, 2013, http://www .thedailybeast.com/articles/2013/09/15/congress-hillary-s-benghazi-investigation -let-top-officials-escape-blame.html.

113 James Rosen, "State Department's Benghazi Review Panel Under Investigation, Fox News confirms," FoxNews.com, May 2, 2013, http://www.foxnews .com/politics/2013/05/02/state-department-benghazi-review-panel-under -investigation-fox-news-confirms/.

114 "Press Briefing by Press Secretary Jay Carney and Chief Technology Officer Todd Park," WhiteHouse.gov, May 8, 2013, http://www .whitehouse.gov/the-press-office/2013/05/08/press-briefing-press-secretary -jay-carney-and-chief-technology-officer-t.

115 Sharyl Attkisson, "White House Declines to Release Images from Night of Benghazi Attacks," CBSNews.com, November 21, 2012, http://www.cbsnews .com/8301-250_162-57553090/white-house-declines-to-release-images-from -night-of-benghazi-attacks/?tag=socsh.

116 Testimony of Secretary Hillary Clinton before the House Foreign Affairs Committee on January 23, 2013.

117 Paul, "Hold Obama Accountable for Benghazi Cover-up."

118 "Exclusive: Dozens of CIA Operatives on the Ground During Benghazi Attack," CNN.com, August 1, 2013, http://thelead.blogs.cnn.com/2013 /08/01/exclusive-dozens-of-cia-operatives-on-the-ground-during-benghazi -attack/.

119 Jason Howerton, "CBS Reporter: Kerry Tells Congress He Won't Make Benghazi Survivors Available for Questioning, Subpoenas," TheBlaze.com, September 10, 2013, http://www.theblaze.com/stories/2013/09/10/cbs -reporter-kerry-tells-congress-he-wont-make-benghazi-survivors-available -for-questioning-subpoenas-could-be-coming/?utm_source=twitter&utm _medium=story&utm_campaign=Share%20Buttons.

120 "Congress Interviewing 'Dozens' of Benghazi Witnesses," CBSNews.com, July 30, 2013, http://www.cbsnews.com/8301-250_162-57596146/congress -interviewing-dozens-of-benghazi-witnesses/?tag=socsh.

121 Kerry Picket, "Clinton Aide Pressured Whistleblowers on Speaking to Chaffetz," Breitbart.com, May 8, 2013, http://www.breitbart.com/Big-Peace/2013/05/08/State-Dept-Told-Benghazi-Witness-Not-to-Talk-to-Chaffetz-Hid-Witness-Whereabouts-from-Public.

122 Andrew Johnson, "Benghazi Whistleblower: I've Been 'Punished' for Speaking Out," NationalReview.com, September 8, 2013, http://www.nationalreview.com/corner/357898/benghazi-whistleblower-ive-been-punished-speaking-out-andrew-johnson.

123 Michael Hastings, "Advisers Urged Obama Early On to Release Comprehensive Benghazi Timeline," BuzzFeed.com, May 21, 2013, http://www.buzzfeed.com/mhastings/advisers-urged-obama-early-on-to-release-comprehensive-bengh.

124 "Hillary Clinton Aide Tells Reporter to 'Fuck Off' and 'Have a Good Life,'" BuzzFeed.com, September 24, 2012, http://www.buzzfeed.com/buzzfeed-politics/hillary-clinton-aide-tells-reporter-to-fuck-off.

125 Dylan Byers, "The Post's Sharyl Attkisson Piece," Politico.com, May 8, 2013, http://www.politico.com/blogs/media/2013/05/the-posts-sharyl-attkisson-piece-163496.html.

126 William Bigelow, "Politico: Media Didn't Ignore Benghazi," Breitbart.com, August 6, 2013, http://www.breitbart.com/Big-Journalism/2013/08/05/Politico-Media-Didn-t-Ignore-Benghazi-revised-w-added-links.

127 Ben Shapiro, "WH: 'Irrelevant' Where Obama Was During Benghazi Attack," Breitbart.com, May 19, 2013, http://www.breitbart.com/Big-Government/2013/05/19/WH-spokesman-Obama-Benghazi-irrelevant.

128 Ben Shapiro, "Shrug: Obama Says Benghazi Attack Isolated Incident, Localized Threat," Breitbart.com, May 23, 2013, http://www.breitbart.com/Big-Peace/2013/05/23/Obama-Benghazi-speech.

129 Ben Shapiro, "Dems: GOP Leading Benghazi 'Witch Hunt' Against Hillary," Breitbart.com, May 12, 2013, http://www.breitbart.com/Big-Government/2013/05/12/Democrats-split-on-Benghazi.

130 Ben Shapiro, "WH: Republicans 'Owe Ambassador Rice an Apology' for Benghazi Criticisms," Breitbart.com, May 19, 2013, http://www.breitbart.com/Big-Government/2013/05/19/WH-GOP-apologize-Rice.

131 Ben Shapiro, "Colbert Mocks Benghazi Hearings as Unimportant," Breitbart.com, May 8, 2013, http://www.breitbart.com/Big-Hollywood/2013/05/08/Colbert-mocks-Benghazi-hearings.

132 Bigelow, "Politico: Media Didn't Ignore Benghazi."

133 Ben Shapiro, "White House Meets Privately with Press to Discuss Benghazi," Breitbart.com, May 10, 2013, http://www.breitbart.com/Big-Peace/2013/05/10/White-House-Benghazi-off-the-record.

134 Ben Shapiro, "White House: Buck Stops with Hillary on Libya," Breitbart .com, October 12, 2012, http://www.breitbart.com/Big-Peace/2012/10/12 /White-House-Buck-Stops-Hillary-Libya.

135 "In Context: Hillary Clinton's 'What Difference Does It Make' Comment," Politifact.com, May 8, 2013, http://www.politifact.com/truth-o-meter/ article/2013/may/08/context-hillary-clintons-what-difference-does-it-m/.

136 Glenn Kessler, "Has Anyone Been 'Fired' Because of the Benghazi Attacks?," WashingtonPost.com, May 22, 2013, http://www.washingtonpost.com/blogs /fact-checker/post/has-anyone-been-fired-because-of-the-benghazi-attacks /2013/05/21/c29657aa-c27b-11e2-914f-a7aba60512a7_blog.html.

137 Josh Rogin, "Kerry Clears Benghazi Officials Clinton Punished," TheDaily Beast.com, August 19, 2013, http://www.thedailybeast.com/articles/2013 /08/19/kerry-clears-benghazi-officials-clinton-punished.html.

138 Ben Shapiro, "Obama to Promote Benghazi Talking Points Manipulator," Breitbart.com, May 24, 2013, http://www.breitbart.com/Big-Peace/2013/05 /24/Obama-Benghazi-Nuland.

139 Meredith Shiner, "Graham, McCain Praise Obama's Pick of Nu-land," RollCall.com, May 24, 2013, http://blogs.rollcall.com/wgdb /graham-mccain-praise-obamas-pick-of-nuland/.

140 Allahpundit, "Bad News: Turns Out It's Sexist and Racist to Criticize Susan Rice for Giving Bad Information to the Public," HotAir.com, November 16, 2012, http://hotair.com/archives/2012/11/16/bad-news-turns-out-its-sexist -and-racist-to-criticize-susan-rice-for-giving-bad-information-to-the-public/.

141 Jeff Poor, "Kirsten Powers calls Obama's Defense of Susan Rice 'Silly, Sexist,' and 'Paternalistic,'" DailyCaller.com, November 15, 2012, http://dailycaller .com/2012/11/15/kirsten-powers-calls-obamas-defense-of-susan-rice-silly -sexist-and-paternalistic/.

142 "D/SecState on 2012 State Department Awards: 32 of Our Very Best," Diplopundit .net, January 15, 2013, http://diplopundit.net/tag/g-kathleen-hill/.

143 State, February 2013 http://digitaledition.state.gov/publication/?i=143879 &p=16.

144 "Press Briefing by Press Secretary Jay Carney," June 11, 2013, http://www.white house.gov/the-press-office/2013/06/11/press-briefing-press-secretary-jay-carney -6112013.

145 Associated Press, "Petraeus Testimony on Benghazi Contradicts Previous House Statement," Guardian (U.K.), November 16, 2012, http:// www.the-guardian.com/world/2012/nov/16/petraeus-testimony-benghazi -contradicts.

146 Elspeth Reeve, "Mike Morell Swears He's Quitting CIA for His Family (Not

Benghazi), for 'Real,'" TheAtlanticWire.com, June 12, 2013, http://www
.theatlanticwire.com/politics/2013/06/mike-morell-cia/66179/.

147 Daniel Halper, "Panetta Steps Down for 'Walnut Farm,' to Deal 'with a Different Set of Nuts," TheWeeklyStandard.com, January 7, 2013, http://www
.weeklystandard.com/blogs/panetta-steps-down-walnut-farm-deal-different
-set-nuts_694105.html.

148 Jessica Chasmar, "Jeb Bush to Award Hillary Clinton with 2013 Liberty
Medal," WashingtonTimes.com, June 27, 2013, http://www.washingtontimes
.com/news/2013/jun/27/jeb-bush-award-hillary-clinton-2013-liberty-medal/.

149 "Hillary Clinton Resigns as 67th Secretary of State Leaving Behind Legacy
of Most Countries Visited," *Daily Mail* (U.K.), February 2, 2013, http://
www.dailymail.co.uk/news/article-2272235/Hillary-Clinton-resigns-67th
-secretary-state-leaving-legacy-countries-visited.html.

150 "Remarks by the President in a Press Conference," WhiteHouse.gov,
August 9, 2013, http://www.whitehouse.gov/the-press-office/2013/08/09
/remarks-president-press-conference.

151 "Judge Kaufman's Statement Upon Sentencing the Rosenbergs," University of Missouri–Kansas City, http://law2.umkc.edu/faculty/projects/ftrials
/rosenb/ROS_SENT.HTM.

152 "Authorization for the Use of Military Force," S.J.Res.23, September 14,
2001, http://news.findlaw.com/hdocs/docs/terrorism/sjres23.enr.html.

153 "Yes We Can: Obama Waives Anti-terrorism Provisions to Arm Syrian rebels," RT.com, September 17, 2013, http://rt.com/usa/obama-terrorist-arms
-supply-966/.

154 Guy Benson, "Lawyer for Benghazi Whistle-blower: The Administration is Obstructing Justice," Townhall.com, May 1, 2013, http://townhall.com/tipsheet/
guybenson/2013/05/01/lawyer-for-benghazi-whistleblower-the-administration
-is-obstructing-justice-n1584304.

Count 2: Involuntary Manslaughter

1 Jonathan Clark, "Elite Team Was Trained to Flush Out Border Bandits," *Nogales International,* December 16, 2010, http://www.nogalesinternational.com
/news/elite-team-was-trained-to-flush-out-border-bandits/article_1197c315
-cebd-5ef7-b1e2-b24877e92407.html.

2 Richard A. Serrano, "Gun Store Owner Had Misgivings About ATF Sting,"
Los Angeles Times, September 11, 2011, http://articles.latimes.com/2011/sep
/11/nation/la-na-atf-guns-20110912.

3 Sari Horwitz, "A Gunrunning Sting Gone Fatally Wrong," Washington
-Post.com, July 25, 2011, http://www.washingtonpost.com/investigations

/us-anti-gunrunning-effort-turns-fatally-wrong/2011/07/14/gIQAH5d6YI _print.html.

4 Edwin Mora, "State Department: Mexican Drug Cartel Activity Is 'Consistent with' Terrorism," CNSNews.com, October 17, 2011, http://www.cnsnews .com/news/article/state-department-mexican-drug-cartel-activity-consistent -terrorism.

5 Janet Pickel, "Middletown Bar Owner Charged After Customer's Fatal Crash," Pennlive.com, February 23, 2009, http://www.pennlive.com/midstate /index.ssf/2009/02/middletown_bar_owner_charged_a.html.

6 "Department of Justice Cartel Strategy, October 2009," WashingtonPost .com, http://www.washingtonpost.com/wp-srv/nation/documents/atf-fast -and-furious-2.html.

7 "January 2010 Phoenix Briefing Paper," WashingtonPost.com, http://www .washingtonpost.com/wp-srv/nation/documents/atf-fast-and-furious-3.html.

8 Katie Pavlich, *Fast and Furious: Barack Obama's Bloodiest Scandal and Its Shameless Cover-Up* (Washington, D.C.: Regnery, 2012), 50–51.

9 Joint Staff Report, "Part I of III: *Fast and Furious: The Anatomy of a Failed Operation,*" Prepared for Rep. Darrell E. Issa and Senator Charles E. Grassley, 112th Congress, July 31, 2012, http://oversight.house.gov/wp-content /uploads/2012/07/7-31-12-FF-Part-I-FINAL-REPORT.pdf.

10 John Solomon, "Gun-Running Sting Blows Up," TheDailyBeast.com, June 15, 2011, http://www.thedailybeast.com/articles/2011/06/15/gun-running -sting-blows-up-house-hearings-on-atf-s-fast-and-furious.html.

11 Horwitz, "A Gunrunning Sting Gone Fatally Wrong."

12 Kim Murphy and Ken Ellingwood, "Mexico Demands Answers on Guns," LATimes.com, March 11, 2011, http://articles.latimes.com/2011/mar/11 /nation/la-naw-mexico-guns-20110311.

13 Horwitz, "A Gunrunning Sting Gone Fatally Wrong."

14 Katie Pavlich, "ATF Managers Lawyer Up, Slam Gun Laws, and Still Deny Gunwalking," Townhall.com, March 21, 2012, http://townhall.com /columnists/katiepavlich/2012/03/21/atf_managers_lawyer_up_slam_gun _laws_and_still_deny_gunwalking/page/full.

15 Horwitz, "A Gunrunning Sting Gone Fatally Wrong."

16 Ibid.

17 Email from David J. Voth to Phoenix Group VII, Subject: Monday Morning Meeting, Strike Force 9:30 a.m., Friday, March 12, 2010, 7:34 p.m., http://www .washingtonpost.com/wp-srv/nation/documents/atf-fast-and-furious-1.html.

18 Email from David J. Voth to Emory Hurley and George Gillett, Subject: No Pressure but Perhaps an Increased Sense of Urgency, Friday, April 2, 2010,

10:31 a.m., http://www.washingtonpost.com/wp-srv/nation/documents/atf-fast-and-furious-1.html.

19 Email exchanges, NPR.org http://www.npr.org/assets/news/2012/01/DOJdocs.pdf.

20 Email from David J. Voth to Hope A. MacAllister, Subject: No More Rose Colored Glasses, Wednesday, December 15, 2010, 6:49 p.m., http://www.grassley.senate.gov/about/upload/Voth-Eban-docs.pdf.

21 Pavlich, *Fast and Furious,* 66–67.

22 Letter from Senator Charles Grassley to ATF Acting Director Kenneth Melson, January 27, 2011, http://grassley.senate.gov/about/upload/Judiciary-01-27-11-letter-to-ATF-SW-Border-strategy.pdf.

23 Letter from Assistant Attorney General Ronald Weich to Senator Charles Grassley, February 4, 2011, http://www.washingtonpost.com/wp-srv/nation/documents/atf-fast-and-furious-1.html.

24 Murphy and Ellingwood, "Mexico Demands Answers on Guns."

25 Katie Pavlich, "Operation Fast and Furious: Designed to Promote Gun Control," Townhall.com, July 13, 2011, http://townhall.com/tipsheet/katiepavlich/2011/07/13/operation_fast_and_furious_designed_to_promote_gun_control.

26 Sari Horwitz and James V. Grimaldi, "U.S. Gun Dealers with the Most Firearms Traced over the Past Four Years," *Washington Post,* December 13, 2010, http://www.washingtonpost.com/wp-dyn/content/article/2010/12/12/AR2010121202667.html.

27 Sharyl Attkisson, "Documents: ATF Used 'Fast and Furious' to Make the Case for Gun Regulations," CBSNews.com, December 7, 2011, http://www.cbsnews.com/8301-31727_162-57338546-10391695/documents-atf-used-fast-and-furious-to-make-the-case-for-gun-regulations/.

28 "Brian Terry Family Sues Officials over Fast and Furious," Associated Press, December 14, 2012, http://www.politico.com//story/2012/12/brian-terry-family-sues-officials-over-fast-and-furious-85110.html.

29 Murphy and Ellingwood, "Mexico Demands Answers on Guns."

30 Sharyl Attkisson, "3 More Murders Linked to Gunwalker," CBSNews.com, September 14, 2011, http://www.cbsnews.com/8301-31727_162-20106253-10391695.html.

31 Murphy and Ellingwood, "Mexico Demands Answers on Guns."

32 Allahpundit, "Report: At Least 200 Murders in Mexico Now Linked to Fast & Furious Weapons," HotAir.com, September 20, 2011, http://hotair.com/archives/2011/09/20/report-at-least-200-murders-in-mexico-now-linked-to-fast-furious-weapons/.

33 Interview with President Barack Obama, Univision, March 23, 2011.

34 Devin Dwyer, "Obama on 'Fast and Furious': 'People Who Have Screwed Up Will Be Held Accountable,'" ABCNews.com, October 18, 2011, http://abcnews.go.com/blogs/politics/2011/10/obama-on-fast-and-furious-people-who-have-screwed-up-will-be-held-accountable/.

35 Pavlich, *Fast and Furious*, 136–37.

36 Letter from Assistant Attorney General Ronald Weich to Senator Charles Grassley, March 2, 2011, http://www.washingtonpost.com/wp-srv/nation/documents/atf-fast-and-furious-1.html.

37 Sharyl Attkisson, "ATF Fast and Furious: New Documents Show Attorney General Eric Holder Was Briefed in July 2010," CBSNews.com, October 3, 2011, http://www.cbsnews.com/8301-31727_162-20115038-10391695.html.

38 Michael F. Walther, Memorandum to the Attorney General Through the Acting Deputy Attorney General, July 5, 2010, http://www.cbsnews.com/htdocs/pdf/pdf_40_43.pdf.

39 Memorandum from Assistant Attorney General Lanny A. Breuer to Attorney General Eric Holder and Acting Deputy Attorney General, November 1, 2010, http://www.cbsnews.com/htdocs/pdf/pdf_65_67.pdf.

40 Email from James Trusty to Jamie Weinstein, RE: OCGS Weekly Report, Monday, October 18, 2010, 9:21 a.m., http://www.cbsnews.com/htdocs/pdf/pdf_64.pdf.

41 Tim Mak, "Issa Subpoenas Holder on Fast & Furious," Politico.com, October 12, 2011, http://www.politico.com/news/stories/1011/65759.html.

42 Pavlich, *Fast and Furious*, 130–31.

43 Richard A. Serrano, "Obama Invokes Executive Privilege over Fast and Furious Documents," LATimes.com, June 20, 2012, http://articles.latimes.com/2012/jun/20/news/la-pn-obama-invokes-executive-privilege-over-fast-and-furious-documents-20120620.

44 Jordy Yager, "Justice Department Report Clears Holder, but Faults DOJ, ATF Officials," TheHill.com, September 19, 2012, http://thehill.com/homenews/administration/250575-report-clears-holder-hits-doj-atf-officials.

45 Richard A. Serrano, "White House Aide Declined to Cooperate in Fast and Furious Probe," *Los Angeles Times*, September 20, 2012, http://articles.latimes.com/2012/sep/20/nation/la-na-fast-furious-20120921.

46 Fred Lucas, "WH Aide Involved in Fast and Furious Was 'Suddenly' Transferred to Iraq; Issa Threatens Subpoena," CNSNews.com, October 1, 2012, http://cnsnews.com/news/article/wh-aide-involved-fast-and-furious-was-suddenly-transferred-iraq-issa-threatens-subpoena.

47 Mary Chastain, "WH Employee with Knowledge of Fast & Furi-

ous Returns from Iraq After IG Clears Holder," Breitbart.com, October 12, 2012, http://www.breitbart.com/Big-Government/2012/10/12 /White-House-Link-To-Fast-and-Furious-Is-Back-In-America.

48 "Transcript: Univision's 'Meet the Candidate' Forum with President Obama," Latinalista.com, September 20, 2012, http://latinalista.com/2012/09/transcript -univisions-meet-the-candidate-forum-with-president-obama.

49 Tom Fitton, *The Corruption Chronicles: Obama's Big Secrecy, Big Corruption, and Big Government* (New York: Threshold Editions, 2012), 287.

50 "Transcript: Univision's 'Meet the Candidate' Forum with President Obama."

51 Pavlich, *Fast and Furious*, 82.

52 "CBS News Confirms Sharyl Attkisson's Computer Hacked," CBSNews .com, June 14, 2013, http://www.cbsnews.com/8301-201_162-57589367 /cbs-news-confirms-sharyl-attkissons-computer-hacked/.

53 Katie Pavlich, "The Smearing of Fast and Furious Whistleblower John Dodson," Townhall.com, October 3, 2012, http://townhall.com/columnists /katiepavlich/2012/10/03/the_smearing_of_fast_and_furious_whistleblower _john_dodson/page/full.

54 Pavlich, *Fast and Furious*, 114–21.

55 "ATF Director Reassigned; U.S. Attorney Out Amid 'Fast and Furious' Uproar," FoxNews.com, August 30, 2011.

56 Chris W. Cox, "'Fast and Furious' Agents Get Promoted," Newsmax.com, August 25, 2011, http://www.newsmax.com/Newsfront/fast-furious-Newell -Voth/2011/08/25/id/408717.

57 Katie Pavlich, "ATF Managers Lawyer Up, Slam Gun Laws, and Still Deny Gunwalking," Townhall.com, March 21, 2012, http://townhall.com /columnists/katiepavlich/2012/03/21/atf_managers_lawyer_up_slam_gun _laws_and_still_deny_gunwalking/page/full.

58 Sharyl Attkisson, "Heads Roll After Fast and Furious Investigation," CBSNews.com, December 5, 2012, http://www.cbsnews.com/8301-201 _162-57557358/heads-roll-after-fast-and-furious-investigation/.

59 Cox, "'Fast and Furious' Agents Get Promoted."

60 Attkisson, "Heads Roll After Fast and Furious Investigation."

61 William La Jeunesse, "Ex-ATF Official's Gun Ends Up at Mexican Cartel Shootout That Killed Beauty Queen," FoxNews.com, December 19, 2012, http://www.foxnews.com/politics/2012/12/19/ex-atf-official-gun-ends-up-at -mexican-cartel-shootout-that-killed-beauty-queen/.

62 Attkisson, "Heads Roll After Fast and Furious Investigation."

63 Ibid.

64 Matthew Boyle, "ATF Official Resigns After Issa, Grassley Nail Him in Congressional Fast and Furious Report," DailyCaller.com, August 2, 2012, http://dailycaller.com/2012/08/02/atf-official-resigns-after-issa-grassley-nail-him-in-congressional-fast-and-furious-report/.

65 Horwitz, "A Gunrunning Sting Gone Fatally Wrong."

66 Evan Perez and Devlin Barrett, "Head of ATF Is Likely to Go," WSJ.com, June 18, 2011, http://online.wsj.com/article/SB10001424052702304453304576392023631543738.html.

67 Horwitz, "A Gunrunning Sting Gone Fatally Wrong."

68 Jerry Markon and Sari Horwitz, "ATF Head Kenneth Melson Reassigned amid Gun-Trafficking Probe," Washington Post, August 30, 2011, http://articles.washingtonpost.com/2011-08-30/politics/35269510_1_kenneth-e-melson-operation-fast-fast-and-furious.

69 "Kenneth E. Melson," George Washington University School of Law website http://www.law.gwu.edu/faculty/profile.aspx?id=3241.

70 Attkisson, "Heads Roll After Fast and Furious Investigation."

71 "Gary G. Grindler," King & Spalding http://www.kslaw.com/people/Gary-Grindler.

72 Jordy Yager, "DOJ Criminal Division Chief Breuer Resigns," TheHill.com, January 30, 2013, http://thehill.com/homenews/administration/280133-doj-criminal-division-chief-breuer-steps-down.

73 "Lanny A. Breuer," Cov.com, http://www.cov.com/lbreuer/.

74 Mike Levine, "Justice Official Leaving for Law School Post After Criticism over 'Fast and Furious' Claim," FoxNews.com, April 25, 2012, http://www.foxnews.com/politics/2012/04/25/top-justice-figure-in-fast-and-furious-leaving-department-to-head-up-law-school/.

75 "ATF Director Reassigned; U.S. Attorney Out Amid 'Fast and Furious' Uproar," FoxNews.com, August 30, 2011, http://www.foxnews.com/politics/2011/08/30/sources-atf-director-to-be-reassigned-amid-fast-and-furious-uproar/.

76 Letter from Dennis K. Burke to President Barack Obama, August 30, 2011, http://www.cbsnews.com/htdocs/pdf/0830burke-resignation-letter.pdf.

77 Department of Justice Office of Public Affairs, "Statement of Attorney General Eric Holder on the Resignation of U.S. Attorney for the District of Arizona Dennis Burke," Tuesday, August 30, 2011, http://www.justice.gov/opa/pr/2011/August/11-ag-1111.html.

78 Charlie Savage, "Ex-U.S. Attorney in Arizona Is Criticized for Leak to Fox," NYTimes.com, May 20, 2013, http://www.nytimes.com/2013/05/21/us/politics/dennis-k-burke-criticized-for-fast-and-furious-leak.html.?_r=0.

79 Sharyl Attkisson, "Family of Border Patrol Agent Brian Terry Sues U.S. Government," CBSNews.com, February 1, 2012, http://www.cbsnews.com /8301-31727_162-57370092-10391695/family-of-border-patrol-agent-brian -terry-sues-u.s-government/.

80 Complaint, *Kent Terry, Sr. and Josephine Terry vs. William Newell, et al.* (2012).

81 "Border Patrol Agent Brian Terry's Family Sues 6 from ATF, Gun Store Owner," AZStarnet.com, December 15, 2012, http://azstarnet.com/news /local/border/border-patrol-agent-brian-terry-s-family-sues-from-atf/article _39a9730f-fdb9-5dd7-9e19-8d00662f4f0a.html.

82 *The Daily Show with Jon Stewart* (Comedy Central), June 21, 2011.

83 *The Daily Show with Jon Stewart* (Comedy Central), June 26, 2012.

84 Taylor Rose, "Author: Documents 'Damning' for Holder," WND.com, April 7, 2013. http://www.wnd.com/2013/04/author-documents-damning-for-holder/.

Count 3: Violation of Internal Revenue Laws

1 Rory Carroll, *Comandante: Hugo Chavez's Venezuela* (New York: Penguin Press, 2013), 176–77.

2 Yolanda Ojeda Reyes, "Firmar Contra Chavez Es Un Acto De Terror Smo," ElUniversal.com, March 21, 2004, http://www.eluniversal.com/2004/03/21 /pol_art_21108A.

3 Carroll, *Comandante*, 103–104, 179.

4 Ibid., 134.

5 Glenn Harlan Reynolds, "Tax Audits Are No Laughing Matter," WSJ.com, May 18, 2009, http://online.wsj.com/article/SB124260113149028331 .html.

6 Jason Scott Smith, *Building New Deal Liberalism: The Political Economy of Public Works, 1933–1956* (Cambridge: Cambridge University Press), 180.

7 "Criminal Tax Manual 17.00—26 U.S.C. §7212(a) 'OMNIBUS CLAUSE,'" Department of Justice, May 2001, http://www.justice.gov/tax /readingroom/2001ctm/17ctax.htm.

8 David Burnham, "Misuse of the IRS: The Abuse of Power," *New York Times*, September 3, 1989, http://www.nytimes.com/1989/09/03/magazine/misuse -of-the-irs-the-abuse-of-power.html.?pagewanted=all&src=pm.

9 John Gizzi, "IRS Political Abuse Started Long Before Tea Party," Newsmax .com, May 13, 2013, http://www.newsmax.com/Newsfront/irs-tea-party -political/2013/05/13/id/504108.

10 Burton W. Folsom, *New Deal or Raw Deal?* (New York: Threshold Editions, 2008), 164.

11 Burnham, "Misuse of the IRS."

12 Gizzi, "IRS Political Abuse Started Long Before Tea Party."

13 J. D. Tuccille, "IRS Has a Long History of Political Abuse," Reason.com, May 13, 2013, http://reason.com/blog/2013/05/13/irs-has-a-long-history-of-political-abus.

14 http://www.forbes.com/sites/kellyphillipserb/2014/01/20/why-justice-matters-the-indictment-trial-of-dr-martin-luther-king-on-tax-charges/.

15 http://www.realclearpolitics.com/lists/irs-scandal/american_communists.html?state=stop.

16 "JFK Used Audits to Silence Critics," WND.com, September 5, 2003, http://www.wnd.com/2003/09/20617/.

17 Burnham, "Misuse of the IRS."

18 Gizzi, "IRS Political Abuse Started Long Before Tea Party."

19 http://www.realclearpolitics.com/lists/irs-scandal/american_communists.html?state=stop.

20 http://www.realclearpolitics.com/lists/irs-scandal/american_communists.html?state=stop.

21 Todd Keister, "The IRS: Destroying Liberty Since Before You Were Born," AmericanThinker.com, May 22, 2013, http://www.americanthinker.com/2013/05/m-the_irs_destroying_liberty_since_before_you_were_born.html.

22 George T. Bell, "Memorandum: The White House, Subject: Opponents List," June 24, 1971, https://en.wikisource.org/wiki/Dealing_with_our_Political_Enemies.

23 "History of IRS Abuse," RealClearPolitics.com, http://www.realclearpolitics.com/lists/irs-scandal/introduction.html.

24 Michael Scherer, "New IRS Scandal Echoes a Long History of Political Harassment," Time.com, May 14, 2013, http://swampland.time.com/2013/05/14/anger-over-irs-audits-of-conservatives-anchored-in-long-history-of-abuse/#ixzz2TMyxsVPZ.

25 Gizzi, "IRS Political Abuse Started Long Before Tea Party."

26 Tom Fitton, *The Corruption Chronicles* (New York: Threshold Editions, 2012), 16–19.

27 "History of IRS Abuse," RealClearPolitics.com, http://www.realclearpolitics.com/lists/irs-scandal/introduction.html.

28 David Mendell, "Obama Lets Opponent Do Talking," ChicagoTribune.com, June 24, 2004, http://www.chicagotribune.com/chi-0406240383jun24,0,6662127.story.

29 Ann Coulter, "Obama's Signature Move: Unsealing Private Records," Hu-

manEvents.com, August 1, 2012, http://www.humanevents.com/2012/08/01/ann-coulter-obamas-signature-move-unsealing-private-records/.

30   Imaeyen Ibanga and Russell Goldman, "America's Overnight Sensation Joe the Plumber Owes $1,200 in Taxes," ABCNews.com, October 16, 2008, http://abcnews.go.com/GMA/Vote2008/story?id=6047360&page=1.

31   Randy Ludlow, "Government Computers Used to Find Information on Joe the Plumber," *Columbus Dispatch,* October 24, 2008, http://www.dispatch.com/content/stories/local/2008/10/24/joe.html.

32   Ibid.

33   "Database Plumbed about 'Joe,'" WashingtonTimes.com, October 26, 2008, http://www.washingtontimes.com/news/2008/oct/26/database-plumbed-about-joe/.

34   Mary Pat Flaherty, "Ohio IG Report: Joe the Plumber's Records Were Improperly Searched," WashingtonPost.com, November 20, 2008, http://voices.washingtonpost.com/44/2008/11/20/ohio_ig_report_joe_the_plumber.html.

35   Associated Press, "Agency Director Resigns After Spying on 'Joe the Plumber' on State Computers," FoxNews.com, December 17, 2008, http://www.foxnews.com/politics/2008/12/17/agency-director-resigns-spying-joe-plumber-state-computers/.

36   Michal Elseth, "'Joe the Plumber' Loses Suit over File-Snooping," Washington Times.com, August 5, 2010, http://www.washingtontimes.com/news/2010/aug/5/joe-the-plumber-loses-suit-over-file-snooping/.

37   Jeffrey M. Jones, "Obama's Initial Approval Ratings in Historical Context," Gallup.com, January 26, 2009, http://www.gallup.com/poll/113968/obama-initial-approval-ratings-historical-context.aspx.

38   Kevin Hecthkopf, "Poll: Obama Approval Rating Dips Slightly," CBSNews.com, September 1, 2009, http://www.cbsnews.com/8301-503544_162-5280405-503544.html.

39   Alexander Burns, "Obama Targets Tea Bags at Town Hall," Politico.com, April 29, 2009, http://www.politico.com/news/stories/0409/21870.html.

40   Julie Percha, "President Obama: GOP Opposition to Stimulus 'Helped to Create the Tea-Baggers,'" ABCNews.com, May 4, 2010, http://abcnews.go.com/blogs/politics/2010/05/president-obama-gop-opposition-to-stimulus-helped-to-create-the-teabaggers/.

41   Kenneth T. Walsh, "Obama Says Race a Key Component in Tea Party Protests," USNews.com, March 2, 2011, http://www.usnews.com/news/articles/2011/03/02/obama-says-race-a-key-component-in-tea-party-protests_print.html.

42   "NBC News Takes on Tea Party 'Terrorists,'" FoxNews.com, July 29, 2011,

http://nation.foxnews.com/nbc-news/2011/07/29/nbc-news-takes-tea-party
-terrorists-theyre-strapped-dynamite-sitting-middle-time-square-rush-hour.

43 Joe Klein, "Republicans' Debt Ceiling Charade Is Downright Dangerous," Time.com, July 28, 2011, http://swampland.time.com/2011/07/28
/republicans-dangerous-debt-ceiling-charade/.

44 "Rightwing Extremism: Current Economic and Political Climate Fueling
Resurgence in Radicalization and Recruitment," U.S. Department of Homeland Security, April 7, 2009, http://michellemalkinblog.files.wordpress.com
/2009/04/hsa-rightwing-extremism-09-04-07.pdf.

45 Eliana Johnson, "E-mails Suggest Collusion Between FEC, IRS to Target
Conservative Groups," NationalReview.com, July 31, 2013, http://www
.nationalreview.com/corner/354801/e-mails-suggest-collusion-between-fec
-irs-target-conservative-groups-eliana-johnson.

46 "Obama's State of the Union address: Criticism of the Supreme Court
Campaign Finance Ruling," LATimes.com, January 27, 2010, http://
latimesblogs.latimes.com/washington/2010/01/obamas-state-of-the-union
-address-criticism-of-the-supreme-court-campaign-finance-ruling.html.

47 Eric Lichtblau, "Republicans See a Political Motive in IRS Audits," NYTimes.com,
October 6, 2010, http://www.nytimes.com/2010/10/07/us/politics/07irs.html.

48 Eliana Johnson, "The Missing Koch Report," NationalReview.com, August 20,
2013, http://www.nationalreview.com/article/356260/missing-koch-report
-eliana-johnson.

49 Lichtblau, "Republicans See a Political Motive in IRS Audits."

50 Jake Tapper and Sunlen Miller, "J'Accuse! President Obama Says Chamber of
Commerce Using Foreign Funds to Influence U.S. Elections," ABCNews.com,
October 7, 2010, http://abcnews.go.com/blogs/politics/2010/10/obama-says
-chamber-of-commerce-using-foreign-funds-to-influence-us-elections/.

51 John Sexton, "Lois Lerner Discusses Political Pressure on the IRS in 2010,"
Breitbart.com, August 6, 2013, http://www.breitbart.com/InstaBlog/2013
/08/06/Lois-Lerner-Discusses-Political-Pressure-on-the-IRS-in-2010.

52 Steven Sloan, "Shulman Says IRS Will Focus on 'High Risk' Return Preparers," BusinessWeek.com, November 15, 2011, http://www
.businessweek.com/news/2011-11-15/shulman-says-irs-will-focus-on-high
-risk-return-preparers.html.

53 "Senate Democrats Urge IRS to Impose Strict Cap on Political Spending by
Nonprofit Groups—Vow Legislation if Agency Doesn't Act," Schumer.Senate
.gov, March 12, 2012, http://www.schumer.senate.gov/Newsroom/record
.cfm?id=336270.

54 Jonathan Weisman, "Scrutiny of Political Nonprofits Sets Off Claim of Ha-

rassment," NYTimes.com, March 6, 2012, http://www.nytimes.com/2012/03/07/us/politics/irs-scrutiny-of-political-groups-stirs-harassment-claim.html.?pagewanted=all&_r=0.

55 "Former IRS Chief Shulman Reportedly Visited White House at Least 157 Times," FoxNews.com, May 30, 2013, http://www.foxnews.com/politics/2013/05/30/former-irs-chief-shulman-reportedly-visited-white-house-at-least-157-times/.

56 Caroline May, "Shulman Never Looked Into IRS Targeting, Though 132 Congressmen Contacted Him," DailyCaller.com, May 22, 2013, http://dailycaller.com/2013/05/22/shulman-never-checked-out-irs-targeting-though-132-congressmen-contacted-him/.

57 "Former IRS Chief Shulman Reportedly Visited White House at Least 157 Times," FoxNews.com, May 30, 2013, http://www.foxnews.com/politics/2013/05/30/former-irs-chief-shulman-reportedly-visited-white-house-at-least-157-times/.

58 "Flashback: Doug Shulman in March 2012: 'There Is Absolutely No Targeting,'" FreeBeacon.com, May 13, 2013, http://freebeacon.com/flashback-doug-shulman-in-march-2012-there-is-absolutely-no-targeting/.

59 "Issa Talks IRS Targeting Investigation, Previews Thursday's Conference Spending Hearing on CNN SOTU," House Committee on Oversight & Government Reform, June 2, 2013 http://oversight.house.gov/release/issa-talks-irs-targeting-investigation-previews-thursdays-irs-conference-spending-hearing-on-cnn-sotu/.

60 Treasury Inspector General for Tax Administration, "Inappropriate Criteria Were Used to Identify Tax-Exempt Applications for Review," Treasury.gov, May 14, 2013, http://www.treasury.gov/tigta/auditreports/2013reports/201310053fr.pdf.

61 "Lois Lerner's Own Words," WSJ.com, September 11, 2013, http://online.wsj.com/article/SB10001424127887324549004579068914192280866.html.?mod=opinion_newsreel.

62 Treasury Inspector General for Tax Administration, "Inappropriate Criteria Were Used to Identify Tax-Exempt Applications for Review."

63 Gregory Korte, "IRS List Reveals Concerns over Tea Party 'Propaganda,'" USAToday.com, September 18, 2013, http://www.usatoday.com/story/news/politics/2013/09/17/irs-tea-party-target-list-propaganda/2825003/.

64 Treasury Inspector General for Tax Administration, "Inappropriate Criteria Were Used to Identify Tax-Exempt Applications for Review."

65 "Lois Lerner's Own Words," WSJ.com, September 11, 2013, http://online.wsj.com/article/SB10001424127887324549004579068914192280866.html.?mod=opinion_newsreel.

66 Patrick Howley, "White House, IRS Exchanged Confidential Taxpayer Info," DailyCaller.com, October 9, 2013, http://dailycaller.com/2013/10/09 /white-house-irs-exchanged-confidential-taxpayer-info/.

67 Patrick Howley, "155 White House Meetings Involved Key IRS Scandal Figures," DailyCaller.com, October 10, 2013, dailycaller.com/2013/10/10 /irs-white-house-officials-that-shared-confidential-taxpayer-info-had-155 -white-house-meetings/.

68 Matthew Boyle, "Romney Donor VanderSloot: I Was Audited Twice by IRS, Once by DOL & Investigated by Former Senate Staffer," Breitbart .com, May 19, 2013, http://www.breitbart.com/Big-Government/2013 /05/19/Businessman-Frank-VanderSloot-I-was-audited-twice-by-IRS-once -by-DOL-investigated-by-Senate-staffer-after-giving-1-million-to-Romney -Super-PAC.

69 Sean Higgins, "Major GOP Donor Sheldon Adelson Scrutinized by IRS," WashingtonExaminer.com, May 14, 2013, http://washingtonexaminer .com/major-gop-donor-sheldon-adelson-scrutinized-by-irs/article/2529649 ?custom_click=rss.

70 Joel B. Pollak, "Obama Now Scapegoating Jewish Donor Adelson," Breitbart .com, August 8, 2012, http://www.breitbart.com/Big-Government/2012/08 /08/Obama-Now-Scapegoating-Jewish-Donor-Adelson.

71 "Conservative Group Claims It Has Proof IRS Leaked Donor List," FoxNews.com, June 4, 2013, http://www.foxnews.com/politics/2013/06/04 /chairman-anti-gay-marriage-group-says-has-proof-irs-leaked-donor-details/.

72 Kim Barker and Justin Elliott, "IRS Office That Targeted Tea Party Also Disclosed Confidential Docs from Conservative Groups," ProPublica .org, May 13, 2013, http://www.propublica.org/article/irs-office-that-targeted -tea-party-also-disclosed-confidential-docs.

73 Paul Sperry, "IRS Gave Black Nonprofits Preferential Treatment," Investors .com, September 6, 2013 http://news.investors.com/ibd-editorials-viewpoint /090613-670166-irs-holder-advised-black-nonprofits-tax-law.htm?p=full.

74 Associated Press, "IRS Admits Bias Against Conservative Political Groups for Tax-Exempt Status," *Guardian* (U.K.), May 10, 2013, http://www.theguardian .com/world/2013/may/10/irs-bias-conservative-tax-status.

75 Gregory Korte, "Planted Question Gambit Backfires on IRS Officials," USAToday.com, May 18, 2013, http://www.usatoday.com/story/news/politics /2013/05/18/irs-scandal-planted-question/2216747/.

76 Aaron Blake, "'I'm Not Good at Math': The IRS's Public Relations Disaster," WashingtonPost.com, May 10, 2013, http://www.washingtonpost .com/blogs/the-fix/wp/2013/05/10/im-not-good-at-math-the-irss-public -relations-disaster/?hpid=z1.

77 Glenn Kessler, "A Bushel of Pinocchios for IRS's Lois Lerner," WashingtonPost.com, May 20, 2013, http://www.washingtonpost.com /blogs/fact-checker/post/a-bushel-of-pinocchios-for-irss-lois-lerner/2013/05 /19/771687d2-bfdd-11e2-9b09-1638acc3942e_blog.html.

78 Juliet Eilperin and Zachary A. Goldfarb, "IRS Officials in Washington Were Involved in Targeting of Conservative Groups," WashingtonPost.com, May 13, 2013, http://www.washingtonpost.com/politics/obama-denounces -reported-irs-targeting-of-conservative-groups/2013/05/13/a0185644-bbdf -11e2-97d4-a479289a31f9_story.html.

79 Julie Bykowicz, "IRS Focus on Tea Parties Stirs Dissent on Health Care Law," Bloomberg.com, May 13, 2013, http://www.bloomberg.com /news/2013-05-14/irs-focus-on-tea-parties-stirs-dissent-on-health-care-law .html.

80 C. J. Ciaramella, "Target Acquired," FreeBeacon.com, May 16, 2013, http:// freebeacon.com/target-acquired/.

81 Korte, "Planted Question Gambit Backfires on IRS officials."

82 C. J. Ciaramella, "Chilling Effect," FreeBeacon.com, May 14, 2013, http:// freebeacon.com/chilling-effect/.

83 Alana Goodman, "IRS Crosses Green Line," FreeBeacon.com, May 30, 2013, http://freebeacon.com/irs-crosses-green-line/.

84 Carol D. Leonnig, "IRS Stalled Conservative Groups, but Gave Speedy Approval to Obama Foundation," WashingtonPost.com, May 16, 2013, http:// www.washingtonpost.com/politics/irs-stalled-conservative-groups-but-gave -speedy-approval-to-obama-foundation/2013/05/16/90c53e8a-be57-11e2 -89c9-3be8095fe767_story.html.

85 Chris Moody, "Conservative Group Says IRS Approved Nonprofit Status After Applying with 'Liberal-Sounding Name,'" Yahoo! News, May 15, 2013, http://news.yahoo.com/blogs/ticket/conservative-activist-green-name -gets-irs-stamp-approval-193457897.html.

86 Eilperin and Goldfarb, "IRS Officials in Washington Were Involved in Targeting of Conservative Groups."

87 "IRS Official Who Oversaw Unit Targeting Tea Party Now Heads Obama Care Office," FoxNews.com, May 17, 2013, http://www.foxnews.com /politics/2013/05/17/second-irs-official-to-leave-amid-tea-party-scandal/.

88 Eilperin and Goldfarb, "IRS Officials in Washington Were Involved in Targeting of Conservative Groups."

89 "Sen. Durbin Defends Asking IRS to Target Conservative Group," Breitbart .com, May 26, 2013, http://www.breitbart.com/Big-Government/2013/05 /26/Durbin-defends-letter-IRS.

90 Bykowicz, "IRS Focus on Tea Parties Stirs Dissent on Health Care Law."

91 Becket Adams, "Obama During Surprise News Conference: We've Fired the Acting IRS Commissioner Over Tea Party Scandal," TheBlaze .com, May 15, 2013, http://www.theblaze.com/stories/2013/05/15/watch-live -president-obama-addresses-the-irs-scandal/.

92 "Obama: Acting IRS Chief Steven Miller Resigns," Politico.com, May 15, 2013, http://www.politico.com/story/2013/05/obama-acting-irs-chief -resigns-91441.html.

93 Kelly Phillips Erb, "IRS Hearing Marks End of Their Worst. Week. Ever but Congress Signals More Hearings Are on the Way," Forbes.com, May 20, 2013, http://www.forbes.com/sites/kellyphillipserb/2013/05/20/irs-hearing -marks-end-of-their-worst-week-ever-but-congress-signals-more-hearings-are -on-the-way/.

94 "Testimony of the Honorable J. Russell George, Treasury Inspector General for Tax Administration," Hearing Before the Committee on Ways and Means, U.S. House of Representatives, May 17, 2013, http://www.scribd .com/doc/142597193/George-Testimony-IRS-Hearings.

95 Tom Cohen, "IRS Official in Charge of Targeting Unit Takes the 5th," CNN.com, May 23, 2013, http://www.cnn.com/2013/05/22/politics /irs-targeting.

96 Patrick Howley, "IRS Supporters 0-for-3 on Putting Scandal to Rest," DailyCaller .com, July 8, 2013, http://dailycaller.com/2013/07/08/irs-supporters-0-for -3-on-putting-scandal-to-rest/?print=1.

97 Kelly Phillips Erb, "IRS Issues Initial Report and Action Plan Following Tax Exempt Organization Scandal," Forbes.com, June 24, 2013, http://www .forbes.com/sites/kellyphillipserb/2013/06/24/irs-issues-initial-report-and -action-plan-following-tax-exempt-organization-scandal/.

98 Treasury Inspector General for Tax Administration, "Inappropriate Criteria Were Used to Identify Tax-Exempt Applications for Review."

99 "Issa Talks IRS Targeting Investigation, Previews Thursday's Conference Spending Hearing on CNN SOTU," House Committee on Oversight & Government Reform, June 2, 2013, http://oversight.house.gov/release/issa -talks-irs-targeting-investigation-previews-thursdays-irs-conference-spending -hearing-on-cnn-sotu/.

100 Jonathon M. Seidl, "Unraveling Narrative? New Transcripts Reveal 'Low-Level' IRS Officials Naming Names of Those in DC Who Oversaw Targeting," TheBlaze.com, June 6, 2013, http://www.theblaze.com/stories/2013/06/06 /unraveling-narrative-new-transcripts-reveal-low-level-irs-officials-naming -names-of-those-who-oversaw-targeting/.

101 "IRS Chief Counsel's Office Demanded Information on 2010 Election Activity of Tea Party Applicants," Oversight.House.Gov, July 17, 2013, http://oversight.house.gov/release/irs-chief-counsels-office-demanded-information-on-2010-election-activity-of-tea-party-applicants/.

102 Seidl, "Unraveling Narrative?"

103 Bernie Becker, "Issa Vows IRS Hearing Will Show DC Involvement in Tea Party Targeting," TheHill.com, July 18, 2013, http://thehill.com/blogs/on-the-money/domestic-taxes/312001-issa-hearing-will-show-dc-involvement-in-irs-controversy.

104 "IRS Chief Counsel's Office Demanded Information on 2010 Election Activity of Tea Party Applicants," Oversight.House.Gov, July 17, 2013, http://oversight.house.gov/release/irs-chief-counsels-office-demanded-information-on-2010-election-activity-of-tea-party-applicants/.

105 Dana Bash, "First on CNN: IRS Collects Docs from 88 Employees in Investigation," CNN.com, May 31, 2013, http://politicalticker.blogs.cnn.com/2013/05/31/first-on-cnn-irs-collects-docs-from-88-employees-in-investigation/.

106 Leticia Domenech, "IRS Scandal Shows No Signs of Slowing Down," HNGN.com, May 29, 2013, http://www.hngn.com/articles/3891/20130529/irs-scandal-shows-signs-slowing-down-more-evidence-fuels-anti.htm.

107 Stephen Ohlemacher, "IRS Supervisor in DC Scrutinized Tea Party Cases," Associated Press, June 16, 2013, http://news.yahoo.com/irs-supervisor-dc-scrutinized-tea-party-cases-222846717.html.

108 Ed O'Keefe, "Issa: 'This Is More Important than Any One Election,'" WashingtonPost.com, May 22, 2013, http://www.washingtonpost.com/blogs/post-politics/wp/2013/05/22/the-houses-irs-hearing-live-updates/?hpid=z1#liveblog-entry-42560.

109 Eliana Johnson, "Did the IRS Fire Holly Paz?," NationalReview.com, June 13, 2013, http://www.nationalreview.com/corner/350990/did-irs-fire-holly-paz-eliana-johnson.

110 Siobhan Hughes, "Rep. Issa Asks IG for Broader IRS Review," WSJ.com, July 29, 2013, http://blogs.wsj.com/washwire/2013/07/29/rep-issa-asks-ig-for-broader-irs-review/.

111 Rebekah Metzler, "House Panel Scrutinizes IRS Inspector General Report," USNews.com, July 18, 2013, http://www.usnews.com/news/articles/2013/07/18/house-panel-scrutinizes-irs-inspector-general-report.

112 Fred Lucas, "Gowdy Denounces IRS, Democrats for Ever-Shifting Defense in Tea Party-IRS Scandal," CNSNews.com, July 19, 2013, http://www

.cnsnews.com/news/article/gowdy-denounces-irs-democrats-ever-shifting-defense-tea-party-irs-scandal.

113 David Nakamura, "Carney Acknowledges 'Legitimate Criticisms' of White House's IRS Response," WashingtonPost.com, May 22, 2013, http://www.washingtonpost.com/blogs/post-politics/wp/2013/05/22/the-houses-irs-hearing-live-updates/.

114 Rich Noyes, "Broadcast Networks Drop the Ball on Obama's Smarmy 'Phony Scandal' Mantra," Newsbusters.org, August 9, 2013, http://newsbusters.org/blogs/rich-noyes/2013/08/09/broadcast-networks-drop-ball-obama-s-smarmy-phony-scandal-mantra.

115 "Carney Identifies Which Scandals Obama Thinks Are Phony: Benghazi and IRS," RealClearPolitics.com, July 31, 2013, http://www.realclearpolitics.com/video/2013/07/31/carney_identifies_which_scandals_obama_thinks_are_phony_benghazi_and_irs.html.

116 Paul Bedard, "IRS Agent: Tax Agency Is Still Targeting Tea Party Groups," WashingtonExaminer.com, August 9, 2013, http://washingtonexaminer.com/irs-agent-tax-agency-is-still-targeting-tea-party-groups/article/2534044.

117 Justin Sink, "Schock: IRS Can't Stop Illegal Behavior," TheHill.com, August 17, 2013, http://thehill.com/blogs/blog-briefing-room/news/317507-schock-irs-cant-stop-illegal-behavior.

118 Bernie Becker, "Van Hollen to Join Lawsuit Against IRS," TheHill.com, August 20, 2013, http://thehill.com/blogs/on-the-money/domestic-taxes/317937-van-hollen-campaign-finance-advocates-to-sue-irs.

119 Tom Tillison, "Homeland Security Monitors Tea Party at Florida IRS Protest," BizPacReview.com, May 21, 2013, http://www.bizpacreview.com/2013/05/21/homeland-security-monitors-tea-party-at-florida-irs-protest-71096.

120 Kelly Phillips Erb, "Defying Directive, IRS Set to Pay Out $70 Million In Employee Bonuses," Forbes.com, June 20, 2013, http://www.forbes.com/sites/kellyphillipserb/2013/06/20/defying-directive-irs-set-to-pay-out-70-million-in-employee-bonuses/.

121 "Price: 16,000 IRS Agents Will Enforce Obama Health Care Law," Politifact.com, June 29, 2012, http://www.politifact.com/georgia/statements/2012/jul/10/tom-price/price-16000-irs-agents-will-enforce-obama-health-c/.

122 Eliana Johnson, "IRS Source: Lerner Placed on Administrative Leave," NationalReview.com, May 23, 2013, http://www.nationalreview.com/corner/349199/irs-source-lerner-placed-administrative-leave-eliana-johnson.

123 Deirdre Shesgreen, "House Panel Moves to Force IRS Official to Testify,"

USAToday.com, June 28, 2013, http://www.usatoday.com/story/news/politics/2013/06/28/oversight-committee-irs-lois-lerner-issa/2471943/.

124 Katie Pavlich, "After Taking the Fifth, Lois Lerner Wants Immunity over IRS Scandal," Townhall.com, July 3, 2013, http://townhall.com/tipsheet/katiepavlich/2013/07/03/after-taking-the-fifth-lois-lerner-wants-immunity-over-irs-scandal-n1633351.

125 Angela Hunt, "Lois Lerner's Summer Vacation," WSJ.com, July 25, 2013, http://online.wsj.com/article/SB10001424127887323610704578627880966088710.html.

126 Johnson, "Did the IRS Fire Holly Paz?"

127 "IRS Official Who Oversaw Unit Targeting Tea Party Now Heads ObamaCare office," FoxNews.com, May 17, 2013, http://www.foxnews.com/politics/2013/05/17/second-irs-official-to-leave-amid-tea-party-scandal/.

128 Patrick Howley, "Separate from Shulman, IRS official Sarah Hall Ingram Recorded 165 White House Visits," DailyCaller.com, June 5, 2013, http://dailycaller.com/2013/06/05/irs-official-sarah-hall-ingram-recorded-165-white-house-visits-never-overlapped-with-shulman/.

129 Aaron Blake, "Shulman: 'I Feel Very Comfortable with My Actions,'" WashingtonPost.com, May 22, 2013 http://www.washingtonpost.com/blogs/post-politics/wp/2013/05/22/the-houses-irs-hearing-live-updates/.

130 Erb, "Defying Directive, IRS Set to Pay Out $70 Million In Employee Bonuses."

131 Allahpundit, "ABC: Yes, It's True, the Acting IRS Commissioner Was Preparing to Leave in a Few Weeks Anyway," HotAir.com, May 16, 2013, http://hotair.com/archives/2013/05/16/abc-yes-its-true-the-acting-irs-commissioner-was-preparing-to-leave-in-a-few-weeks-anyway/.

132 Eliana Johnson, "Report: IRS Lawyer Who Oversaw Tea-Party Targeting Said to Be Retiring," NationalReview.com, June 6, 2013, http://www.nationalreview.com/corner/350390/report-irs-lawyer-who-oversaw-tea-party-targeting-said-be-retiring-eliana-johnson.

133 Stephen Dinan, "Officials Thought Obama Wanted Crackdown on Tea Party Groups, Worried About Negative Press," WashingtonTimes.com, September 17, 2013, http://www.washingtontimes.com/news/2013/sep/17/report-irs-staff-acutely-aware-tea-party-antipathy/?utm_source=RSS_Feed&utm_medium=RSS.

134 Adan Salazar, "DoD Training Manual: 'Extremist' Founding Fathers 'Would Not Be Welcome in Today's Military,'" Infowars.com, August 24, 2013, http://www.infowars.com/dod-training-manual-suggests-extremist-founding-fathers-would-not-be-welcome-in-todays-military/.

135 Ben Wolfgang, "IRS Continues to Hound Tea Party Patriots, Demands More

Data for Tax-Exempt Status," WashingtonTimes.com, August 29, 2013, http://www.washingtontimes.com/news/2013/aug/29/irs-continues-to-hound-tea-party-patriots/.

136 "Big Government Meets Big Data," Economist.com, January 8, 2013, http://www.economist.com/blogs/schumpeter/2013/01/tax-evasion-italy.

137 Angus Roxburgh, *Strongman: Vladimir Putin and the Struggle for Russia* (New York: I. B. Tauris, 2013), 78.

138 Meghashyam Mali, "Poll: 76 Percent Want Special Prosecutor to Investigate IRS Scandal," TheHill.com, May 30, 2013, http://thehill.com/blogs/blog-briefing-room/news/302479-poll-76-percent-want-special-prosecutor-to-investigate-irs-scandal.

139 Dana Blanton, "Fox News Poll: Phony Scandals? Not to Voters," FoxNews.com, August 8, 2013 http://www.foxnews.com/politics/2013/08/08/fox-news-poll-phony-scandals-not-to-voters/.

Count 4: Unauthorized Disclosure of Information

1 "Osama Bin Laden Dead: Obama Speech Video and Transcript," HuffingtonPost.com, May 2, 2011, http://www.huffingtonpost.com/2011/05/02/osama-bin-laden-dead-obama-speech-video-transcript_n_856122.html.

2 "Remarks by the Vice President at the Atlantic Council's 50th Anniversary Dinner," WhiteHouse.gov, May 4, 2011, http://www.whitehouse.gov/the-press-office/2011/05/04/remarks-vice-president-atlantic-councils-50th-anniversary-dinner.

3 Jeffrey T. Kuhner, "Who Betrayed Navy SEAL Team 6?," WashingtonTimes.com, August 9, 2013, http://www.washingtontimes.com/news/2013/aug/9/kuhner-who-betrayed-navy-seal-team-6/.

4 Bob Cusack, "Congress to Probe Lethal Crash That Killed SEAL Team 6 Members," TheHill.com, July 24, 2013, http://thehill.com/homenews/house/313039-congress-to-probe-lethal-seal-crash.

5 "Helicopter Crash in Afghanistan Reportedly Kills Members of SEAL Team 6," FoxNews.com, August 6, 2011, http://www.foxnews.com/world/2011/08/06/afghan-president-31-americans-killed-in-helicopter-crash/.

6 Cusack, "Congress to Probe Lethal Crash That Killed SEAL Team 6 Members."

7 Fox News Insider, "Parents of Slain Navy SEAL: Obama Admin Put a Target on Our Son's Back," FoxNewsInsider.com, May 10, 2013, http://foxnewsinsider.com/2013/05/10/parents-navy-seal-aaron-vaughn-blast-biden-2011-helicopter-crash-killed-their-son.

8 Ann E. Marimow, "A Rare Peek into a Justice Department Leak Probe,"

Washington Post, May 19, 2013, http://articles.washingtonpost.com/2013
-05-19/local/39376688_1_press-freedom-justice-department-records.

9   Aaron Blake, "Holder: I Didn't Lie About James Rosen," WashingtonPost
.com, June 20, 2013, http://www.washingtonpost.com/blogs/post-politics
/wp/2013/06/20/holder-i-didnt-lie-about-james-rosen/.

10 Michael Isikoff, "DOJ Confirms Holder OK'd Search Warrant for Fox News
Reporter's Emails," NBCNews.com, May 27, 2013, http://investigations
.nbcnews.com/_news/2013/05/23/18451142-doj-confirms-holder-okd-search
-warrant-for-fox-news-reporters-emails.

11 Jack Mirkinson, "Obama Administration Doubled Down on Theory
That James Rosen Was a Potential Criminal," HuffingtonPost.com, May
24, 2013, http://www.huffingtonpost.com/2013/05/24/james-rosen-obama
-criminal-secret-warrant_n_3333424.html.

12 Josh Feldman, "Fox's Bret Baier Reveals That DOJ Also Seized Phone Records for
James Rosen's Parents," Mediaite.com, May 21, 2013, http://www.mediaite.com/tv
/foxs-bret-baier-reveals-that-doj-also-seized-phone-records-for-james-rosens
-parents/.

13 Blake, "Holder: I Didn't Lie About James Rosen."

14 "U.S.: CIA Thwarts New al-Qaeda Underwear Bomb," Associated Press,
May 8, 2012, http://usatoday30.usatoday.com/news/washington/story
/2012-05-07/al-qaeda-bomb-plot-foiled/54811054/1.

15 Mark Sherman, "Gov't Obtains Wide AP Phone Records in Probe,"
Associated Press, May 13, 2013, http://bigstory.ap.org/article/govt
-obtains-wide-ap-phone-records-probe.

16 Mark Hosenball, "Exclusive: Did White House Spin Tip a Covert
Op?," Reuters, May 18, 2012, http://www.reuters.com/article/2012/05/18
/us-usa-security-plot-spin-idUSBRE84H0OZ20120518.

17 Sherman, "Gov't Obtains Wide AP Phone Records in Probe."

18 Michael Calderone, Sam Stein, and Ryan J. Reilly, "AP Phone Records Seized by
Justice Department as War on Leaks Continues," HuffingtonPost.com,
May 13, 2013, http://www.huffingtonpost.com/2013/05/13/ap-phone
-records-doj-leaks_n_3268932.html.

19 Sherman, "Gov't Obtains Wide AP Phone Records in Probe."

20 Dana Milbank, "Obama, the Uninterested President," Washingtonpost.com,
May 14, 2013, http://articles.washingtonpost.com/2013-05-14/opinions
/39254536_1_phone-records-president-obama-press-secretary.

21 Chris Lawrence, Barbara Starr, and Tom Cohen, "Embassies Close as U.S. Issues Global Travel Alert Due to Threat," CNN.com, August 3, 2013, http://
www.cnn.com/2013/08/03/politics/us-embassies-close-duplicate-2.

22 Eli Lake and Josh Rogin, "Exclusive: Al Qaeda Conference Call Intercepted by U.S. Officials Sparked Alerts," TheDailyBeast.com, August 7, 2013, http://www.thedailybeast.com/articles/2013/08/07/al-qaeda-conference-call-intercepted-by-u-s-officials-sparked-alerts.html.

23 Barbara Starr, Chris Lawrence, and Tom Cohen, "Intercepted al Qaeda Message Led to Shuttering Embassies, Consulates," CNN.com, August 4, 2013, http://www.cnn.com/2013/08/04/politics/us-embassies-close.

24 Lara Jakes and Adam Goldman, "Terrorists Turn to Online Chat Rooms to Evade U.S.," Associated Press, August 14, 2013, http://bigstory.ap.org/article/terrorists-turn-online-chat-rooms-evade-us.

25 Jo Becker and Scott Shane, "Secret 'Kill List' Tests Obama's Principles," NYTimes.com, May 29, 2012, http://www.nytimes.com/2012/05/29/world/obamas-leadership-in-war-on-al-qaeda.html.?pagewanted=all.

26 Greg McNeal, "Obama's Self-Serving Leaks, His Selective Outrage, and the Need for a Special Counsel," Forbes.com, June 8, 2012, http://www.forbes.com/sites/gregorymcneal/2012/06/08/obamas-self-serving-leaks-his-selective-outrage-and-the-need-for-a-special-counsel/.

27 Suzanne Kelly, "Feinstein: 'Avalanche of Leaks,'" CNN.com, June 6, 2012, http://security.blogs.cnn.com/2012/06/06/feinstein-avalanche-of-leaks/.

28 Daniel Stone, "Obama on National Security Leaks: It Wasn't Me," TheDailyBeast.com, June 8, 2012, http://www.thedailybeast.com/articles/2012/06/08/obama-on-national-security-leaks-it-wasn-t-me.html.

29 Gregory Kane, "What a Piece of anti-Semitic Work is Rev. Jeremiah Wright," WashingtonExaminer.com, March 15, 2012, http://washingtonexaminer.com/what-a-piece-of-anti-semitic-work-is-rev.-jeremiah-wright/article/37269.

30 Pamela Geller with Robert Spencer, *The Post-American Presidency: The Obama Administration's War on America* (New York: Threshold Editions, 2010), 76.

31 John Podhoretz, "Derrick Bell in 1994: 'Jewish Neoconservative Racists,'" CommentaryMagazine.com, March 9, 2012, http://www.commentarymagazine.com/2012/03/09/derrick-bell-jewish-neoconservative-racists/.

32 Michael Medved, "Obama's 'Undivided Jerusalem'—More Meaningless Words?," Townhall.com, June 11, 2008, http://townhall.com/columnists/michaelmedved/2008/06/11/obamas_undivided_jerusalem_-_more_meaningless_words/page/full.

33 Ben Shapiro, "The Jewish Case Against Barack Obama," Townhall.com, October 15, 2008, http://townhall.com/columnists/benshapiro/2008/10/15/the_jewish_case_against_barack_obama/page/full.

34 "Obama: No Green Light for Israel to Attack Iran," CNN.com, July 7, 2009, http://edition.cnn.com/2009/POLITICS/07/07/obama.israel.iran/.

35 "Saudi Arabia Gives Israel Clear Skies to Attack Iranian Nuke Sites," *Times of London*, June 12, 2010, http://www.thetimes.co.uk/tto/news/world/middleeast/article2552397.ece.

36 Mark Landler and Steven Lee Myers, "Obama Sees '67 Borders as Starting Point for Peace Deal," NYTimes.com, May 19, 2011, http://www.nytimes.com/2011/05/20/world/middleeast/20speech.html.?pagewanted=all.

37 Benjamin Joffe-Walt, "Is Israel Arming in Saudi Arabia?," JPost.com, June 27, 2010, http://www.jpost.com/Middle-East/Is-Israel-arming-in-Saudi-Arabia.

38 Benjamin Netanyahu, "Netanyahu's Address to U.S. Congress, May 2011," CFR.org, May 24, 2011, http://www.cfr.org/israel/netanyahus-address-us-congress-may-2011/p25073.

39 Michael Barbaro, "A Friendship Dating to 1976 Resonates in 2012," NYTimes.com, April 7, 2012, http://www.nytimes.com/2012/04/08/us/politics/mitt-romney-and-benjamin-netanyahu-are-old-friends.html.?pagewanted=all&_r=0.

40 David Ignatius, "Is Israel Preparing to Attack Iran?," WashingtonPost.com, February 2, 2012, http://articles.washingtonpost.com/2012-02-02/opinions/35443465_1_israeli-attack-israelis-fear-israelis-doubt.

41 Seymour M. Hersh, "Our Men in Iran?," NewYorker.com, April 6, 2012, http://www.newyorker.com/online/blogs/newsdesk/2012/04/mek.html.

42 Mark Perry, "Israel's Secret Staging Ground," ForeignPolicy.com, Marcy 28, 2012, http://www.foreignpolicy.com/articles/2012/03/28/israel_s_secret_staging_ground?page=full.

43 Brad Knickerbocker, "Attacking Iran: Did U.S. Just Torpedo Israeli Deal for a Base in Azerbaijan?," CSMonitor.com, March 29, 2012, http://www.csmonitor.com/USA/Foreign-Policy/2012/0329/Attacking-Iran-Did-US-just-torpedo-Israeli-deal-for-a-base-in-Azerbaijan.

44 Viola Ginger and Tony Capaccio, "Iran's Centrifuge 'Workshops' Complicate Raid Planning," Bloomberg.com, March 28, 2012, http://www.bloomberg.com/news/2012-03-28/iran-s-centrifuge-workshops-add-to-difficulties-facing-israel.html.

45 Alexander Marquardt, "Israelis Suspect Obama Media Leaks to Prevent Strike on Iran," ABCNews.com, March 29, 2012, http://abcnews.go.com/blogs/headlines/2012/03/obama-administration-media-campaign-to-stop-israeli-strike-on-iran/.

46 David E. Sanger, "Obama Order Sped Up Wave of Cyberattacks Against Iran," NYTimes.com, June 1, 2012, http://www.nytimes.com/2012/06/01/world/middleeast/obama-ordered-wave-of-cyberattacks-against-iran.html.?pagewanted=all.

47 Greg McNeal, "Obama's Self-Serving Leaks, His Selective Outrage, and the Need for a Special Counsel," Forbes.com, June 8, 2012, http://www.forbes.com/sites/gregorymcneal/2012/06/08/obamas-self-serving-leaks-his-selective-outrage-and-the-need-for-a-special-counsel/.

48 Rowan Scarborough, "In Classified Cyberwar Against Iran, Trail of Stuxnet Leak Leads to White House," WashingtonTimes.com, August 18, 2013, http://www.washingtontimes.com/news/2013/aug/18/trail-of-stuxnet-cyberwar-leak-to-author-leads-to-/?page=all.

49 Sharona Schwartz, "Report: Obama Administration Apologizes for Another National Security Leak," TheBlaze.com, May 19, 2013, http://news.yahoo.com/report-obama-administration-apologizes-another-national-security-leak-182208023.html.

50 Stuart Winer, "U.S. Spills Israeli Missile Defense Secrets," TimesofIsrael.com, June 4, 2013, http://www.timesofisrael.com/us-leaks-israeli-arrow-3-missile-secrets/.

51 "U.S. Sources: Israel Behind Latakia Attack," YNetNews.com, July 13, 2013, http://www.ynetnews.com/articles/0,7340,L-4404336,00.html.

52 Michael R. Gordon, "Some Syria Missiles Eluded Israeli Strike, Officials Say," NYTimes.com, July 31, 2013, http://www.nytimes.com/2013/08/01/world/middleeast/syrian-missiles-were-moved-before-israeli-strike-officials-say.html.?ref=middleeast.

53 Jonathan S. Tobin, "More Dangerous Administration Leaks," CommentaryMagazine.com, August 8, 2013, http://www.commentarymagazine.com/2013/08/01/more-dangerous-administration-leaks-syria-russia-israel-missiles/.

54 Jonathan S. Landay and Marisa Taylor, "Experts: Obama's Plan to Predict Future Leakers Unproven, Unlikely to Work," McClatchyDC.com, July 9, 2013, http://www.mcclatchydc.com/2013/07/09/196211/linchpin-for-obamas-plan-to-predict.html.#.UiPpLWDrOR-.

55 Adam Kredo, "Shamai Leibowitz Sentenced for Leaking FBI Secret," *Jewish Chronicle*, June 3, 2010, http://thejewishchronicle.net/view/full_story/7789457/article-Shamai-Leibowitz-sentenced-for-leaking-FBI-secret.

56 Matt Apuzzo, "State Department Contractor Steven Kim Charged with Leaking Secrets to Press," Associated Press, August 27, 2010, http://www.huffingtonpost.com/2010/08/27/steven-kim-state-department-contractor-charged-leak_n_697734.html.

57 Andrea Shalal-Esa, "Advice for Snowden from a Man Who Knows: 'Always Check Six,'" Reuters, June 11, 2013, http://www.reuters.com/article/2013/06/11/us-usa-security-nsa-drake-idUSBRE95A12X20130611.

58 Greg Miller, "Former CIA Officer Jeffrey A. Sterling Charged in Leak Probe," Washingtonpost.com, January 6, 2011, http://www.washingtonpost .com/wp-dyn/content/article/2011/01/06/AR2011010604001.html.

59 Marc Ambinder, "Leaks Aren't 'In,' Clapper Tells Intelligence Community," TheAtlantic.com, August 28, 2010, http://www.theatlantic.com/politics /archive/2010/08/leaks-arent-in-clapper-tells-intelligence-community/62195/.

Count 5: Deprivation of Rights Under Color of Law

1 George W. Bush, "Address to Congress and the American People following the September 11, 2001, Attacks," September 20, 2001, http://www.history2u .com/bush_war_on_terror.htm.

2 "President Bush Signs Anti-Terrorism Bill," PBS.org, October 26, 2001, http:// www.pbs.org/newshour/updates/terrorism/july-dec01/bush_terrorismbill.html.

3 Toby Harnden, "Barack Obama and John McCain on 9/11: Statements then and now," Telegraph.co.uk, September 12, 2008, http://blogs.telegraph .co.uk/news/tobyharnden/5213537/Barack_Obama_and_John_McCain_on _911_Statements_then_and_now/.

4 Marc Ambinder, "Obama Embraces Patriot Act; As Senator, He Was Skeptical," TheAtlantic.com, September 15, 2009, http://www.theatlantic.com/politics/archive /2009/09/obama-embraces-patriot-act-as-senator-he-was-skeptical/26614/.

5 Glenn Greenwald, "On Prism, Partisanship, and Propaganda," TheGuardian .com, June 14, 2013, http://www.theguardian.com/commentisfree/2013/jun /14/nsa-partisanship-propaganda-prism.

6 Ben Shapiro, "The Day America Lost the War on Terror," Townhall.com, January 28, 2009, http://townhall.com/columnists/benshapiro/2009/01/28 /the_day_america_lost_the_war_on_terror.

7 "Obama Speech on Drone Policy," NYTimes.com, May 23, 2010, http:// www.nytimes.com/2013/05/24/us/politics/transcript-of-obamas-speech-on -drone-policy.html.?pagewanted=all&_r=0.

8 "Conspiracy Against Rights," Department of Justice, http://www.justice.gov /crt/about/crm/241fin.php.

9 Glenn Kessler, "James Clapper's 'Least Untruthful' Statement to the Senate," WashingtonPost.com, June 12, 2013, http://www.washingtonpost.com /blogs/fact-checker/post/james-clappers-least-untruthful-statement-to-the-senate /2013/06/11/e50677a8-d2d8-11e2-a73e-826d299ff459_blog.html.

10 Andy Greenberg, "NSA Chief Denies Wired's Domestic Spying Story (Fourteen Times) in Congressional Hearing," Forbes.com, March 20, 2012, http://www.forbes.com/sites/andygreenberg/2012/03/20/nsa-chief-denies -wireds-domestic-spying-story-fourteen-times-in-congressional-hearing/.

11 Andy Greenberg, "Watch Top U.S. Intelligence Officials Repeatedly Deny NSA Spying on Americans over the Last Year," Forbes.com, June 6, 2013, http://www.forbes.com/sites/andygreenberg/2013/06/06/watch-top-u-s-intelligence-officials-repeatedly-deny-nsa-spying-on-americans-over-the-last-year-videos/.

12 Glenn Greenwald, "NSA Collecting Phone Records of Millions of Verizon Customers Daily," *Guardian* (U.K.), June 5, 2013, http://www.theguardian.com/world/2013/jun/06/nsa-phone-records-verizon-court-order.

13 Barton Gellman and Laura Poitras, "U.S., British Intelligence Mining Data from Nine U.S. Internet Companies in Broad Secret Program," *Washington Post,* June 6, 2013, http://www.washingtonpost.com/investigations/us-intelligence-mining-data-from-nine-us-internet-companies-in-broad-secret-program/2013/06/06/3a0c0da8-cebf-11e2-8845-d970ccb04497_print.html.

14 Ewen MacAskill, "NSA Paid Millions to Cover Prism Compliance Costs for Tech Companies," *Guardian,* August 22, 2013, http://www.theguardian.com/world/2013/aug/23/nsa-prism-costs-tech-companies-paid.

15 Ellen Nakashima, "Obama Administration Had Restrictions on NSA Reversed in 2011," WashingtonPost.com, September 7, 2013, http://www.washingtonpost.com/world/national-security/obama-administration-had-restrictions-on-nsa-reversed-in-2011/2013/09/07/c26ef658-0fe5-11e3-85b6-d27422650fd5_story.html.

16 Gellman and Poitras, "U.S., British Intelligence Mining Data from Nine U.S. Internet Companies in Broad Secret Program."

17 "NSA Slides Explain the PRISM Data-Collection Program," WashingtonPost.com, July 6, 2013, http://www.washingtonpost.com/wp-srv/special/politics/prism-collection-documents/.

18 "Privacy Scandal: NSA Can Spy on Smart Phone Data," Spiegel.de, September 7, 2013, http://www.spiegel.de/international/world/privacy-scandal-nsa-can-spy-on-smart-phone-data-a-920971.html.

19 Emma Roller, "This Is What Section 215 of the Patriot Act Does," Slate.com, June 7, 2013, http://www.slate.com/blogs/weigel/2013/06/07/nsa_prism_scandal_what_patriot_act_section_215_does.html.

20 Barton Gellman, Aaron Blake, and Greg Miller, "Edward Snowden Comes Forward as Source of NSA Leaks," WashingtonPost.com, June 9, 2013, http://www.washingtonpost.com/politics/intelligence-leaders-push-back-on-leakers-media/2013/06/09/fff80160-d122-11e2-a73e-826d299ff459_story.html.

21 Glenn Greenwald and Ewen MacAskill, "Boundless Informant: The NSA's Secret Tool to Track Global Surveillance Data," TheGuardian.com, June 11, 2013, http://www.theguardian.com/world/2013/jun/08/nsa-boundless-informant-global-datamining.

22 Dan Roberts and Spencer Ackerman, "Obama Defiant over NSA Revelations Ahead of Summit with Chinese Premier," TheGuardian .com, June 7, 2013, http://www.theguardian.com/world/2013/jun/07 /obama-nsa-revelations-chinese-summit.

23 Mary Bruce, "Obama: 'Nobody Is Listening to Your Phone Calls,'" ABC-News.com, June 7, 2013, http://abcnews.go.com/blogs/politics/2013/06 /obama-nobody-is-listening-to-your-phone-calls/.

24 Amy Davidson, "The NSA's Dirty Dishes: Obama's Press Conference," NewYorker.com, August 9, 2013, http://www.newyorker.com/online/blogs /closeread/2013/08/nsa-dirty-dishes-obama-press-conference.html.

25 Greenwald, "On Prism, Partisanship, and Propaganda."

26 Jonathan Easley, "Obama Tells Leno: 'We Don't Have a Domestic Spying Pro-gram,'" TheHill.com, August 6, 2013, http://thehill.com/blogs/blog-briefing -room/news/315871-obama-we-dont-have-a-domestic-spying-program.

27 "Transcript: President Obama's News Conference," NPR.org, August 9, 2013, http://www.npr.org/2013/08/09/210574114/transcript-president-obamas -news-conference.

28 Barton Gellman, "NSA Broke Privacy Rules Thousands of Times per Year, Audit Finds," Washington Post, August 15, 2013, http://www.washingtonpost.com /world/national-security/nsa-broke-privacy-rules-thousands-of-times-per -year-audit-finds/2013/08/15/3310e554-05ca-11e3-a07f-49ddc7417125_print. html.

29 Mark Hosenball and Tabassum Zakaria, "NSA Collected 56,000 Emails by Americans a Year: Documents," Reuters.com, August 21, 2013, http://www.reuters.com/article/2013/08/22/us-usa-security-nsa-id USBRE97K14Y20130822.

30 "Obama: NSA 'Inadvertently, Accidentally' Pulled Emails of Americans," CBSLocal.com, August 23, 2013, http://washington.cbslocal.com/2013/08 /23/obama-nsa-inadvertently-accidentally-pulled-emails-of-americans/.

31 Kimberly Dozier, "NSA Admits Rare Willful Surveillance Violations," As-sociated Press, August 23, 2013, http://news.yahoo.com/nsa-admits-rare -willful-surveillance-violations-211422017.html.

32 Niels Lesniewski, "NSA Violations 'Just the Tip of a Larger Iceberg,' Say Wyden, Udall," RollCall.com, August 16, 2013, http://blogs.rollcall.com /wgdb/nsa-violations-just-the-tip-of-a-larger-iceberg-say-wyden-udall/.

33 Carol Leonnig, "Court: Ability to Police U.S. Spying Program Limited," Washing-ton Post, August 15, 2013, http://www.washingtonpost.com/politics/court-ability -to-police-us-spying-program-limited/2013/08/15/4a8c8c44-05cd-11e3-a07f -49ddc7417125_story.html.

34 Mark Hosenball and Tabassum Zakaria, "NSA Collected 56,000 Emails by Americans a Year: Documents."

35 Adam Serwer, "NSA Violated the Law and Misled Its Court Chaperone," MSNBC.com, August 22, 2013, http://tv.msnbc.com/2013/08/22/nsa-violated-the-law-misled-its-secret-court-chaperone/.

36 Eric Lichtblau and Michael S. Schmidt, "Other Agencies Clamor for Data NSA Compiles," NYTimes.com, August 3, 2013, http://www.nytimes.com/2013/08/04/us/other-agencies-clamor-for-data-nsa-compiles.html.?partner=rss&emc=rss&_r=2&.

37 Scott Shane and Colin Moynihan, "Drug Agents Use Vast Phone Trove, Eclipsing NSA's," NYTimes.com, September 1, 2013, http://www.nytimes.com/2013/09/02/us/drug-agents-use-vast-phone-trove-eclipsing-nsas.html.?pagewanted=all.

38 Sam Sacks, "Obama's NSA Review Board Proving the Cynics Right," RT.com, August 27, 2013, http://rt.com/op-edge/obama-nsa-high-level-group-064/.

39 Tom Kludt, "Greenwald: Snowden Charges Show Obama's 'Vindictive Mentality,'" TalkingPointsMemo.com, June 22, 2013, http://livewire.talkingpointsmemo.com/entry/greenwald-snowden-charges-show-obamas-vindictive-mentality.

40 "Kerry: NSA Leaker Snowden 'Betrayed His Country,'" UPI.com, June 25, 2013, http://www.upi.com/Top_News/World-News/2013/06/25/Kerry-NSA-leaker-Snowden-betrayed-his-country/UPI-48331372174535/.

41 Nancy Benac, "Obama Recasts Edward Snowden as 'Hacker' in Effort to Downplay Him," Associated Press, June 28, 2013, http://www.huffingtonpost.com/2013/06/28/obama-edward-snowden-hacker_n_3515562.html.

42 Jonathan Weisman, "Boehner Calls Snowden a Traitor," NYTimes.com, June 11, 2013, http://thecaucus.blogs.nytimes.com/2013/06/11/boehner-calls-snowden-a-traitor/?_r=0.

43 "Cheney Defends NSA Programs, Says Snowden a 'Traitor,' Obama 'Lacks Credibility,'" FoxNews.com, June 16, 2013, http://www.foxnews.com/politics/2013/06/16/cheney-defends-us-surveillance-programs-says-snowden-traitor-obama-lacks/.

44 Jeremy Herb and Justin Sink, "Sen. Feinstein Calls Snowden's NSA Leaks an 'Act of Treason,'" TheHill.com, June 10, 2013, http://thehill.com/blogs/defcon-hill/policy-and-strategy/304573-sen-feinstein-snowdens-leaks-are-treason.

45 Davidson, "The NSA's Dirty Dishes: Obama's Press Conference."

46 Emily Bazelon, "Is Edward Snowden a Traitor?," Slate.com, June 11, 2013, http://www.slate.com/articles/news_and_politics/jurisprudence/2013/06/edward_snowden_and_daniel_ellsberg_is_the_nsa_leaker_a_traitor.html.

47 Aubrey Bloomfield, "6 Worst Reactions to Edward Snowden's NSA Leaks," PolicyMic.com, http://www.policymic.com/articles/48143/6-worst-reactions-to-edward-snowden-s-nsa-leaks.

48 Lucia Graves, "Mike Rogers: Glenn Greenwald 'Doesn't Have a Clue' About NSA Surveillance," HuffingtonPost.com, June 9, 2013, http://www.huffingtonpost.com/2013/06/09/mike-rogers-glenn-greenwald_n_3411864.html.

49 "Glenn Greenwald's Partner Detained at Heathrow Airport for NineHours," TheGuardian.com, August 18, 2013, http://www.theguardian.com/world/2013/aug/18/glenn-greenwald-guardian-partner-detained-heathrow.

50 Natasha Lennard, "U.S. Knew in Advance About Greenwald Partner's Detention," Salon.com, August 19, 2013, http://www.salon.com/2013/08/19/u_s_knew_in_advance_about_greenwalds_partner_detention/.

51 Kyle Stock, "A Federal Top-Secret Club That's Not Very Secret or Federal," Businessweek.com, June 10, 2013, http://www.businessweek.com/articles/2013-06-10/a-federal-top-secret-club-thats-not-very-secret-or-federal.

52 Nicole Blake Johnson, "Agencies Struggle to Launch Insider Threat Program," FederalTimes.com, September 3, 2013, http://www.federaltimes.com/article/20130903/IT01/309030002/Agencies-struggle-launch-insider-threat-programs.

53 Cheryl K. Chumley, "CIA finds 1 in 5 Flagged Job Applicants Come from Hamas, Hezbollah, al Qaeda," WashingtonTimes.com, September 2, 2013, http://www.washingtontimes.com/news/2013/sep/2/cia-finds-1-5-job-applicants-hail-hamas-hezbollah-/.

54 Brett Logiurato, "GOP Congressman: The Government's Phone Tracking Has Stopped a Terrorist Attack in the U.S. in 'the Last Few Years,'" BusinessInsider.com, June 6, 2013, http://www.businessinsider.com/mike-rogers-nsa-phone-tracking-obama-terrorist-attack-2013-6.

55 Tim Mak and Burgess Everett, "Dianne Feinstein on NSA: 'It's Called Protecting America,'" Politico.com, June 6, 2013, http://www.politico.com/story/2013/06/dianne-feinstein-on-nsa-its-called-protecting-america-92340.html.

56 Tal Kopan, "Lindsey Graham 'Glad' NSA Tracking Phones," Politico.com, June 6, 2013, http://www.politico.com/story/2013/06/lindsey-graham-nsa-tracking-phones-92330.html.?hp=l1.

57 Chris Moody, "Lindsey Graham: 'If I Thought Censoring the Mail Was Necessary, I Would Suggest It,'" Yahoo.com, June 11, 2013, http://news.yahoo.com/blogs/ticket/lindsey-graham-thought-censoring-mail-necessary-suggest-182932835.html.

58 Scott Shane, "Phone Calls Discussing Jihad Prompted Russian Warning on Tsarnaev," NYTimes.com, April 27, 2013, http://www.nytimes.com/2013/04/28/us/jihad-discussions-led-to-warning-on-tamerlan-tsarnaev.html.

59 "Russian Official: U.S. 'Ignored Boston Bombers Warning,'" Associated Press, June 4, 2013, http://www.independent.co.uk/news/world/americas /russian-official-us-ignored-boston-bombers-warning-8644560.html.

60 Josh Gerstein, "FBI Knew Earlier of Boston Bombing Suspect," Politico .com, June 15, 2013, http://www.politico.com/blogs/under-the-radar/2013 /06/fbi-knew-earlier-of-boston-bombing-suspect-166313.html.

61 Brendan Sasso, "NRA Joins ACLU Lawsuit, Claims NSA Starting 'Gun Regis-try,'" TheHill.com, September 4, 2013, http://thehill.com/blogs/hillicon-valley /technology/320357-nra-claims-nsa-illegally-created-a-gun-database.

62 Glenn Kessler, "James Clapper's 'Least Untruthful' Statement to the Sen-ate," WashingtonPost.com, June 12, 2013, http://www.washingtonpost.com /blogs/fact-checker/post/james-clappers-least-untruthful-statement-to-the -senate/2013/06/11/e50677a8-d2d8-11e2-a73e-826d299ff459_blog.html.

63 Bruce, "Obama: 'Nobody Is Listening to Your Phone Calls.'"

64 "NSA Spying on Americans is Illegal," ACLU.org, December 29, 2005, https://www.aclu.org/technology-and-liberty/nsa-spying-americans-illegal.

65 Ellen Nakashima and Ann E. Marimow, "Judge: NSA's Collecting of Phone Records is Probably Unconstitutional," WashingtonPost.com, December 16, 2013, http://www.washingtonpost.com/national/judge-nsas-collecting-of -phone-records-is-likely-unconstitutional/2013/12/16/6e098eda-6688-11e3 -a0b9-249bbb34602c_story.html.

66 Steven Nelson, "Judge Orders NSA to Stop Collecting Phone Records," USNews.com, December 16, 2013, http://www.usnews.com/news/articles /2013/12/16/judge-orders-nsa-to-stop-collecting-phone-records.

Count 6: Bribery

1 "Executive Order," White House Office of the Press Secretary, January 21, 2009, http://www.whitehouse.gov/the-press-office/ethics -commitments-executive-branch-personnel.

2 Angie Drobnic Holan, "Waiver for Former Defense Lobbyist Moves the Needle," Politifact.com, January 23, 2009, http://www.politifact .com/truth-o-meter/promises/obameter/promise/240/tougher-rules-against -revolving-door-for-lobbyists/.

3 Angie Drobnic Holan, "Defense, Treasury Appointees Have Con-flicts," Politifact.com, February 5, 2009, http://www.politifact.com /truth-o-meter/promises/obameter/promise/240/tougher-rules-against-revolving -door-for-lobbyists/.

4 Angie Drobnic Holan, "Former Lobbyist in the White House? It's Okay if They Say It's Okay," Politifact.com, March 17, 2009, http://www.politifact

.com/truth-o-meter/promises/obameter/promise/240/tougher-rules-against
-revolving-door-for-lobbyists/.

5　Brian Ross and Rhonda Schwartz, "The Rezko Connection: Obama's Achilles
Heel?," ABCNews.com, January 10, 2008, http://abcnews.go.com/Blotter
/rezko-connection-obamas-achilles-heel/story?id=4111483.

6　Larry Bell, "Chicago Corruption Trials and the Sounds of Silence," American Thinker
.com, December 2, 2011, http://www.americanthinker.com/2011/12/chicago
_corruption_trials_and_the_sounds_of_silence.html.

7　D'Angelo Gore, "Michelle Obama's Salary," FactCheck.org, May 17, 2009,
http://www.factcheck.org/2009/05/michelle-obamas-salary/.

8　Lynn Sweet, "Sweet Scoop: Obama, After Initial Refusal, Releases All Ear-
mark Requests," SunTimes.com, March 13, 2008, http://blogs.suntimes
.com/sweet/2008/03/sweet_scoop_obama_after_initia.html.

9　Gore, "Michelle Obama's Salary."

10　Bruce Japsen, "University of Chicago Hospital to Trim 7% of Budget,"
ChicagoTribune.com, January 10, 2009, http://articles.chicagotribune
.com/2009-01-10/news/0901090286_1_new-pavilion-trim-first-lady-michelle
-obama.

11　Joe Stephens, "Obama's Lawyer Connected to Controversial Program,"
Washingtonpost.com, January 9, 2009, http://voices.washingtonpost.com
/44/2009/01/first-ladys-lawyer-helped-with.html.?wprss=the-trail.

12　Ed Morrissey, "Jeremiah Wright Claims Obama Ally Offered $150,000
Bribe in 2008 to Shut Up," HotAir.com, May 13, 2012, http://hotair.com
/archives/2012/05/13/jeremiah-wright-claims-obama-ally-offered-150000
-bribe-in-2008-to-shut-up/.

13　Jeff Poor, "Book Says U. of Chicago Medical Center VP Bribed Jeremiah
Wright," DailyCaller.com, May 14, 2012, http://dailycaller.com/2012/05/14
/book-reveals-obama-ally-who-bribed-jeremiah-wright-to-stay-quiet/.

14　"HHS Sends $6 Million to Program Run by Obama Buddy," InvestmentWatchBlog
.com, May 14, 2012, http://investmentwatchblog.com/hhs-sends-6-million
-to-program-run-by-obama-buddy/#.T7G3mu0Tvx4.

15　"2008: Unions Spent $400 Million to Elect Obama," Politifact.com,
February 24, 2011, http://www.politifact.com/truth-o-meter/statements
/2011/mar/15/republican-national-committee-republican/rnc-said-unions
-raised-400-million-obama-2008/.

16　"Mallory Factor Exposes Big Labor's War on America," FrontPageMag
.com, March 4, 2013, http://frontpagemag.com/2013/frontpagemag-com
/mallory-factor-exposes-big-labors-war-on-america/.

17　Newt Gingrich, "Once, We Would Have Called It a Scandal,"

HumanEvents.com, June 10, 2009, http://www.humanevents.com/2009/06 /10/once-we-would-have-called-it-a-scandal/.

18 Jeff Poor, "UAW Gave $1 Million+ to Pro-Bailout Congressmen; Media Focus on Anti-Bailout Interests," Newsbusters.org, December 15, 2008, http://newsbusters.org/blogs/jeff-poor/2008/12/15 /uaw-gave-1-million-pro-bailout-congressmen-media-focus-anti-bailout-inter.

19 Kris Maher, "SEIU Campaign Spending Pays Political Dividends," WSJ.com, May 16, 2009, http://online.wsj.com/article/SB124243785248026055 .html.

20 Barack Obama, "Remarks to the United Auto Workers Conference in Dubuque, Iowa," American Presidency Project, November 13, 2007, http:// www.presidency.ucsb.edu/ws/index.php?pid=77020.

21 John Tamny, "The Unions Didn't Bankrupt Detroit, but Great American Cars Did," Forbes.com, July 21, 2013, http://www.forbes .com/sites/johntamny/2013/07/21/the-unions-didnt-bankrupt-detroit-but -great-american-cars-did/.

22 Kevin Hassett, "Auto Union Drove GM to Trouble," Marketplace.org, March 30, 2009, http://www.marketplace.org/topics/business/auto-union-drove-gm -trouble.

23 Doug Altner, "What Explains GM's Problems With the UAW?," Forbes .com, May 20, 2013, http://www.forbes.com/sites/realspin/2013/05/20 /what-explains-gms-problems-with-the-uaw/.

24 Todd Zywicki, "The Auto Bailout and the Rule of Law," NationalAffairs .com, Spring 2011, http://www.nationalaffairs.com/publications/detail/the -auto-bailout-and-the-rule-of-law.

25 Associated Press, "Report: Obama Sparked GM Bankruptcy," SanduskyRegister.com, August 17, 2013, http://www.sanduskyregister .com/article/4435371.

26 Rory Cooper, "Meet GM's Bondholders: Chris Crowe," Heritage .org, May 18, 2009, http://blog.heritage.org/2009/05/18/meet-gms-bondholders -chris-crowe/.

27 Porter Stansberry, "GM and the Truth About One of America's Biggest Bankruptcies," DailyWealth.com, June 21, 2012, http://www.dailywealth .com/2125/gm-americas-biggest-bankruptcy.

28 Barbara Hollingsworth, "U.S. Taxpayers Still Down $19.1B from Obama's General Motors Bailout," CNSNews.com, August 21, 2013, http://www.cnsnews.com/news/article/us-taxpayers-still-down-191b-obamas -general-motors-bailout.

29 Patrice Hill, "GM's Union Recovering After Stock Sale," WashingtonTimes

.com, November 25, 2010, http://www.washingtontimes.com/news/2010/nov/25/gms-union-on-road-to-recovery-after-stock-sale/?page=1.

30 Zywicki, "The Auto Bailout and the Rule of Law."

31 Eamon Javers, "Obama Picks a Fight with 'Speculators,'" Politico.com, April 30, 2009, http://www.politico.com/news/stories/0409/21935.html.

32 Christopher Jensen, "Chrysler Bankruptcy and Product Liability," NYTimes.com, May 20, 2009, http://wheels.blogs.nytimes.com/2009/05/20/chrysler-bankruptcy-and-product-liability/.

33 Andrew Seidman, "Obama Administration Favored Union Worker Pensions in GM Bailout, House Republicans Say," *Los Angeles Times,* June 23, 2011, http://articles.latimes.com/2011/jun/23/business/la-fi-gm-bailout-review-20110623.

34 Zywicki, "The Auto Bailout and the Rule of Law."

35 Hollingsworth, "U.S. Taxpayers Still Down $19.1B from Obama's General Motors Bailout."

36 James Sherk and Todd Zywicki, "Sherk and Zywicki: Obama's United Auto Workers Bailout," WSJ.com, June 13, 2012, http://online.wsj.com/article/SB10001424052702303768104577462650268680454.html.

37 Lynn Sweet, "Sweet Column: Obama Cheered at SEIU, Union Weighing Whether to Endorse," SunTimes.com, September 18, 2007, http://blogs.suntimes.com/sweet/2007/09/sweet_column_obama_cheered_at.html.

38 Susan Davis, "SEIU's Stern Tops White House Visitor List," WSJ.com, October 30, 2009, http://blogs.wsj.com/washwire/2009/10/30/seius-stern-tops-white-house-visitor-list/.

39 Maher, "SEIU Campaign Spending Pays Political Dividends."

40 "President Obama Announces Recess Appointments to Key Administration Positions," White House Office of the Press Secretary, March 27, 2010, http://www.whitehouse.gov/the-press-office/president-obama-announces-recess-appointments-key-administration-positions.

41 "NLRB Office of Public Affairs—News Releases—a/k/a 'Bias Score-card,'" NRTW.org, August 30, 2013, http://www.nrtw.org/en/nlrb-watch/nlrbs-bias-scorecard.

42 Steven Greenhouse, "Labor Board Drops Case Against Boeing," NYTimes.com, December 9, 2011, http://www.nytimes.com/2011/12/10/business/labor-board-drops-case-against-boeing.html.

43 "Lafe Solomon 'Did What IAM Bosses Told Him To,'" NRTWC.org, January 3, 2012, http://nrtwc.org/lafe-solomon-did-what-iam-bosses-told-him-to-2/.

44 Kevin Bogardus, "For NLRB lawyer Lafe Solomon, Boeing Action Was No Laughing Matter," TheHill.com, February 3, 2012, http://thehill

.com/business-a-lobbying/208459-for-nlrb-lawyer-boeing-action-no-laughing
-matter-.

45 Kyung M. Song, "NLRB's Top Lawyer Still Feels Fallout from Boeing, Union Case," SeattleTimes.com, February 19, 2012, http://seattletimes.com /html./businesstechnology/2017551565_solomon20.html.

46 Greenhouse, "Labor Board Drops Case Against Boeing."

47 Editorial, "The NLRB's Boeing Sham," WSJ.com, December 12, 2011, http://online.wsj.com/article/SB100014240529702038331045770705727 68248242.html.

48 Melanie Trottman, "Obama Renominates Solomon to Be Top NLRB Lawyer," WSJ.com, May 24, 2013, http://blogs.wsj.com/washwire/2013/05/24 /obama-renominates-solomon-to-be-top-nlrb-lawyer/.

49 "Another Court Finds NLRB Recess Appointments Invalid, New Members Nominated," Associated Builders and Contractors Inc., July 24, 2013, http://www.abc.org/NewsMedia/Newsline/tabid/143/entryid/1244/another -court-finds-nlrb-recess-appointments-invalid-new-members-nominated.aspx.

50 Greg Stohr, "Obama's Recess Appointments Draw Supreme Court Scrutiny," Bloomberg.com, June 24, 2013, http://www.bloomberg.com/news/2013 -06-24/obama-s-recess-appointments-draw-supreme-court-scrutiny.html.

51 "Richard F. Griffin Jr.," NLRB.gov, http://www.nlrb.gov/who-we-are/board /richard-griffin, and "Sharon Block," NLRB.gov, http://www.nlrb.gov/who -we-are/board/sharon-block.

52 Josh Hicks, "How Obama's NLRB Nominees Became Central to Senate Filibuster Deal," WashingtonPost.com, July 17, 2013, http://www .washingtonpost.com/blogs/federal-eye/wp/2013/07/17/how-obamas-nlrb -nominees-became-central-to-the-senates-filibuster-deal/.

53 "Obama Economic Speech: Warns of Dire Consequences Without Stimulus," Associated Press, February 9, 2009, http://www.huffingtonpost.com /2009/01/08/obama-economic-speech-war_n_156171.html.

54 "More Obama Stimulus Fraud," JudicialWatch.org, August 11, 2009, http:// www.judicialwatch.org/blog/2009/08/more-obama-stimulus-fraud/.

55 Wynton Hall, "Richer Democratic States with Lower Unemployment Got Bulk of Obama Stimulus," Breitbart.com, April 20, 2012, http://www .breitbart.com/Big-Government/2012/04/20/richer-democratic-states-with -lower-unemployment-got-bulk-of-obama-stimulus.

56 Ashton Ellis, "Transparently Corrupt: Links Between Obama's Campaign Donors, Stimulus, and Energy Loans," CFIF.org, April 18, 2012, http://cfif .org/v/index.php/commentary/44/1390-transparently-corrupt-links-between -obamas-campaign-donors-stimulus-and-energy-loans.

57 Fred Schulte, "Obama Rewards Big Bundlers with Jobs, Commissions, Stimulus Money, Government Contracts, and More," PublicIntegrity.org, June 15, 2011, http://www.publicintegrity.org/node/4880.

58 Matthew Daly, "George Kaiser, Obama Donor, Discussed Solyndra Loan with White House, Emails Show," Associated Press, November 9, 2011, http://www.huffingtonpost.com/2011/11/09/george-kaiser-solyndra_n_1084568.html.

59 David Mildenberg and Peter Robison, "Kaiser Charity Sought Solyndra Plant After Billionaire Founder Aided Obama," Bloomberg.com, September 26, 2011, http://www.bloomberg.com/news/2011-09-26/oil-billionaire-s-charity-backing-obama-sought-solyndra-in-tulsa.html.

60 Joe Stephens and Carol D. Leonnig, "White House Pushed $500 Million Loan to Solar Company Now Under Investigation," WashingtonPost.com, September 13, 2011, http://www.washingtonpost.com/politics/white-house-pushed-500-million-loan-to-solar-company-now-under-investigation/2011/09/13/gIQAr3WbQK_story.html.

61 Aaron Task, "Peter Schweizer: Solyndra Is 'Tip of the Iceberg' of 'Very Suspicious' Govt. Loans," Yahoo.com, November 18, 2011, http://finance.yahoo.com/blogs/daily-ticker/peter-schweizer-solyndra-tip-iceberg-very-suspicious-govt-184151321.html.

62 "Stimulus-Funded Solar Firm Cancels IPO," FreeBeacon.com, April 13, 2012, http://freebeacon.com/stimulus-funded-solar-firm-cancels-ipo/.

63 Carol D. Leonnig, "Another Obama Fundraiser Is Investor in Car Company That Won Federal Loan," WashingtonPost.com, October 28, 2011, http://articles.washingtonpost.com/2011-10-28/politics/35280008_1_solyndra-loan-loan-program-jonathan-silver.

64 Chris Woodyard, "Van Maker VPG, Backed by DOE Loans, Shuts Down," USAToday.com, May 8, 2013, http://www.usatoday.com/story/money/cars/2013/05/08/vpg-auto-fisker-solyndra-tesla-doe-loan/2143201/.

65 "Growing Solyndra Green Scandal Is Just One of Many," Investors.com, February 23, 2012, http://news.investors.com/ibd-editorials/022312-602121-new-obama-green-stimulus-scandals-surface.htm.

66 Veronique De Rugy, "Assessing the Department of Energy Loan Guarantee Program," Mercatus Center at George Mason University, June 19, 2012, http://mercatus.org/publication/assessing-department-energy-loan-guarantee-program.

67 "Barack Obama (D): Top Contributors," OpenSecrets.org http://www.opensecrets.org/pres08/contrib.php?cid=N00009638.

68 "General Electric Making 'Bank' off Obama's 'Green' Stimulus Money," Greencorruption.blogspot.com, July 12, 2012, http://greencorruption

.blogspot.com/2012/07/general-electric-making-bank-off-obamas.html.#
.Ui4072DrOR-.

69 Lachlan Markey, "Lawsuit Alleges 'Corruption and Negligence' at Department
of Energy," Heritage.org, November 16, 2012, http://blog.heritage.org/2012
/11/16/lawsuit-alleges-corruption-and-negligence-at-department-of-energy/.

70 "EPA Gives Info for Free to Big Green Groups 92% of Time; Denies 93%
of Fee Waiver Requests from Biggest Conservative Critics," CEI.org, May
14, 2013, http://cei.org/news-releases/epa-gives-info-free-big-green-groups
-92-time-denies-93-fee-waiver-requests-biggest-con.

71 "Former EPA Chief Lisa Jackson Returns to Familiar Hot Seat," Politico
.com, September 9, 2013 http://www.politico.com/story/2013/09/lisa-jackson
-returns-to-familiar-hot-seat-96420.html.

72 Ed Morrissey, "The List of Payoffs That Got Reid His Cloture Vote," Hotair
.com, December 22, 2009, http://hotair.com/archives/2009/12/22
/the-list-of-payoffs-that-got-reid-his-cloture-vote/.

73 Dr. Milton R. Wolf, "Obamacare Waiver Corruption Must Stop,"
WashingtonTimes.com, May 20, 2011, http://www.washingtontimes.com
/news/2011/may/20/obamacare-waiver-corruption-must-stop/.

74 John Hayward, "Congress Gets Its Illegal Obamacare Waiver," HumanEvents
.com, August 5, 2013, http://www.humanevents.com/2013/08/05/congress-gets
-its-illegal-obamacare-waiver/.

75 Jim McElhatton, "Labor Department Spends Stimulus Funds for Ads
During Olbermann, Maddow Shows," *Washington Times*, August 21, 2012,
http://www.washingtontimes.com/news/2012/aug/21/stimulus-funds-spent
-obama-ads-olbermann-maddow/.

76 Paul Connor, "Labor Unions Primary Recipients of Obamacare Waivers," DailyCaller.com, January 6, 2012, http://dailycaller.com/2012/01/06
/labor-unions-primary-recipients-of-obamacare-waivers/.

77 Ben Shapiro, *Primetime Propaganda: The True Hollywood Story of How the
Left Took Over Your TV* (New York: Harper Collins, 2011), 295.

78 Jeff Zeleny, "Obama Raises $11 Million in Hollywood," NYTimes
.com, September 17, 2008, http://thecaucus.blogs.nytimes.com/2008/09/17
/obama-raises-11-million-in-hollywood/?_r=0.

79 Ben Shapiro, "ObamaCare Propaganda—Hollywood-Style," FrontPageMag
.com, July 25, 2013, http://frontpagemag.com/2013/ben-shapiro/hollywoods
-obamacare-propaganda/.

80 "Fiscal Cliff Deal: Hollywood Gets Tax Incentive Extension," Breitbart.com,
January 1, 2013, http://www.breitbart.com/Big-Hollywood/2013/01/01
/hollywood-loophole-fiscal-cliff.

81 "Trust in Government," Gallup.com http://www.gallup.com/poll/5392
    /trust-government.aspx.

Count 7: Obstruction of Justice

1   Evan McMurry, "Attorney Mark O'Mara: 'If George Zimmerman Was
    Black, He Would Never Have Been Charged with a Crime,'" Mediaite.com,
    July 13, 2013, http://www.mediaite.com/tv/defense-attorney-if-george-
    zimmerman-was-black-he-would-never-have-been-charged-with-a-crime/.

2   Ben Shapiro, *Bullies: How the Left's Culture of Fear and Intimidation Silences
    America* (New York: Threshold Editions, 2013), 90–91

3   "Flashback: Obama Called for 'Soul Searching,' Investigations in Trayvon
    Martin Case," Breitbart.com, March 23, 2012 http://www.breitbart.com
    /Breitbart-TV/2013/04/15/FLASHBACK-Obama-Called-For-Soul-Searching
    -Investigations-In-Trayvon-Martin-Case.

4   Jerry Seper, "Justice Department Defends Fla. 'Peacekeeper' Rallies,"
    WashingtonTimes.com, July 11, 2013, http://www.washingtontimes.com/news
    /2013/jul/11/justice-department-defends-fla-peacekeeper-rallies/?page=all.

5   "Judicial Watch Releases Audio of DOJ Helping Trayvon Protesters," Breitbart
    .com, July 11, 2013, http://www.breitbart.com/Big-Government/2013/07
    /11/Judicial-watch-peacekeepers-Sanford.

6   Cheryl K. Chumley, "Ex–Justice Department Official: Agency Tainted by 'Racial
    Favoritism,'" WashingtonTimes.com, July 23, 2013, http://www.washingtontimes
    .com/news/2013/jul/23/ex-justice-department-official-agency-tainted-raci/.

7   Chuck Ross, "Legal Experts: DOJ's Zimmerman Tip Line Merely Gives
    Impression That Agency Is Acting," DailyCaller.com, July 21, 2013, http://
    dailycaller.com/2013/07/21/legal-experts-dojs-zimmerman-tip-line-merely
    -gives-impression-that-agency-is-acting/.

8   Ben Shapiro, "DOJ Asks Civil Rights Groups, General Public for 'Tips' on
    Zimmerman," Breitbart.com, July 16, 2013, http://www.breitbart.com/Big
    -Government/2013/07/16/DOJ-phone-call-Zimmerman.

9   "Obama Trayvon Martin Speech Transcript: President Comments on George
    Zimmerman Verdict," HuffingtonPost.com, July 19, 2013, http://www
    .huffingtonpost.com/2013/07/19/obama-trayvon-martin-speech-transcript
    _n_3624884.html.

10 "Protection of Government Processes—Omnibus Clause—18 U.S. Code
    §1503," Department of Justice, http://www.justice.gov/usao/eousa/foia
    _reading_room/usam/title9/crm01724.htm.

11 J. Christian Adams, "Inside the Black Panther case," WashingtonTimes

.com, June 25, 2010, http://www.washingtontimes.com/news/2010/jun/25/inside-the-black-panther-case-anger-ignorance-and-/.

12 Benny Johnson, "Don't Miss the Connection: Obama 'Delivered' to Office by Black Panthers, Holder 'Owes Them Some Favors,'" TheBlaze.com, May 22, 2012, http://www.theblaze.com/stories/2012/05/22/dont-miss-the-connection-obama-and-holder-delivered-to-office-by-black-panthers-owe-them-some-favors/.

13 J. Christian Adams, "Return of the New Black Panthers," Breitbart.com, November 6, 2012, http://www.breitbart.com/Big-Government/2012/11/06/Return-of-the-New-Black-Panther.

14 Lee Stranahan, "New Black Panther: Never Contacted by Obama DOJ Over Zimmerman Threats," Breitbart.com, July 11, 2013, http://www.breitbart.com/Big-Government/2013/07/11/New-Black-Panther-on-Trayvon-We-were-not-contaced-by-the-Justice-Department.

15 Tracy Jan, "Harvard Professor Gates Arrested at Cambridge Home," Boston.com, July 20, 2009, http://www.boston.com/news/local/breaking_news/2009/07/harvard.html.

16 Foon Rhee, "Obama: Cambridge Police Acted 'Stupidly' in Gates Arrest," Boston.com, July 22, 2009, http://www.boston.com/news/politics/politicalintelligence/2009/07/obama_cambridge.html.

17 Peter Baker, Helene Cooper, and Jeff Zeleny, "What a White House Beer Says About Race and Politics," NYTimes.com, July 30, 2009, http://thecaucus.blogs.nytimes.com/2009/07/30/what-a-white-house-beer-says-about-race-and-politics/?_r=0.

18 Huma Khan, "President Obama Fires Controversial Inspector General," ABCNews.com, June 12, 2009, http://abcnews.go.com/blogs/politics/2009/06/president-obama-fires-controversial-inspector-general/.

19 Ibid.

20 Byron York, "Gerald Walpin Speaks: The Inside Story of the AmeriCorps Firing," WashingtonExaminer.com, March 16, 2012, http://washingtonexaminer.com/gerald-walpin-speaks-the-inside-story-of-the-americorps-firing/article/135584.

21 "The White House Fires a Watchdog," WSJ.com, June 17, 2009, http://online.wsj.com/article/SB124511811033017539.html.

22 Michelle Malkin, "AmeriCorps's Favorite Scandal-Plagued Mayor: Friend of the Obamas Kevin Johnson," Creators Syndicate, June 29, 2011, http://michellemalkin.com/2011/06/29/americorpss-favorite-scandal-plagued-mayor/.

23 David Jackson, "Obama: Military Sexual Assaults Are 'Outrage,'" USAToday .com, May 8, 2013, http://www.usatoday.com/story/theoval/2013/05/08 /obama-hagel-sexual-assaults-in-military/2143695/.

24 Paige Lavender, "Obama Military Sexual Assault Comments Were 'Unlaw-ful Command Influence,' Judge Says," HuffingtonPost.com, June 15, 2013, http://www.huffingtonpost.com/2013/06/15/obama-military-sexual-assault _n_3447523.html.

25 Erik Slavin, "Judge: Obama Sex Assault Comments 'Unlawful Command Influ-ence,'" Stripes.com, June 14, 2013, http://www.stripes.com/judge-obama-sex -assault-comments-unlawful-command-influence-1.225974.

26 "Hagel Aims to Blunt Obama Remarks on Military Sexual Assault," CBSNews .com, August 15, 2013, http://www.cbsnews.com/8301-250_162-57598734 /hagel-aims-to-blunt-obama-remarks-on-military-sexual-assault/.

27 Eamon Javers, "Inside Obama's Bank CEOs Meeting," Politico.com, April 3, 2009, http://www.politico.com/news/stories/0409/20871.html.

28 Nina Easton, "What's Really Behind SEIU's Bank of America Protests?," Money.cnn.com, May 19, 2010, http://money.cnn.com/2010/05/19/news /companies/SEIU_Bank_of_America_protest.fortune/.

29 Daniel Halper, "Obama on Occupy Wall Street: 'We Are on Their Side,'" WeeklyStandard.com, October 18, 2011, http://www.weeklystandard.com /blogs/obama-occupy-wall-street-we-are-their-side_598251.html.

30 Robert Yoon, "Goldman Sachs Was Top Obama Donor," CNN.com, April 20, 2010 http://www.cnn.com/2010/POLITICS/04/20/obama.goldman .donations/index.html.

31 Peter J. Boyer and Peter Schweizer, "Why Can't Obama Bring Wall Street to Justice?," TheDailyBeast.com, May 6, 2012, http://www.thedailybeast.com /newsweek/2012/05/06/why-can-t-obama-bring-wall-street-to-justice.html.

32 Karen Mracek and Thomas Beaumont, "Goldman Reveals Where Bailout Cash Went," USAToday.com, July 26, 2010, http://usatoday30.usatoday .com/money/industries/banking/2010-07-24-goldman-bailout-cash _N.htm.

33 Jenny Anderson, "Goldman Sachs Alters Its Bonus Policy to Quell Uproar," NYTimes.com, December 10, 2009, http://www.nytimes.com/2009/12/11 /business/11goldman.html.?_r=0.

34 Jason Ryan, "DOJ Will Not Prosecute Goldman Sachs in Financial Crisis Probe," ABCNews.com, August 9, 2012, http://abcnews.go.com /blogs/politics/2012/08/doj-will-not-prosecute-goldman-sachs-in-financial -crisis-probe/.

35 Boyer and Schweizer, "Why Can't Obama Bring Wall Street to Justice?,"

TheDailyBeast.com, May 6, 2012, http://www.thedailybeast.com/newsweek
/2012/05/06/why-can-t-obama-bring-wall-street-to-justice.html.

36 Peter J. Boyer and Peter Schweizer, "Why Can't Obama Bring Wall Street to
Justice?"

37 Glenn Greenwald, "The Real Story of How 'Untouchable' Wall Street Execs Avoided
Prosecution," *Guardian* (U.K.), January 23, 2013, http://www.businessinsider
.com/why-wall-street-execs-werent-prosecuted-2013-1.

38 Sarah Kliff, "Budget Request Denied, Sebelius Turns to Health Executives
to Finance Obamacare," WashingtonPost.com, May 10, 2013, http://www
.washingtonpost.com/blogs/wonkblog/wp/2013/05/10/budget-request-denied
-sebelius-turns-to-health-executives-to-finance-obamacare/.

39 Shapiro, *Bullies*, 217.

40 Scott Wilson and Joel Achenbach, "BP Agrees to $20 Billion Fund for Gulf Oil
Spill Claim," WashingtonPost.com, June 17, 2010 http://www.washingtonpost
.com/wp-dyn/content/article/2010/06/16/AR2010061602614.html.

41 Kristina Wong, "President Obama Says Arizona's 'Poorly-Conceived' Immigration
Law Could Mean Hispanic-Americans Are Harassed," ABCNews.com,
April 27, 2010, http://abcnews.go.com/blogs/politics/2010/04/president-obama
-says-arizonas-poorlyconceived-immigration-law-could-mean-hispanicamericans
-are-haras/.

42 Randal C. Archibold, "Arizona Enacts Stringent Law on Immigration,"
NYTimes.com, April 23, 2010, http://www.nytimes.com/2010/04/24/us
/politics/24immig.html.?_r=0.

43 "Napolitano Admits She Hasn't Read Arizona Immigration Law in 'Detail,'"
FoxNews.com, May 18, 2010, http://www.foxnews.com/politics/2010/05
/18/napolitano-admits-read-arizona-immigration-law/.

44 Elise Foley, "Obama Administration to Stop Deporting Younger Undocu-
mented Immigrants and Grant Work Permits," HuffingtonPost.com, June
15, 2012, http://www.huffingtonpost.com/2012/06/15/obama-immigration
-order-deportation-dream-act_n_1599658.html.

45 Mytheos Holt, "'He's a DREAMer. Release Him': Immigration Officials
Outline Disturbing Changes Under New Obama Executive Order," TheBlaze
.com, July 26, 2012, http://www.theblaze.com/stories/2012/07/26/hes-a
-dreamer-release-him-immigration-officials-outline-disturbing-changes-under
-new-obama-executive-order/#.

46 *Gonzales v. Raich*, 545 U.S. 1 (2005).

47 Kevin Johnson and Raju Chebium, "Justice Dept. Won't Challenge State
Marijuana Laws," USAToday.com, August 29, 2013, http://www.usatoday
.com/story/news/nation/2013/08/29/justice-medical-marijuana-laws/2727605/.

48 Michael F. Cannon, "Yes, Delaying Obamacare's Employer Mandate Is Illegal," CATO.org, July 8, 2013, http://www.cato.org/blog/yes-delaying-obamacares -employer-mandate-illegal.

49 Deroy Murdock, "Obama Squirrels Away His Links to ACORN," NationalReview .com, October 16, 2008, http://www.nationalreview.com/articles/226000/obama -squirrels-away-his-links-acorn/deroy-murdock.

50 Carol D. Leonnig, "Some Criticize SEIU for Its ACORN Connections," WashingtonPost.com, October 6, 2009, http://articles.washingtonpost .com/2009-10-06/news/36850132_1_acorn-office-seiu-president-andy-stern -seiu-locals.

51 Michelle Malkin, "More Left-Wing Voter Fraud Allegations Against ACORN," MichelleMalkin.com, March 13, 2008, http://michellemalkin .com/2008/03/13/more-left-wing-voter-fraud-allegations-against-acorn/.

52 Michelle Malkin, "The ACORN Obama Knows," MichelleMalkin .com, June 25, 2008, http://michellemalkin.com/2008/06/25/the-acorn -obama-knows/.

53 Zach Carter, "ACORN, in New GOP Budget Bill, Would Be Defunded Again, Even Though It No Longer Exists," HuffingtonPost.com, March 5, 2013, http://www.huffingtonpost.com/2013/03/05/acorn-gop-budget-bill _n_2810345.html.

54 "Obama Violated ACORN Funding Ban with Housing Grant to Offshoot, Watchdog Says," FoxNews.com, July 6, 2011, http://www.foxnews.com /politics/2011/07/06/obama-violates-acorn-funding-ban-with-housing-grant -to-offshoot-watchdog-says/.

55 Matthew Vadum, "Obama Gives $446 Million to ACORN Veteran," FrontPageMag.com, June 12, 2012, http://frontpagemag.com/2012/matthew -vadum/obama-gives-446-million-to-acorn-veteran/.

56 David Martosko, "Nonprofit Executive Overseeing the White House's Obamacare Youth Video Contest is the Disgraced ACORN Group's Former Top Lobbyist," *Daily Mail* (U.K.), August 19, 2013, http://www.dailymail .co.uk/news/article-2397611/Nonprofit-executive-overseeing-White-Houses -Obamacare-youth-video-contest-disgraced-ACORN-groups-lobbyist.html.

57 "Judicial Watch Releases Special Report: 'The Rebranding of ACORN,'" JudicialWatch.org, September 28, 2011, http://www.judicialwatch.org /press-room/press-releases/judicial-watch-releases-special-report-"the-rebranding -of-acorn"/.

58 Josh Gerstein, "President Barack Obama: 'Due Process' in Drone Strikes," Politico.com, September 7, 2012, http://www.politico.com/blogs/under-the -radar/2012/09/obama-us-seeks-due-process-in-drone-strikes-134889.html.

59 Jo Becker and Scott Shane, "Secret 'Kill List' Proves a Test of Obama's Principles and Will," NYTimes.com, May 29, 2012, http://www .nytimes.com/2012/05/29/world/obamas-leadership-in-war-on-al-qaeda.html .?pagewanted=all.

Conclusion

1 Ed Morrissey, "Obama: Say, There *Was* a Little 'Sloppiness' in State Department Security, Huh?," HotAir.com, December 31, 2012, http://hotair.com/archives/2012/12/31/obama-say-there-was-a-little-sloppiness -in-state-department-security-huh/.

2 Josh Gerstein, "Barack Obama Vows Action on Fast and Furious Gun Program," Politico.com, October 18, 2011, http://www.politico.com/news /stories/1011/66289.html.

3 Billy Hallowell, "'Outrageous': Obama Vows Full Investigation, Account-ability Amid IRS Intimidation Furor," TheBlaze.com, May 13, 2013, http:// www.theblaze.com/stories/2013/05/13/obama-vows-full-investigation-of -outrageous-irs-intimidation-people-have-to-be-held-accountable-i-will-not -tolerate-it/.

4 Fred Lucas, "Obama Calls for DOJ Review of Leak Investigations," CNSNews.com, May 23, 2013, http://www.cnsnews.com/news/article /obama-calls-doj-review-leak-investigations.

5 Deep Harm, "Obama Appoints James Clapper to Oversee 'Independent' NSA Review,'" DailyKos.com, August 12, 2013, http://www.dailykos.com /story/2013/08/13/1230832/-Obama-appoints-James-Clapper-to-oversee -independent-NSA-review.

6 "Memorandum for the Heads of Executive Departments and Agencies: Trans-parency and Open Government," WhiteHouse.gov, http://www.whitehouse .gov/the_press_office/TransparencyandOpenGovernment.

7 "Remarks by the President on Trayvon Martin," WhiteHouse.gov, July 19, 2013, http://www.whitehouse.gov/the-press-office/2013/07/19/remarks-president -trayvon-martin.

8 Ed Morrissey, "Obama: Sacked Consulate and Dead Ambassador 'Bumps in the Road,'" HotAir.com, September 24, 2012, http://hotair.com/archives /2012/09/24/obama-sacked-consulate-and-dead-ambassador-bumps-in-the -road/.

9 Fred Lucas, "WH Clarifies: Obama Told CNN Espanol in March He Heard About 'Fast and Furious' 'On the News,'" CNSNews.com, October 5, 2011, http://cnsnews.com/news/article/wh-clarifies-obama-told-cnn-espanol-march -he-heard-about-fast-and-furious-news.

10 Katie Pavlich, "Obama on IRS Scandal: I've Got No Patience with It,"

Townhall.com, May 13, 2013, http://townhall.com/tipsheet/katiepavlich /2013/05/13/obama-on-irs-scandal-ive-got-no-patience-with-it-n1593814.

11 Dana Milbank, "Obama, the Uninterested President," WashingtonPost.com, May 14, 2013, http://articles.washingtonpost.com/2013-05-14/opinions /39254536_1_phone-records-president-obama-press-secretary.

12 Margaret Hartmann, "Obama to Leno, 'We Don't Have Domestic Spying,'" NYMag.com, August 7, 2013, http://nymag.com/daily/intelligencer/2013 /08/obama-to-leno-we-dont-have-domestic-spying.html.

13 David Jackson, "Top Obama Aides Say They Knew Nothing of Solyndra," USAToday.com, September 23, 2011, http://content.usatoday.com /communities/theoval/post/2011/09/top-obama-aides-deny-knowledge-of -solyndra/1#.UjaSHmDrOR8.

14 Ben Johnson, "Obama Doesn't Comment on Ongoing Trials—Unless They Involve Trayvon Martin," LifeSiteNews.com, April 15, 2013, http://www.lifesitenews .com/blog/obama-doesnt-comment-on-ongoing-trials-unless-they-involve -trayvon-martin/.

15 Stephen J. Dubner, "How Biased Is the Media? Bring Your Questions for the Author of *Left Turn*," Freakonomics.com, August 2, 2011, http://freakonomics.com/2011/08/02/how-biased-is-the-media-bring-your -questions-for-the-author-of-left-turn/.

16 Thomas Jefferson, *Notes on the State of Virginia*, 1784, http://press-pubs .uchicago.edu/founders/documents/v1ch10s9.html.

17 *Rotella v. Wood*, 147 F.3d 438 (2000).

18 Arie J. Lipinski, "Combating Government Corruption: Suing the Federal Government Via a Proposed Amendment to the Civil RICO Statute," *Valparaiso University Law Review* 46, no. 1 (Fall 2011): 169–210.

INDEX

★

spying on, 126–28
and targeting of anti-Americans with
drone strikes, 201–2
See also surveillance programs
civil liberties/rights
and New Black Panther Party case, 186
surveillance programs and, 139, 140,
150, 156
Zimmerman–Trayvon Martin case and,
178–84
See also Patriot Act; surveillance
programs
Civil Rights Act (1964), 141
Civil Rights Division, 185
Clapper, James, 3, 136, 142, 143, 155, 207
Clarke, Richard, 149
CleanUpATF.org, 77–78
Cleaver, Emanuel, 104
Clinton, Bill, 8, 90–91, 158, 203, 204
Clinton, Hillary Rodham and Assad-Syria
events, 23
awards for, 55–56
and Ben Ali–Tunisia events, 22
Benghazi attack and, 3, 18, 32, 35–36,
41, 44, 47, 48, 49–50, 53, 58
Congress/Senate testimonies of, 32, 47,
49
elections of 2012 and, 185
elections of 2016 and, 18, 52
and gunrunning in Syria, 30
and "Innocence of Muslims" video, 38
and IRS activities, 91
and Israeli-U.S. relations, 130
and leaks, 134
Libyan uprising and, 24, 25, 28, 32
and Mubarak-Egypt events, 23
New Black Panthers and, 185
resignation of, 55–56
Travelgate and, 90
closing arguments
about Benghazi, 56–59
about bribery, 176–77
about Fast and Furious Operation,
82–84
about IRS activities, 116–17
about leaks, 137
about manslaughter, 82–84
against Obama administration, 210–14
about obstruction of justice, 200–202
about surveillance programs, 154–56
CNBC, 95
CNN
Benghazi story and, 50, 53, 209

and IRS activities, 111
and Israel-Iran relations, 129
and Israel-U.S. relations, 134
and leaks about al-Qaeda operations,
127
and Snowden case, 151
and surveillance programs, 147
COINTELPRO, 89
Colbert, Stephen, 52–53
Cole, James, 73
command responsibility principle, 4
Commentary magazine, 134–35
Committee for Truth in Politics, 99
Community Relations Service (CRS),
Justice Department, 182
Competitive Enterprise Institute, 173
Concerned Women for America, 91
Congress, U.S.
ACORN and, 199
and AmeriCorps/Walpin case, 189, 190
appointments and, 166, 168
authorizations from, 26–27
and auto bailouts, 164
and Benghazi, 1, 3, 34, 35, 44, 45, 46,
47, 48–49, 50, 52, 53, 55
and briefing about bin Laden's death,
120
and Clapper-NSA surveillance case, 3
decline in power of, 12
elections of people to, 212
and Energy Department activities, 171
and Fast and Furious Operation, 65,
68, 70, 72–73, 75, 77, 78, 79–80,
83
immigration and, 196–97
impeachments in, 212
and IRS activities, 89, 90, 98, 100,
109–10, 111–12, 113, 115
and Libya events, 26–27, 28, 29
monitoring of programs by, 144–45
Netanyahu's visit to, 130
Obama and, 10, 11, 26–27, 57, 166,
168, 196–97
Obamacare and, 2, 94, 174, 195, 198
RICO Act, 5, 15
role of, 13
and Sebelius's solicitation of donations
for Obamacare, 2
surveillance programs and, 144–45, 146,
148, 154, 155
and targeting of journalists, 122–23
and what can be done about government, 212–13

282 ★ INDEX

Holder, Eric (cont.)
and targeting of U.S. citizens with drone strikes, 201
and Wall Street businesses, 194
Zimmerman–Trayvon Martin case and, 184
Hollywood
Obamacare and, 175
Obama's relations with, 175–76, 206
Homeland Security Department (DHS), U.S., 28, 67, 96, 114, 149
Hoover, J. Edgar, 15, 89, 90, 211
Hoover, William, 79
Horner, Christopher, 173
Horowitz, Michael E., 74, 75
House Emerging Threats and Capabilities Subcommittee (House Armed Services Committee), 142
House Oversight and Government Reform Committee
Benghazi and, 37, 39, 46, 50–51
and Fast and Furious Operation, 70, 73
and IRS activities, 100–101, 103, 111, 116
House Ways and Means Committee: and IRS activities, 113–14
Housing Development Authority, Illinois, 199
Housing and Urban Development (HUD), U.S. Department of: ACORN and, 199
Howard, Andre, 61, 69, 81
Hudson, Jennifer, 175
Hull, Blair, 92
Hull, Carter, 111, 116
Human Rights Campaign, 104
Hurley, Emory, 66–67, 69, 78, 80, 81
Hurricane Katrina, 13

Ideological Organizations Project, 89
Iger, Bob, 175
Ignatius, David, 107, 131
illegal gratuity, 159–60, 176
Illinois Housing Development Authority, 199
Immelt, Jeffrey, 172, 175
immigration, 11, 12, 60–61, 196–97, 208
Immigration and Customs Enforcement, U.S.: and Fast and Furious Operation, 68
impeachments, 212
Ingraham, Laura, 76
Ingram, Sarah Hall, 102, 115

"Innocence of Muslims" (YouTube video), 38, 41, 42–47, 55
Institute for National Security Studies, 132
Interior, U.S. Department of, 176
Internal Revenue Code. See Internal Revenue Service
Internal Revenue Service (IRS) accountability/transparency of, 105–9
aftermath of targeting by, 113–16, 155
and blame, 105, 110–11, 112, 116
BOLO list of, 101–2, 110
charges concerning the, 87–116
climate of retaliation at, 97–100
closing argument about activities of, 116–17
cover-up for targeting by, 109–12
Democratic reactions to, 108
employee bonuses at, 114–16
investigations/reports about, 89, 90, 93–94, 98, 100, 105, 108, 109–10, 111–12, 113–14, 115, 116
liberal groups and, 107
litigation against, 213
and media as willing accomplices, 209–10
Obama as unaware of scandal about, 11, 107–9
Obamacare and, 115
opening arguments about, 86–87
public opinion concerning, 117
targeting of conservative groups/opposition by, 2, 98–117, 155, 204, 206, 209–10
as tool of intimidation and oppression, 116
as weapon of political retribution, 88–89
White House comments about activities of, 11, 108, 112, 113, 207, 208
International Association of Machinist and Aerospace Workers, 166
Internet: and surveillance programs, 143–44, 148
intimidation, criminal: definition of, 184
investigations/reports
about AIG bailout, 193–94
and AmeriCorps/Walpin case, 189, 190
about Benghazi, 1, 3, 47–50, 52, 53, 54, 56, 58
and blame, 3, 13
about Fast and Furious Operation, 65, 68, 71–76, 78–79, 80, 81
about IRS activities, 89, 90, 93–94, 98, 100, 105, 108, 109–10, 111–12, 113–14, 115, 116

phony scandals and, 3
about Rezko, 160
about shooting of Navy SEALs, 121
about surveillance programs, 142, 147,
 149
about terrorism, 96
Iran
 Ahmadinejad's election in, 21–22
 Bush administration and, 22
 Israeli relations with, 129–34, 205
 leaks about, 129–34, 136, 205
 nuclear program of, 129–34, 136, 205
 Obama's diplomacy overtures to, 22
Iraq
 al-Qaeda in, 21, 25
 AQIM in, 25
 and Armitage-Plame incident, 205
 due process and, 202
 Obama's call for pullout from, 21
Irey, Elmer, 88
Islam: Obama's views about, 20–21
Israel
 Iranian relations with, 129–34, 205
 leaks about, 128–36, 205
 Syrian relations with, 134
Israeli Defense Forces (IDF), 132
Issa, Darrell, 37, 70, 72–73, 74, 78, 80,
 190, 209

Jackson, David, 14
Jackson, Jesse, Jr., 207
Jackson, Lisa, 173
Jaffer, Jameel, 148
Jarrett, Valerie, 160
Jefferson, Thomas, 13–14, 211
Jewish community, 107, 128–29. See also Israel
jihad, 31–32
Jobs and Family Services, Ohio Department
 of, 93
Johnson, Kevin, 188–89, 201
Johnson, Lyndon Baines "LBJ," 89, 90
Joint Chiefs of Staff: Benghazi and, 40
Jones, B. Todd, 77
Jones-Kelley, Helen E., 93–94
Jones, Paula, 91
Jones, Terry, 38
Jordan, 30
journalists
 Justice Department targeting of, 2, 12,
 14, 122–23, 125–26, 137, 155, 205,
 208, 210
 Obama administration hostility toward,
 14, 122, 207

See also specific person or organization
JPMorgan Chase, 194
Judd, Brandon, 61
Judicial Watch, 75–76, 83, 90–91, 94, 117,
 169, 182, 200
Justice, U.S. Department of
 and AIG–Goldman Sachs case, 193–94
 AmeriCorps/Walpin case and, 190 and
 AP case, 2, 14, 125–26, 210
 BuShitler and, 13
 and Fast and Furious Operation, 63–64,
 65, 68, 70, 71–76, 77–78, 79–81, 83
 and HHS fund-raising, 195
 immigration laws and, 196
 and IRS activities, 88, 98, 108
 marijuana laws and, 197
 as most corrupt branch of government,
 / 206, 212
 and New Black Panther Party case, 185,
 186, 187
 Obama administration appointments
 to, 170
 and obstruction of justice issues, 184
 and race issues, 141
 RICO Act and, 6–7, 15, 212
 and Rosen–Fox News case, 14, 122–23
 Snowden case and, 150
 targeting of journalists by, 2, 12, 14,
 122–23, 125–26, 137, 155, 205,
 208, 210
 White House comments about, 12, 71,
 73, 75, 184
 Zimmerman–Trayvon Martin case and,
 180, 181, 182–83, 206
 See also Holder, Eric

Kaiser, George, 170–71
Kaufman, Brett Max, 154
Kaufman, Irving, 57
Kennedy, Edward "Ted," 168
Kennedy, John F. "JFK," 89–90, 116, 203,
 204
Kennedy, Patrick, 36, 40, 55
Kentucky 9/12 Project, 100
Kerry, John, 54, 150
Kessler, Glenn, 105–6
Keyes, Alan, 92
Keys, Alicia, 175
Khalidi, Rashid, 128
Kiestand, Kevin, 190
"kill list": for al-Qaeda, 127–28
Kilpatrick, Bernard, 5
Kilpatrick, Kwame, 5–6

Lott, John, Jr., 169
low-level employees
  and Benghazi, 48, 110
  blame on, 3–4, 13, 48, 78, 105, 110–11,
    134, 212
  and Fast and Furious Operation, 78, 110
  and IRS activities, 105, 110–11
  and prosecuting the Obama administra-
    tion, 4
Lynn, William J. III, 158, 159

MacAllister, Hope, 65, 67, 79
Maddow, Rachel, 95, 174
Madoff, Bernie, 6
mafia, 15–16, 64, 116
Magariaf, Mohamed, 47
Maher, Bill, 95
Mali, 31–32
Malkin, Michelle, 198–99
Malley, Robert, 129
Mammoth Oil, 176
Manning, Bradley, 19
manslaughter
  Arizona statute about, 60, 82
  Benghazi case and, 19–20, 37
  charges about, 61–82
  closing argument about, 82–84
  definition of, 60
  elements of, 62, 82
  involuntary, 19–20, 37, 60–84
  opening argument about, 60–61
  reckless disregard and, 60, 62, 82
  See also Fast and Furious Operation
marijuana laws, 197
Martin, Jenny Beth, 107
Martin, Trayvon, 178–84
Mason, Karol, 170
Matthews, Chris, 14
Matvienko, Valentina, 153
Maxwell, Raymond, 54
McCain, John, 54, 93, 133, 193
McClatchy news service, 135
McClellan, John, 210–11
McConnell, Mitch, 109
McDonough, Denis, 20
McGavin, Joe, 199
McInerney, Thomas, 170
McNeal, Greg, 127
McPeak, Merrill, 129
media
  Bush administration relations with, 13
  and Fast and Furious Operation, 76–78
  and freedom of the press, 14–15

hacking of, 77
importance of, 13–14
IRS activities and, 102, 106–7, 116
leftist leanings of, 13
Obama administration and, 14–15,
  209–10, 211
Obamacare and, 175
as willing accomplices, 209–10, 211
and Zimmerman–Trayvon Martin case,
  180
See also specific journalist or organization
"Media Trackers," 107
Meet the Press (NBC-TV), 45
Mellon, Andrew, 88
Melson, Ken, 63, 64, 74, 77, 79–80
Merkley, Jeff, 9
Mexico
  Chamber of Deputies in, 70
  knowledge about Fast and Furious in,
    66, 70
  See also drug cartels, Mexican
Microsoft, 143
middle class: Obama's commitment to, 3
military, U.S.: sexual assaults in, 191–92
Miller, Steven, 104, 108–9, 116
Mills, Cheryl, 51
Minnesota Democratic Farmer Labor Party,
  96
Miranda, David, 151
Mitchell, Steven R., 171
Monaco, Lisa, 67
Moonves, Les, 175
Moran, Jim, 91
Morell, Michael, 55, 149
Morgan, Piers, 53
Morgenthau, Henry, Jr., 88, 89
Morsi, Mohammed, 23, 31
Mossad, 131
motive: and conviction of crime, 20
Mourad, Greg, 167
MSNBC, 2, 95, 104, 174
Mubarak, Hosni, 21, 23, 24
Mueller, Robert, 63, 153
Muhammad, James J., 186
Muhammad, Mikhail, 186
Muhammad (prophet), 38
Mujahideen-e-Khalq (MEK), 131
Mullen, Mike, 48, 49
Muslim Brotherhood, 21, 23, 31

Nadler, Jerrold, 26
Nakoula, Nakoula Basseley, 44
Napolitano, Janet, 68, 71–72, 83, 114, 196

as transformative figure, 10
worship of, 8–10
Obama (Barack) administration
case against, 1–16
closing arguments against, 210–14
Congress and, 10, 11, 26–27, 57, 166,
168, 196–97
as criminal enterprise, 4
logo of, 8
media and, 14–15
motive of, 211
prosecution of, 4–7, 15–16, 211–13
responsibility of, 4
Supreme Court and, 10
transparency of, 82–83, 207
what can be done about, 211–14
See also specific person, department, agency,
or topic
Obama, Michelle, 8, 159, 160–61, 189
Obamacare (Affordable Care Act)
business community and, 194–95
contraceptive mandate of, 102–3
elections of 2014 and, 198
employer mandate for, 197–98
funding for, 195
Hollywood and, 175
IRS activities and, 115
labor unions and, 174–75, 206
launching of push for, 94
and Obama approval ratings, 9
obstruction of justice and, 194–95,
197–98
Sebelius's solicitation of donations for,
2, 195
and Shulman's visits to White House,
100
stimulus package and, 173–76
waivers for, 198, 206
website for, 11–12
White House comments about, 11–12
youth video contest for, 199–200
Obamob, 15–16
Obeidi, Mohamed, 37
obstruction of justice
ACORN and, 198–200
AmeriCorps/Walpin case and, 188–90
BP case and, 195
charges about, 184–200
closing arguments about, 200–202
and HHS fund-raising, 195
immigration and, 196–97
and New Black Panther Party, 180,
185–88, 201, 210

Obamacare and, 194–95, 197–98
opening arguments about, 178–84
RICO Act and, 83–84, 201
sexual improprieties cases and, 190–92
U.S. code about, 178, 184
Wall Street and, 192–95
Zimmerman case and, 178–84, 185,
186, 201, 206, 208, 210
Occupy Wall Street, 193, 210
Office of the Inspector General (OIG), 190
Office of Intelligence and Operations
Coordination (Homeland Security
Department), 67
Office of Management and Budget, U.S.,
171
Office of National Drug Control Policy,
149
Office of Personnel Management, U.S., 174
O'Keefe, James, 199
Olbermann, Keith, 174
Olympic Games program, 132–33
O'Mara, Mark, 179, 184
omnibus clause (Internal Revenue Code),
88, 117
"One Light" project, 107
The Onion, Carney parody in, 2
opening arguments
about Benghazi attack, 18
about bribery, 158–59
about IRS activities, 86–87
about leaks, 118–21
about manslaughter count, 60–61
about obstruction of justice, 178–84
about surveillance programs, 139–41
Ordinary People Society, 186
O'Reilly, Kevin, 74–75
Oswald, Lee Harvey, 90
Overton, Spencer, 170

Pakistan, 29, 44, 52
Palestine Liberation Organization (PLO),
128
Palestinian Authority, 107
Palestinians, 130
PalTalk, 143
Pan American Petroleum, 176
Panetta, Leon
Benghazi and, 40, 41–42, 55
and bin Laden killing, 119
and Israeli-Iran-U.S. relations, 131, 133
resignation of, 55
Patriot Act, 139–41, 142, 143, 144, 148,
155–56, 205